The Cocker Spaniel

POPULAR DOGS' BREED SERIES

BASSET HOUND	*George Johnston*
BEAGLE	*Thelma Gray*
BOXER	*Elizabeth Somerfield*
CAIRN TERRIER	*J.W.H. Beynon, Alex Fisher, Peggy Wilson and Doreen Proudlock*
CAVALIER KING CHARLES SPANIEL	*Mary Forwood*
CHIHUAHUA	*Thelma Gray*
COCKER SPANIEL	*Veronica Lucas-Lucas and Joyce Caddy*
COLLIE	*Margaret Osborne and Aileen Speding*
DACHSHUND	*E. Fitch Daglish, Amyas Biss and Jeff Crawford*
DALMATIAN	*Eleanor Frankling, Betty Clay and Marjorie Cooper*
DOBERMANN	*Fred Curnow and Jean Faulks*
FOX TERRIER	*Elsie Williams*
GERMAN SHEPHERD DOG	*J. Schwabacher, Thelma Gray and Madeleine Pickup*
GOLDEN RETRIEVER	*Joan Tudor*
GREAT DANE	*Jean Lanning*
IRISH SETTER	*Janice Roberts*
LABRADOR RETRIEVER	*Lorna, Countess Howe and Geoffrey Waring*
MONGREL	*Angela Patmore*
OLD ENGLISH SHEEPDOG	*Ann Davis*
POODLE	*Clara Bowring, Alida Monro and Shirley Walne*
PUG	*Susan Graham Weall*
ROTTWEILER	*Judy and Larry Elsden*
SCOTTISH TERRIER	*Dorothy Caspersz and Elizabeth Meyer*
SHETLAND SHEEPDOG	*Margaret Osborne*
SHIH TZU	*Audrey Dadds*
SPRINGER SPANIEL	*Dorothy Moorland Hooper and Ian B. Hampton*
STAFFORDSHIRE BULL TERRIER	*John F. Gordon*
WELSH CORGI	*Charles Lister-Kaye and Dickie Albin*
WEST HIGHLAND WHITE TERRIER	*D. Mary Dennis and Catherine Owen*
YORKSHIRE TERRIER	*Ethel and Vera Munday*

THE COCKER SPANIEL

VERONICA LUCAS-LUCAS

Revised by Joyce Caddy

POPULAR DOGS
London Sydney Auckland Johannesburg

Popular Dogs Publishing Co. Ltd

An imprint of Century Hutchinson

Brookmount House, 62–65 Chandos Place
Covent Garden, London WC2N 4NW.

Century Hutchinson Australia (Pty) Ltd
88–91 Albion Street, Surrey Hills, NSW 2010

Century Hutchinson New Zealand Limited
191 Archers Road, PO Box 40-086, Glenfield, Auckland 10

Century Hutchinson South Africa (Pty) Ltd
Po Box 337, Bergvlei 2012, South Africa

First published (as *The Popular Cocker Spaniel*) 1953
Revised editions 1956, 1959, 1964
Revised editions (as *The Cocker Spaniel*) 1967, 1971, 1974,
1976, 1979, 1984, 1988

Set in Baskerville by BookEns, Saffron Walden, Essex

Printed and bound in Great Britain by Anchor Brendon Ltd,
Tiptree, Essex

British Library Cataloguing in Publication Data
Lucas-Lucas, Veronica
The Cocker spaniel.—11th ed.
1. Cocker spaniels. Care
I. Title II. Caddy, Joyce
636.7′52

ISBN 0 09 173578 5

CONTENTS

ACKNOWLEDGEMENTS

The line drawing illustrating the Standard of the Cocker on page 44 is reproduced by kind permission of the Cocker Spaniel Club and the pedigree of Ch. Invader of Ware on pages 28 and 29 is reproduced with the kind permission of the late Mr H.S. Lloyd.

ILLUSTRATIONS

Between pages 80 and 81

Sh. Ch. Sixshot Woodywoodpecker
Bred and owned by Mrs V. Lucas-Lucas

Sh. Ch. Sixshot Otto the Owl
Bred and owned by Mrs V. Lucas-Lucas

Ch. Colinwood Silver Lariot
Bred by Miss H.M. Allen
Owned by Mr A.W. Collins

Ch. Lucklena Musical Maid
Bred and owned by Mr A.S. Mansfield

Ch. Craigleith Cinderella
Bred and owned by Mrs M. Robinson

Sh. Ch. Crosbeian Thornfalcon Flamenco
Bred by Miss B. Seymour Nichols
Owned by Mrs D.M. Trench

Sh. Ch. Sixshot Dan the Duck
Bred and owned by Mrs V. Lucas-Lucas

Sh. Ch. Courtdale Flag Lieutenant
Bred by Mrs G. Anstey
Owned by Mrs S.G. Jones

Between pages 112 and 113

Sh. Ch. Astrawin Amusing
Bred and owned by Mr and Mrs Wise

Sixshot Gobble the Turkey
Bred and owned by Mrs V. Lucas-Lucas

Sh. Ch. Val of Locknell
Bred and owned by Mrs M. Cameron

Sh. Ch. Lochranza Strollaway
Bred by Misses J. Macmillan and Miss J. Coull
Owned by Miss J. Macmillan

Sh. Ch. Olanza Pipistrelle
Bred and owned by Miss P. Becker

AUTHOR'S INTRODUCTIONS

I have written this book chiefly for the novice, and hope it will be of some little help, and save him from making the many mistakes I made when I began breeding and showing. It is written in simple language for the benefit of everyone who keeps or intends to keep a cocker as a show dog or pet, and who, it is hoped, will each find in it information of practical value. Readers who have no knowledge of the origin and ancestry of the cocker will, I trust, find the description I have given enlightening.

The close association I have had with cockers has naturally led to a keen interest in their development and welfare. I have always loved the cocker spaniel since my childhood days. We lived in the country and my father had quite a variety of gun-dogs, but they were not show dogs and were kept entirely for the gun.

My favourite was always the little cocker and when I left home I took one with me. He missed his companions so much that I decided to buy a little bitch puppy to keep him company. It so happened I chose one from an 'Of Ware' sire. She not only turned out to be a winner, but was the basis of my strain; from her I bred Sixshot Bunting, who was mated to Woodcock Othello (full brother to Treetops Treasure Trove) and out of this mating came Sixshot Ring Ouzel, who did a lot of good winning, including best black bitch at Crufts. I then mated Ouzel to Woodcock Ringleader and this mating produced Sixshot Mavis, who also did a lot of winning and afterwards became Treetops Temptress, the dam of Treetops Turtle Dove. I had previously mated Mavis to Bazel Otto and from this mating came the famous red bitch Sixshot Brown Owl who, when mated to Treetops Terrific, produced one of the most famous black dogs ever, Sixshot Black Swan. He in turn sired Sixshot Willy Wagtail who, when mated to Sixshot

Nightingale, produced Sh. Ch. Sixshot Woodywoodpecker. The dogs I have mentioned above are the ones which will be remembered by cocker breeders.

I would like to thank the kind friends in the following list for helping me with pedigrees, dates, etc.: Mr H.S. Lloyd, Judge Townsend Scudder (USA), Mr Frank Williams, Mr H.C. Wicks, Miss M. Barker (New Zealand). Mr P.R.A. Moxon, who must be recognized as one of our great authorities on the training of gundogs, has kindly written a Chapter on *The Cocker Spaniel as a Gundog*, which is a very pleasing addition.

1953

In this new edition I have made some additions to the text and introduced several new kennels in Chapter 2 and new C.C. winners in Chapter 5. New photographs of recent Certificate winners have also been included.

1956

For this third edition, Chapters 2 and 5 have again been revised and a list of British Cocker Champions and Show Champions from 1948 to 1958 has been added as an appendix. I have also brought the illustrations up-to-date.

1959

There is little for me to add to the fourth edition. A few new photographs now appear; where necessary the text has been revised, and Chapters 2 and 5 have again been brought up-to-date, as has the appendix.

1964

I was very pleased to be asked to revise this book once again before it is launched under the new title of *The Cocker Spaniel.* I have made cuts in matter that is now out of date and made certain additions; four photographs have been replaced and the appendix brought up-to-date. Mr F. Andrew Edgson, MRCVS has kindly contributed an entirely fresh chapter on some commoner health problems.

1967

This book has again been revised for this sixth edition. I have replaced six photographs and brought the appendices up-to-date.

1971

What I wrote in the first edition still stands as the general principles of dog breeding and Kennel procedure do not alter. I have, however, replaced four of the photographs and again brought Appendices A and C up-to-date. I am grateful to both Peter Moxon and Andrew Edgson for checking their chapters, neither of which requires revision.

1974

This is the eight edition of *The Cocker Spaniel*. The general plan of the book remains unchanged, but additional photographs have been included, and the text and appendices brought up-to-date.

1976

For the ninth time this work, originally written in 1953, is entering upon a new revised edition, with the inclusion of some new photographs and the latest Show Champion winners.

1979

The book of the Cocker Spaniel has enjoyed a remarkable circulation in Great Britain and abroad. In this tenth edition, new photographs have been added and the text brought up-to-date.

1984 V.L.-L.

Reviser's note:
When I first started to show cockers at Championship Shows in the early 1950s, Mrs Lucas-Lucas was one of those whose dogs I admired most. In her later years she did not show, but she changed little and retained the respect and affection of

everyone in the cocker world. Her death was a great loss to the breed for which she had done so much. Her book has always been a popular one with cocker spaniel owners both here and abroad, and I hope that, having undertaken the task of bringing it up-to-date, the new edition will be as well received as its predecessors.

1988 Joyce Caddy

COCKER LOVE

There's a love that lingers always
Deep within my heart–
It's the love for cocker spaniels,
Here's how it got its start.
Bought a puppy, silky-coated,
Eyes of brown that looked at me
Like he thought I was an idol,
Showed his trust and faith in me.
Stubby tail that wagged 'Hello, there!'
Every time he heard my step
Fitted his mood right with my moods–
Quiet, or a lot of pep.
Ears that gracefully extended
Quite a ways toward the ground–
Chasing after balls; retrieving
Anything he found around.
Gentle always with the children
As he grew from puppyhood
Into just the kind of dog folks
Liked throughout the neighbourhood.
I'm a hunter and I love it,
So did that first cocker pup–
Didn't really have to train him,
He just seemed to pick it up.
Years have passed, but still that puppy
In my heart has left his trace,
For every time I lose a cocker
Another one must take its place.

VERA PAGE

1

Early History of the Cocker Spaniel

The cocker spaniel is always a merry little dog at work or play. At all times he shows his pleasure by the continual wag of his tail, and he is never so happy as when putting up game for the guns, or retrieving a fallen bird from land, water or hedgerow. How far the spaniel goes back in history would be hard to say, but it has been mentioned in early writings as far back as the 14th century. In the early days all breeds of spaniels came under one heading, 'Spaniels'. The name 'cocker' or 'cocking spaniel' came into being about 1800. At this period they were used a great deal for woodcock shooting, being able to work through dense cover where one of the larger breeds could not penetrate. The cocker spaniel was first entered in the Kennel Club Stud Book as a separate breed in 1893.

Until the year 1901 the weight limit was 25 lb, but in that year the limit was abolished by the Spaniel Club on a resolution proposed by Colonel Cane, seconded by Mr James Farrow and confirmed by the Kennel Club. This gave the breeders more scope. Before this a spaniel could be a cocker, and if he put on weight he became a field spaniel. In other words, dogs from the same litter could be of two different classes: under 25 lb cockers and over 25 lb field spaniels.

The popularity of the cocker spaniel is world-wide, no doubt due to his versatility. He is equally suitable as a gundog, showman or companion. In the time of the Stuarts he was used for falconry, a sport indulged in largely on the Fens, and enjoyed by the leaders of venery and fashion in Europe; this was at its zenith in England during the reign of Charles II. George Tumberville, in his *Booke of Faulconorie* published in 1575, wrote, 'Howe necessary a thing a spanell is to Falconrie.'

which goes to prove that even in those very early days the spaniel was a sporting dog.

In the 14th century Chaucer mentions a spaniel in *The Wyf of Bathe's Prologue*. About 200 years later, in 1570, Dr Cains wrote, in his history of the *Englishe Dogges* that the 'Spaniell whose skynnes are white, and if marcked with any spottes they are commonly red . . .' Another writer of this period, John Evelyn, records in his diary, on July 8th, 1647, at La Charite, 'I lost my faithful spaniel Piccoli who had followed me from Rome, it seems he had been taken up by some of the Governor's pages or footmen without recovery, which was a great displeasure to me.' In a fifth edition of *The Dogs of British Islands*, published in 1888, 'Stonehenge' wrote: 'The modern Field spaniel should be the best made all round shooting dog, for he is expected to perform equally well on land and in water, in covert, hedgerow or turnips. He is also called on to return whilst he must be thoroughly steady, reliable under all circumstances, however trying to his nature, and he must never tire.' In order to attain this marvellous combination of powers and varied qualifications our modern breeders have crossed the old-fashioned cocker with the Sussex, and then by careful selection as to size, points and colour they have established a breed. Thus we learn that before 1886 the blood of the Sussex variety of spaniels had been added to the cocker admixture of bloods of other varieties of spaniels, and it was producing what 'Stonehenge' characterized as 'a marvellous combination of powers and varied qualifications.' In the early days, a strain of working cockers was bred in Devonshire, which were hardy and good with the gun, and all along the Devon coast you would find many of these little dogs, eager to accompany any sportsman on a day's shooting, although they were not good retrievers on the whole, which perhaps was just as well as these dogs turned out by the dozen. Their breeding was not studied, except by a few, and yet they seemed to follow a certain type; the principal colours were blue and liver roans, liver and white, and the solids were chiefly liver, with a few reds.

I remember attending a shooting party in Devonshire; with a full gale blowing a cock pheasant shot coming down wind had fallen across water. All the dogs had refused to go across, but one little cocker bitch unhesitatingly swam the water, and brought back the bird. This was the best retrieve I had ever seen with a dog of this size. It must be said that whilst modern show cockers have the instinct for, and are capable of working well in the field, those with pedigrees based on field-trial stock are the real stars of the breed where working is concerned.

Early Breeding

The founder of the modern cocker was Mr James Farrow, who did so much towards the standardization of the breed with his original Obo, who was cocker bred for several generations, and later by Obo's great-grandson Champion Ted Obo, who was by Frank Obo out of Champion Lily Obo. Mr Isaac Sharpe made history for cockers when the first field trails in this country, confined to all spaniels, was run at Sutton Scarsdale in 1889. The stake was won with the cocker Stylish Pride owned by Mr Sharpe. The first cocker to qualify as a Field Trial Champion was Colonel Heseltone's Field Trial Champion Walhampton Judy, who was sired by Champion Rufus Bowdler out of Jum Jum and bred by Mr A. E. Halsey in 1905, trained and handled by Mr John Kent. It was a great event for the cocker spaniel in 1909 when Mr Phillips' Robena obtained her working qualifying certificate in the field as well as obtaining three show Challenge Certificates, thus making her a full champion.

Foundation of Cocker Spaniel Breed Clubs and Breed Council

A milestone in history was made when the Cocker Spaniel Club was formed in 1902 by a few enthusiastic breeders and from then onwards great steps have been made towards the betterment of the cocker. After the First World War the cocker spaniel really came into its own, and nowadays the entries for the breed are amongst the highest at Championship Shows. In the year 1914 only 400 registrations were made at the Kennel Club but in 1939 the registration figure jumped to 5,372 and in 1947 the peak figure of 27,000 was reached. This has now steadied down to about 7,000 per year registered, with an unknown number being merely 'recorded' under a later Kennel Club system.

The Cocker Spaniel Club is still regarded as the parent club of the breed and its annual Championship Show takes its place with Crufts as the two top shows of the year.

It was 21 years before the next breed club – the Midland Cocker Spaniel Club – was formed, and the popularity of the breed can be gauged by the fact that there are now 24, all very well supported. In March 1968 a number of the clubs got together to form a Cocker Spaniel Council to meet together to discuss matters of interest to the breed, and 23 of the clubs now meet twice a year for this purpose. This goes to show how popular the cocker spaniel has become and how this little dog has captured the hearts of so many; he is undoubtedly a staunch favourite, as the registration figure exceeds any other breed of spaniel.

Rawdon B. Lee in 'Modern Dogs'

I have read with great interest the chapter written on the cocker spaniel by Rawdon B. Lee in *Modern Dogs* in the year 1897 and thought it would be of interest to cocker enthusiasts to transcribe some of it here. Rawdon Lee had a very poor opinion of the cocker as a show dog, and also as a gundog, which makes rather amusing reading as it is quite contradictory to what has really happened, when we think of the cocker of today, often topping entries at championship shows and with the highest spaniel registration at the Kennel Club; and to see him work is a joy. I have often been amazed to see a cocker bringing to hand a struggling wounded rabbit or cock pheasant. Most cockers have the ability to work, but unfortunately so few of us have the space or time to train them, therefore their natural instinct as a gundog is lost. Cockers are fortunately adaptable little creatures and are equally happy as a companion.

> 'This, the smallest of our race of sporting spaniels, is retrograding rather than progressing, and hardy, cheerful little dog though he be, sportsmen have found that a bigger

dog can do his duties better, even to working rough covert, and it is not a general thing for a cocker to retrieve a rabbit or a hare; indeed, some cockers I have had would not retrieve at all, nor did I blame them, for retrieving is a duty to be performed by a more powerful dog. The prizes offered for the cocker on the show bench are not of particular value, nor do they carry sufficient honour, to make it worth the while of anyone breeding him for such purpose alone, so as a matter of fact, this once-favoured little dog is not growing with the times in the manner which savours of success. Only the larger exhibitions give him classes of his own, and the prizes then do not always go to the genuine article. The cocker of the olden time I should take to be the connecting link between the working and the toy spaniels. We have been told that the Blenheims at Marlborough House were excellent dogs to work the coverts for cock and pheasant, and excepting in colour there is in reality not much difference in appearance between the older orange and white toys (not as they are today, with their abnormally short noses, round skulls and enormous eyes) and the liver and white cockers H. B. Chalon drew for Daniel's *Rural Sports* in 1801. Two of Chalon's little spaniels have just sprung a woodcock, and charming specimens they are, not too low on the leg, nor over-done in the matter of ears, but sprightly little dogs, evidently under 20 lb weight and of a type we do not find today. Many of us lament the growing scarcity of this variety as he was to be found fifty years ago and more. Modern breeders tell us they have provided us with a better and handsomer animal. It is an open question whether they have done the former; I acknowledge they have done the latter. Some few years ago I became the possessor of a brace of black cockers, the most beautiful little spaniels imaginable. How they were bred I am not aware; this I do know, that wherever they went they were admired more than any other dogs; not in the show ring – they never appeared there – but in the streets and the country generally. At that time I was shooting a good deal, and had ample opportunity of entering them to game of every kind. As sporting dogs they were comparatively useless, for they were noisy, headstrong, not at all careful, and would pass half a dozen rabbits or pheasants whilst they were putting up three or four. My terriers could beat their heads off, and a cross bred spaniel I had at that time could have outworked a big team of them. Of course, this must not be taken as an implication that all these modern extremely pretty black cockers are equally useless, but from others I have seen at work I did not take mine to have been an especially unfortunate brace.

The coats of some of them are not adapted to protect the hide of the dog from being pierced by those sharp thorns and prickly brambles that are to be found in every ordinary covert.

Some parts of Wales and Devonshire have produced the old working type of cocker, mostly liver and white in colour, higher on the leg than an ordinary field spaniel, not so long in ears, with a close coat, not too fine, usually inclining to be a wavy and curly on the hindquarters, and a head finer in the muzzle than the ordinary spaniel would seem to possess, and with a character of its own. Some years ago Dr Boulton was exhibiting his Rhea, a black specimen which won a great many prizes. She, however, had little or no strain of the cocker in her, and what excellence she possessed came from the same blood that ran in the pedigree of Bullock's Nellie and other celebrities of her day.

Perhaps the best class of cockers I have ever seen was benched at Manchester in 1892. There were fourteen of them, of many types, but amongst them specimens of both the old and modern style. Mr H.J. Price of Long Ditton had an excellent team, his Ditton Brevity and Gaiety being particularly excellent, the one a blue and white, the other a tricolour. Mr Carew-Gibson of Fareham, in Grove Rose and Merry Belle, had a brace of beauties, also of the old type, and his first-named won chief prize; but other leading honours of third and reserve were given to miniature modern spaniels, both black, but certainly not like Rose and Brevity, that took first and second honours. Mr Phillips' Rivington Merry Legs was another of the pure strain, a black and white that I believe came from Exeter; and at the most recent Manchester show, that in 1897, the latter exhibitor benched a brace of beauties, Rivington Bee and Rivington Sue by Bruton Victor Busy, which won leading honours in their group.

I have particularly drawn attention to these classes at Manchester in proof, if such were needed, that there still remains material in the country to popularize the old-fashioned breed of cocker and I fancy this would soon be done would judges, in making their awards, stick to one type and throw out those dogs that showed unusually heavy bone, long bodies, heavy heads and over-sized ears. And I may go further than this and say that I never yet saw a good and perfectly characteristic cocker that had a flat coat, was entirely black, or of that bright liver colour found in the Sussex. The correct colours are a mixed roan, or a dull brown and white, or black and white and brown, but the latter have white on the chest and often enough white feet also. Mr J.F. Farrow of Ipswich owns an excellent strain of small black spaniels, one or two of which are of the cocker type of which I approve. Some of them are miniature specimens of the black field spaniel, and from which they are bred, but his Frank Obo, Ted Obo, and Lily Obo are quite of the correct old-fashioned type. Mr J.W. Caless, Shipston-on-Stour, Mr H. Singleton, Leamington Spa, and Miss F. Canham, Forest Gate, own some of the best specimens of the day, their Brutus, Floss, Ladas, and Liko Joko usually winning when they appear in the ring. In weight the cocker ought not to exceed 25 lb at the very most and bitches 20 lb or less are the desirable size. As I have already hinted, they should not be so high on the leg, so long in the body, so heavy in the ears, or so heavy in the muzzle as an ordinary field spaniel, and may be taken as sharp, active little creatures, always busy when at work, and especially smart in driving rabbits from a gorse covert or other rough place.'

The Cocker and the Stage

The cocker has also achieved success on the stage. Tuppenny of Ware made a name for himself in *The Barretts of Wimpole Street* at the Queen's Theatre, London, and whilst on tour Lupin of Ware and Restless of Ware made a great hit in the same part. When the film version was remade in 1957 by MGM, John Holmes' Flush appeared in the role.

Among our English novelists none appears to be such a great lover of the cocker as John Galsworthy, whose black cocker spaniel is commemorated in a delightfully illustrated book, *Memories*. The character of the cocker named John in the novel *The Country House* is one of the finest studies of a dog in our English literature.

The Kennel Club

The high standard the cocker spaniel has attained in the British Isles has been made possible by the Kennel Club, which was founded in April 1873. Its first home was Victoria Street, Westminster, but the headquarters at the present time is 1–4 Clarges Street, London W1Y 8AB. It is generally agreed that the world's first officially recognized dog show took place in Newcastle-upon-Tyne in 1859 and placings at that show are detailed in the first Kennel Club Stud Book. The first show held 'under the patronage of the Kennel Club' was at Crystal Palace in 1873, and very soon afterwards the first Kennel Club Stud Book was issued. It has continued to be published annually ever since.

A rule was then introduced that no dog could be exhibited at any show under the jurisdiction of the Kennel Club without it being registered, and that no registered dog could be shown at a non-authorized show.

About this time the Kennel Club began publishing the *Kennel Gazette*, which included a record of registrations, transfers, and all matters dealing with dogs. The current system is that a monthly edition of *Kennel Gazette* deals with administration, shows, etc., and a quarterly publication, the *Breed Records Supplement*, details all registrations, transfers, export pedigrees issued, Junior Warrant winners, etc. All these steps help to insure the dog world against the fraudulent exhibitor and breeder, and anyone found guilty of discreditable conduct in a matter arising out of dogs is rightly suspended from exhibiting or registering a dog.

The Kennel Club has in its possession trophies worth several thousand pounds, many of which are put up for competition annually. The work of the Kennel Club is of the greatest importance to the canine world and as a governing body its responsibility cannot be over-estimated.

Since that first one at Crystal Palace in 1873, the Kennel Club has continued to run a show annually with the exceptions of the war years and 1954 when an electrician's strike caused the show to be cancelled. Today the Kennel Club show is known as Crufts, and is held at Earls Court. When Charles Cruft died, Mrs Cruft decided to carry on. Later, when she retired, the Kennel Club was approached with a suggestion that it take over the show so that the name should be preserved. This was agreed, and today Crufts is the most famous show in the world.

The following is a list of the number of cocker spaniels registered annually at the Kennel Club since 1953:

1953	8,129	1970	7,121
1954	7,356	1971	6,825
1955	7,275	1972	8,255
1956	7,071	1973	8,193
1957	6,434	1974	8,254
1958	6,515	1975	7,210
1959	6,943	1976	3,336
1960	6,374	1977	2,256
1961	6,758	1978	6,310
1962	6,559	1979	9,415
1963	6,514	1980	9,891
1964	6,263	1981	8,009
1965	6,259	1982	7,697
1966	5,229	1983	8,064
1967	5,625	1984	6,235
1968	5,944	1985	7,619
1969	6,465	1986	7,121

Changes in the registration system whereby puppies may be recorded rather than registered (i.e. no name given to them) means that present-day figures are much understated when related to the number of pedigree cocker spaniel puppies born. The new system of registration/recording was brought in from April 1976.

2

History of the Colours: the Breed Standard

The History of the Particolours

Between the years 1850 and 1860 Mr Burdett owned a black and tan spaniel named Frank. He was mated to a black and white bitch called Venus, owned by Mr Mousley. This mating produced a dog named Bob, which our great authority, Mr H.S. Lloyd, states was the forerunner of the cocker spaniel as we know it on the show bench today. Most particoloured cockers as well as the blacks seem to have descended from the Obo strain. Mr C.A. Phillips, of the Rivington cockers, owned many blue roans and black and whites, including Champions Rivington Dazzle and Rivington Robena. The late Mr R. Lloyd bred a bitch Braeside Bizz which was mated to a black dog Viceroy. This pair appears to have possessed a lot of type, and the mating produced Braeside Bustle, who was one of the first dogs to transmit his blue roan colour regularly to his progeny. There are very few of the coloured cockers that cannot be traced back to this outstanding sire, and there is little doubt that his progeny laid the foundation of many of our leading dogs of today.

Between the year 1900 and the First World War, many good particolour cockers were bred. Mr De Courcy Peel, of the Bowdler strain, was well to the fore and owned a string of champions including Champion Ben Bowdler, who was sired by Braeside Bustle, also Champion Bob Bowdler, Champion Dixon Bowdler, and the great sire Champion Rufus Bowdler, who sprang into prominence at this time by siring three champions. Mr E.C. Spencer's Doony was another strain which helped the breed considerably. Doony Flirt was mated to Champion Ben Bowdler and this mating produced the blue roan Champion Doony Swell, who played a big part as a sire before the First World War. Mr Gordon George's Fairholme Rally has been marked by the memorable success he scored as a sire, giving his offspring length of head which was so much needed in the early days. Rally was also a conspicuous field trial winner. Another great dog which had a remarkable influence at stud was Corncrake. His sire was Dyrons Bluecoat and his dam Rocklyn Betsy. Corncrake was himself a certificate winner in 1916 and was also the sire of many certificate winners. Between the two world wars we were rich in particolours; one of the first well-known dogs of that period was Champion Fulmer Ben, who won no fewer than 20 Challenge Certificates; he was owned by Mrs Fytche. There was also Mr Dickinson's Southernwood Critic, who as an inmate of the Rocklyn Kennel caused a sensation by winning the cup two years following the Kennel Club Show for best dog of all breeds. Then we had Mr Lloyd's Champion Invader of Ware, who was one of the greatest show and stud dogs of all time. Invader not only sired hundreds of winners but stamped his progeny with his great personality to a marked degree.

The 'Of Ware' dogs dominated the 1930s with Challenge Certificates being won by Luckystar (31), Whoopee (56), Silver Templa (19), Sir Galahad (18), Masterman (6) and Whip Hand (4). From 1937 to 1939 the beautiful tricolour bitch Exquisite Model of Ware won 50 of the 61 bitch Challenge Certificates on offer before her career was cut short by the start of the war.

Lucky Star and Exquisite Model both achieved the top honour in dog showing by winning Best in Show at Crufts. Mr Lloyd wrote that Sir Galahad of Ware was the best dog he ever owned. Sir Galahad figures on both sides of nearly all the pedigrees of Challenge Certificate winning dogs since the war.

The Falconers strain owned by the late Mrs Jamieson Higgens took a very prominent place in the show world and did a great amount towards bringing the particolour up to its present-day standard. Mrs Jamieson Higgens was a great personality, whose passing left a grievous gap in the cocker world. Some of her best-known certificate winners were Falconers Chita, Spangle, Cowslip, Chance, Verdict, Clove, Caution, Confidence, and many others. The Falconers certificate winners followed one another without a break, all of which were home bred and had a definite individuality.

There was little breeding done between the years 1940 and 1945, when the war was in progress. Dog foods became very scarce, transport was difficult, and dog shows were few and far between; therefore many well-known kennels closed down during this period, but as soon as peace was declared everyone started breeding in a bigger way than ever before. To my mind the standard of the cocker today has improved considerably, and shows a marked advance on its predecessors of the show bench.

In the early years after the war, four kennels were outstanding with their particolours – Mr Lloyd's 'Of Ware'; Mr Alf Collins' 'Colinwood'; Mr Joe Braddon's 'Of Ide'; and Mrs Joyce Gold's 'Oxshott'. Tracey Witch of Ware, a blue roan bitch won 50 Challenge Certificates despite a break for maternal duties, and emulated her two pre-war predecessors by twice being Best in Show at Crufts. Ch. Oxshott Marxedes won 28 Challenge Certificates for Mrs Gold and proved to be a very successful sire. Mr Joe Braddon had a number of very high-quality champions, including the All-Breeds Best in Show winner, a striking black and white named Ch. Domino of Ide. The late Mr Collins will always be remembered for producing the first post-war champion – the lovely type black white and tan, Ch. Colinwood Cowboy. But amongst the many Colinwood champions, pride of place must go to Ch. Colinwood Silver Lariot with 57 Challenge Certificates – a record for a long time – and a number of Best in Show awards at Championship Shows.

Top winners in later years included Mrs Joyce Caddy's blue roan dog, International Champion Ouainé Chieftain, with 32 challenge Certificates, two All-Breed Championship Show Best in Show wins, and Crufts Reserve Best in Show in 1970 amongst his award (*see* Pedigree on pages 30–31); Mrs Denise Barney's Show Champion Cilleine Echelon whose 34 Challenge Certificates enabled him to overtake Chieftain as the top winning home-bred dog (*see* Pedigree on pages 32–33); and Mr Gordon Williams' blue roan bitch, Champion Bournehouse Starshine who eclipsed them all in winning 60 Challenge Certificates, and in addition was the dam of two champions.

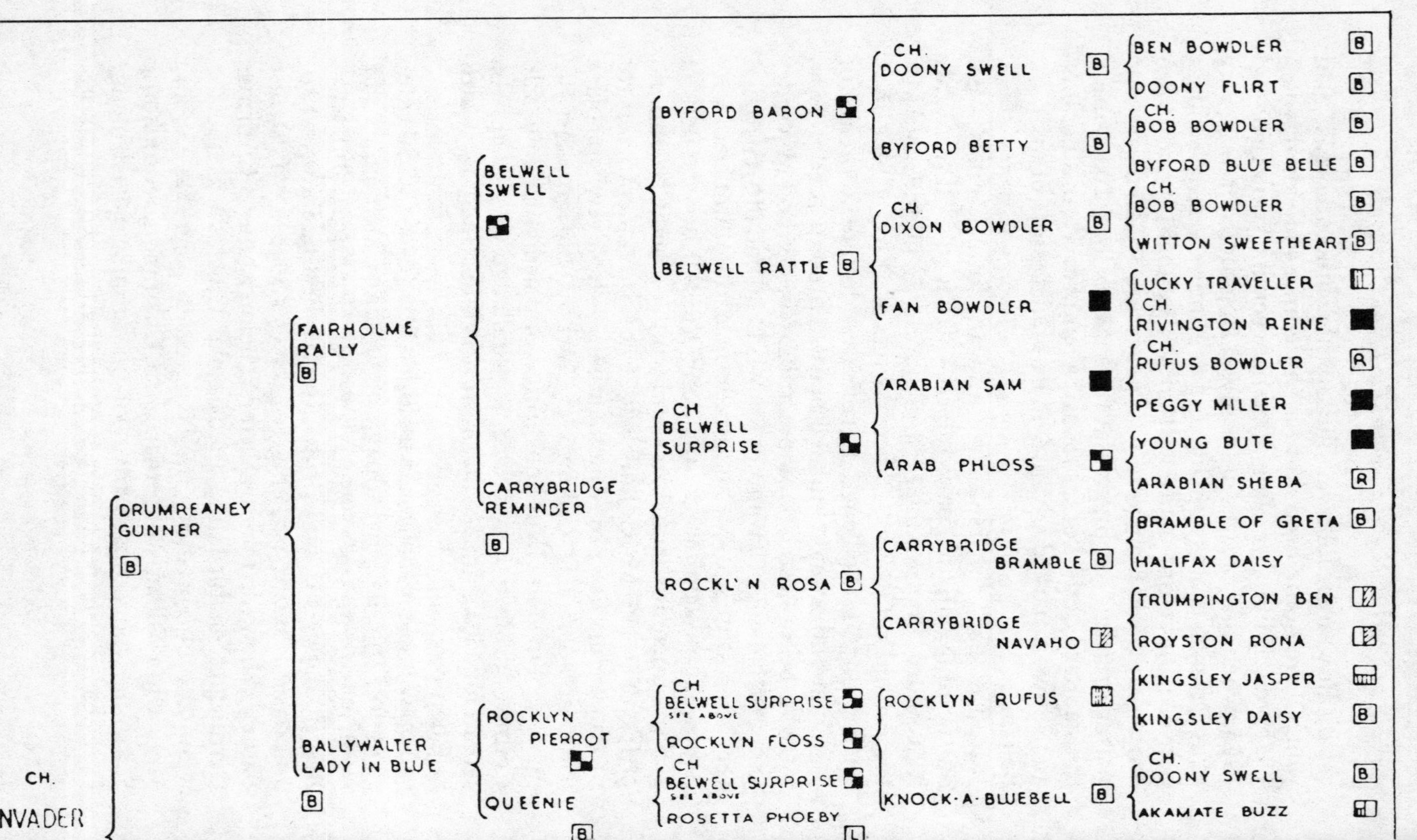
CH. INVADER
DRUMREANEY GUNNER B
FAIRHOLME RALLY B
BELWELL SWELL
BYFORD BARON
CH. DOONY SWELL B
BEN BOWDLER B
DOONY FLIRT B
BYFORD BETTY B
CH. BOB BOWDLER B
BYFORD BLUE BELLE B
BELWELL RATTLE B
CH. DIXON BOWDLER B
CH. BOB BOWDLER B
WITTON SWEETHEART B
FAN BOWDLER
LUCKY TRAVELLER
CH. RIVINGTON REINE
CARRYBRIDGE REMINDER B
CH BELWELL SURPRISE
ARABIAN SAM
CH. RUFUS BOWDLER R
PEGGY MILLER
ARAB PHLOSS
YOUNG BUTE
ARABIAN SHEBA R
ROCKL'N ROSA B
CARRYBRIDGE BRAMBLE B
BRAMBLE OF GRETA B
HALIFAX DAISY
CARRYBRIDGE NAVAHO
TRUMPINGTON BEN
ROYSTON RONA
BALLYWALTER LADY IN BLUE B
ROCKLYN PIERROT
CH BELWELL SURPRISE SEE ABOVE
ROCKLYN FLOSS
ROCKLYN RUFUS
KINGSLEY JASPER
KINGSLEY DAISY B
QUEENIE B
CH BELWELL SURPRISE SEE ABOVE
ROSETTA PHOEBY L
KNOCK-A-BLUEBELL B
CH. DOONY SWELL B
AKAMATE BUZZ

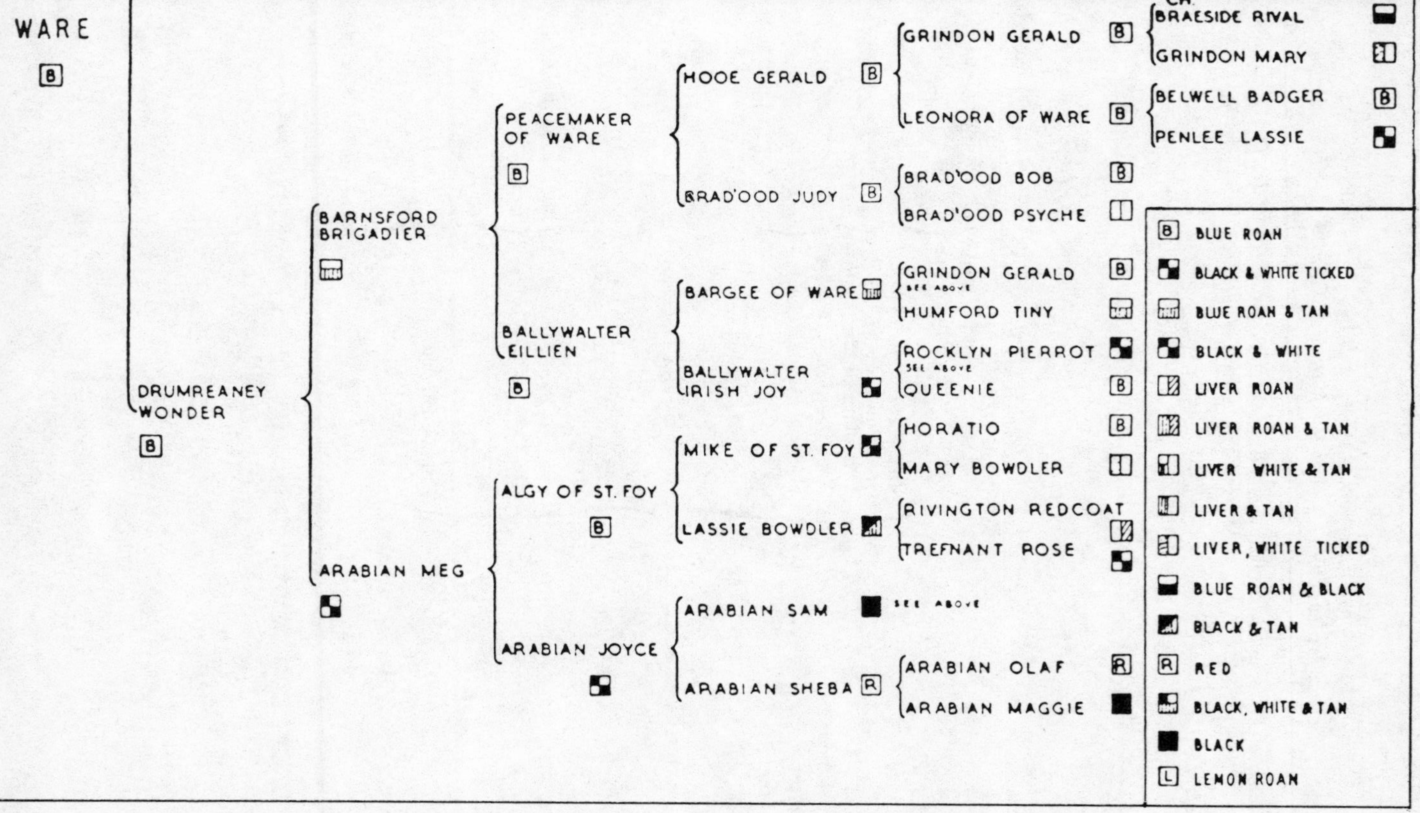
WARE
B
DRUMREANEY WONDER
B
BARNSFORD BRIGADIER
ARABIAN MEG
PEACEMAKER OF WARE
B
BALLYWALTER EILLIEN
B
ALGY OF ST. FOY
B
ARABIAN JOYCE
HOOE GERALD
B
BRAD'OOD JUDY
B
BARGEE OF WARE
BALLYWALTER IRISH JOY
MIKE OF ST. FOY
LASSIE BOWDLER
ARABIAN SAM
SEE ABOVE
ARABIAN SHEBA
R
GRINDON GERALD
B
LEONORA OF WARE
B
BRAD'OOD BOB
B
BRAD'OOD PSYCHE
GRINDON GERALD
SEE ABOVE
B
HUMFORD TINY
ROCKLYN PIERROT
SEE ABOVE
QUEENIE
B
HORATIO
B
MARY BOWDLER
RIVINGTON REDCOAT
TREFNANT ROSE
ARABIAN OLAF
R
ARABIAN MAGGIE
CH.
BRAESIDE RIVAL
GRINDON MARY
BELWELL BADGER
B
PENLEE LASSIE
B
BLUE ROAN
BLACK & WHITE TICKED
BLUE ROAN & TAN
BLACK & WHITE
LIVER ROAN
LIVER ROAN & TAN
LIVER WHITE & TAN
LIVER & TAN
LIVER, WHITE TICKED
BLUE ROAN & BLACK
BLACK & TAN
R
RED
BLACK, WHITE & TAN
BLACK
L
LEMON ROAN

PEDIGREE OF INT. CH. OUAINÉ CHIEFTAIN

Blue roan dog, born 1.2.1968. K.C.S.B. 856 BD
Winner of 32 C.C.s, 7 Gundog Groups, B.I.S. at SK.C.CH.
Show & Paignton Ch. Show, Res. B.I.S. Crufts 1970.
5 Green Stars, I.K.C. Cocker of the Year 1972

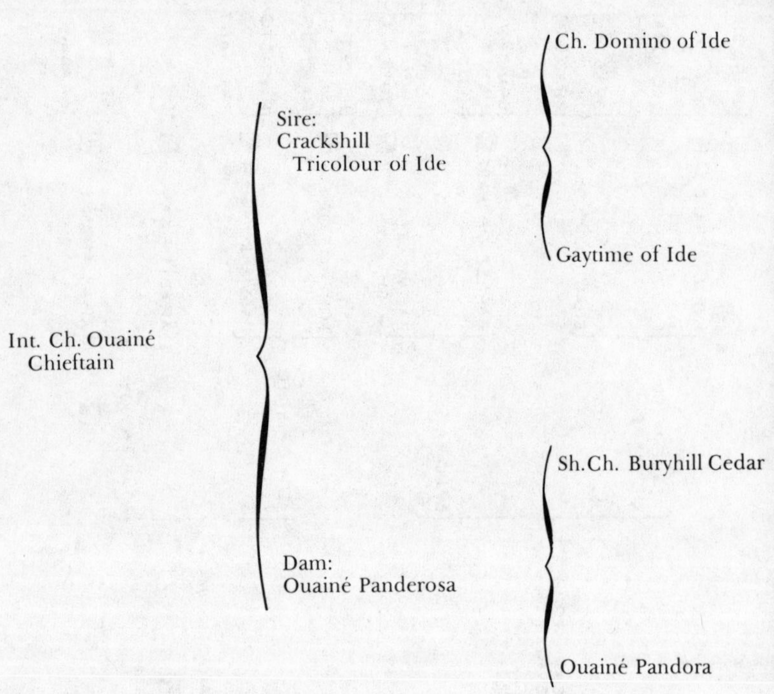

Dog	Parents	Grandparents
Ch. Blue Flash of Ide	Cartref Contender	Harley Courtier
		Cartref Gay Model
	Merryworth Mayflower	Lucky Shandy of Merryworth
		Falconers Coronation
Ch. Rodwood Lass of Sandover	Falconers Mark of Ware	Falconers Workman of Ware
		Falconers Wisdom
	Mareway Marie	Bramble Boy
		Bandoos Lucy Jane
Chayn Janitor	Nostrebor Chayn Weaver	Harley Sandylands Flare
		Chayn Falconers Bertha
	Chayn Jennifer Gay	Falconers Padlock of Ware
		Chayn Sally Peachum
Ch. Rodwood Lass of Sandover	Falconers Mark of Ware	Falconers Workman of Ware
		Falconers Wisdom
	Mareway Marie	Bramble Boy
		Bandoos Lucy Jane
Ch. Valstar Glow of Ide	Ch. Blue Flash of Ide	Cartref Contender
		Merryworth Mayflower
	Cobnar Mist	Cobnar Compact
		Margot of Wyngates
Sh.Ch. Darnmill Dolly Blue	Sh.Ch. Joywyns Blueboy of Ware	Fantee Silver Sentinel
		Cartref Charmer
	Darnmill Buryhill Pipistrelle	Oxshott Marxon
		Buryhill Phoenix
Sh.Ch. Dellah Merrymaker of Wykey	Sh.Ch. Joywyns Blueboy of Ware	Fantee Silver Sentinel
		Cartref Charmer
	Dellah Merry Maid of Wykey	Fop of Wykey
		Wildflower of Wykey
Ouainé Merry Melanie	S.Am.Ch. Thornfalcon Fanfare of Ware	Spellbinder of Ware
		Barings Taffeta of Thornfalcon
	Ouainé Vivid Fairy of Ware	Sh.Ch. Joywyns Blueboy of Ware
		Merry Flirt of Ware

PEDIGREE OF SH. CH. CILLEINE ECHELON

Blue roan dog, born 18.2.1980. K.C.S.B. 0451 BQ

Winner of 36 C.C.s,

5 Gundog Groups, Res. B.I.S. Belfast Ch. Show & Three Counties Ch. Show,

B.I.S. at 3 Gundog Ch. Shows

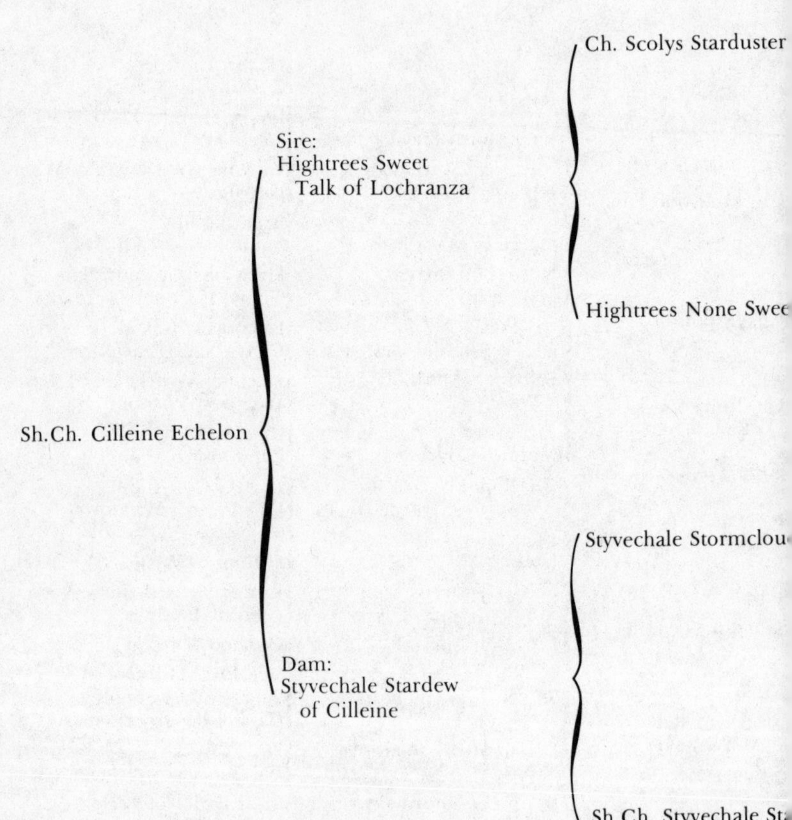

Goldenfields Minstrel Boy	Sh.Ch. Joywyns Blueboy of Ware	Fantee Silver Sentinel
		Cartref Charmer
	Goldenfields Merry Maiden	Mantop Merrylegs
		Goldenfields Merry Miss
Scolys Sweet Solera	Dellah Ouainé Reveller	Sh.Ch. Dellah Merrymaker of Wykey
		Ouainé Merry Melanie
	Scolys Set Fair	Scolys Simon
		Scolys Sagacity
Hightrees Leabank Lance Corporal	Hightrees Forty Secrets	Sh.Ch. Dellah Merrymaker of Wykey
		Hightrees Blue Flicker
	Leabank Blue Mist	Sh.Ch. Dellah Merrymaker of Wykey
		Freshet Flush
Hightrees Scotch Mist	Glencora Gilt Edge	Sh.Ch. Colinwood Cobbler
		Sealrock Skylark
	Hightrees Star Sheen	Hightrees Happy Wanderer
		Hightrees Iris
Sh.Ch. Normanview Thundercloud	Normanview Silver Waters	Normanview Blue Sultan
		Normanview Tricolour
	Normanview Silver Salver	Normanview Dark Knight
		Normanview Bluebird
Styvechale Silver Delight	Ch. Scolys Starduster	Goldenfields Minstrel Boy
		Scolys Sweet Solera
	Styvechale Sleighbells	Styvechale Courtdale Blue Ensign
		Styvechale Stargazer
Scolys Strike Lucky	Leabank Luckstone	Leabank Lexicon
		Leabank Linaria
	Scolys Sunday's Child	Sh.Ch. Courtdale Flag Lieutenant
		Scolys Sweet Solera
Styvechale Sleighbells	Styvechale Courtdale Blue Ensign	Sh.Ch. Courtdale Flag Lieutenant
		Courtdale Chinacraft
	Styvechale Stargazer	Kenricdene Cha Cha
		Styvechale Serana

Pedigree of Champion Invader of Ware

Invader is acknowledged as one of the best blue roan dogs ever, and as a sire was unsurpassed. As a show dog he was exhibited in 88 classes and won 88 First prizes and 12 Challenge Certificates. He worked well in the field, and qualified for his title with flying colours – a dog which will always stand out in cocker history. *See* Pedigree on pages 28–29.

The History of the Red Cocker

The late Mr C. A. Phillips, who was President of the Cocker Spaniel Club, imported in 1896 from America a red cocker named Canadian Red Jacket, and a black cocker Toronto, who also had red breeding in his pedigree. A daughter of Red Jacket was mated to Toronto, producing a black bitch Latcho, and it was through this combination of American blood that Mr and Mrs Trinder under the prefixes 'Arabian' and 'Northwick' produced several red cockers. They were further assisted in establishing a red strain by the use of an imported black dog Hampton Guard, who was bred from a red sire and black dam. At the end of the 1914 war, Mr E. E. Todd, who had been closely associated with Mr Trinder for several years prior to 1914, continued the 'Arabian' strain using Arabian Red Jay for his post-war foundation. In the period of 1920–30 a number of breeders became seriously interested in the development of the red cocker and considerable assistance in the standardization of the colour was given by the late Mr H. S. Lloyd's importation from Canada of the black cocker Broadcaster of Ware, an Obo descendant. His breeding cuts out about 25 years of English blood and goes directly back to the Obo strain. Broadcaster fully justified the wisdom of his importation by siring a big percentage of reds, and imparting supreme quality and type to his progeny, which helped considerably to popularize the red cocker.

Broadcaster was a direct descendant of the original Obo exported from this country to America, which I shall deal with in another chapter. Another dog which did great things for the red cocker was Mr H. S. Lloyd's imported American-bred Robinhurst of Ware. From this blood the majority of reds of today have originated. The enthusiasm of the earlier breeders led to the formation, in May 1928, of the Red and Golden Cocker Spaniel Club with a membership of 24. Mr E. E. Todd was elected secretary, a post he retained for many years. Before the formation of the club there was a fetish for the setter red colour, and it was not uncommon for the dogs of a lighter shade to be penalized at shows as 'poor coloured'. The title Red and Golden Cocker Spaniel Club overcame the prejudice against the golden specimens and there is little doubt that the varying shades did much to popularize the breed as a whole. Looking back over the years, one can appreciate the wisdom of the founders in accepting the standards laid down by the Cocker Club 26 years earlier, and confining themselves solely to the specialization of these colours, with the result that the present-day reds and goldens can hold their own in any colour classes. The club did much valuable work in guaranteeing separate colour classes at the principal open and championship shows, and up to 1929 provided red classes at Crufts confined to members.

Mention should be made of the various prefixes which contributed to the development of the present-day reds and some relevant details are given in the following paragraphs.

The 'Of Sauls' owned by Mrs Southern

The principal influencing red blood was obtained through Lady of Sauls, which was sired by the Canadian imported Broadcaster of Ware. Lady of Sauls mated to Herald of Ware produced Rufus of Sauls, who in turn sired Woodcock Ringleader and Billy of Byfleet, both of whom greatly contributed to the improvement of the reds.

The Lightwater prefix owned by Mrs Pelham Sutton

This strain also had a big say in reds, and comprised a mixture of Pinbrook, Dyrons and Broadcaster blood.

The 'Padsons' owned by Miss Stubberfield and Mrs Spencer

This kennel will be remembered by the black stud dog Joker of Padson, which was sired by Blackcock of Lightwater ex

Youlden Firefly. Joker of Padson was the sire of the famous Bazel Otto, who also sired many reds.

The Byfleet strain founded in 1926 by Mrs M. K. Acton

Mrs Acton purchased two red bitches, Golden Emblem of Byfleet, who was sired by Pinbrook Bungy ex Sunshine of Lightwater, and Owlsmoor Pimpernel by Broadcaster of Ware ex Echo Busy Bee. Mating Golden Emblem to Ottershaw Lorenza she bred Benjamin of Byfleet and Ottershaw Bingo. Owlsmoor Pimpernel was mated to Bovington Red Lacquer and Delia of Byfleet. Brae of Brambletye and Ottershaw Pimpernel resulted from these matings. Mrs Acton later mated Owlsmoor Pimpernel to Rufus of Sauls and bred Billy of Byfleet, who in turn was mated to a bitch Sporting Susan, who had Robinburst of Ware blood on both sides. This produced Daffodil of Byfleet. It was then decided to try to make an improvement in the heads of the reds, so Daffodil was mated to the blue Luckystar of Ware, who possessed red blood coming through his grandfather Invader of Ware, Invader's granddam Arabian Meg being bred through two generations of Arabian Reds. Two reds, Stardust of Byfleet (winner of five Challenge Certificates) and Lodestar of Sorrelsun, resulted from the Luckystar and Daffodil mating. Lodestar of Sorrelsun was mated to Fay of Sorrelsun and produced Cleo of Byfleet, winner of three Challenge Certificates. Fay was by Woodcock Ringleader out of Benita of Byfleet, who was by Benjamin of Byfleet out of Delia of Byfleet. The offspring of the aforementioned dogs were interbred with occasional outcross matings to Woodcock Ebony, Waldiff Copper, and Treetops Talkie, and produced a large number of winners, including Deidre of Byfleet, Cara of Byfleet, Maro of Byfleet, Golden Glory of Byfleet, Jeanette of Byfleet and Beauty of Byfleet, Ottershaw Inego and Ottershaw Cedar, etc.

The Dorswick cockers founded in 1929 by Mrs Wicks

Mrs Wicks obtained from Mrs Acton Jeanette of Byfleet ex Barbara of Byfleet and Golden Glory of Byfleet by Lodestar of Sorrelsun ex Deidre of Byfleet as her foundation stock. Jeanette of Byfleet mated to Treetops Tenor produced Treetops Tarentella, dam of Treetops Taurus and Treetops

Tyrian, and from a mating to Treetops Trivet produced Alpheus of Dorswick and Frolic of Dorswick. Alpheus mated to Golden Glory of Byfleet produced Daylight of Dellcroft (dam of Treetops Torchbearer) and Armida of Dorswick, dam of Treetops Turkey Trot, one of the foundation bitches of the Lochranza strain. Alpheus was also the sire of Aingarth Daffodil, foundation bitch of the Aingarth strain. Frolic of Dorswick was the dam of Golden Miller of Dorswick, founder of the Donnett strain. Among other well-known dogs bred in the kennels were Brynful Barka, Treetops Tender, winner of three Challenge Certificates, Treetops Truculent and Treetops Traveller, C.A.C. winners, France; Sixshot Peggy Puffin, Germany, and Sixshot Sugar Bird, etc. Ten generations were bred under the Dorswick prefix, and the breeding was confined to dogs possessing the same blood-lines as the foundation dogs of the Byfleet strain. Mrs Wicks had not been seen in the show ring for some years until she made a very successful 'come back' in 1952 with her red dog Dorswick Golden Feather, a son of Sixshot Woodywoodpecker, who quickly won his junior warrant.

Prefixes of some of the Red and Golden Breeders, 1922–39, who did so much towards the success and popularity that the red and golden cocker of today has achieved:

Arabian	Mr E. E. Todd	Ottershaw	Mr W. S. Hunt
Beaunash	Mrs Cluckie	Overdale	Mr J. G. Abell
Bethersden	Mrs Adams	Padson	Miss Stubberfield and Mrs Spencer
Brambletye	Mrs R. Gow		
Dellcroft	Mrs L. Childs	Pinbrook	Mr W. H. Edwards
Dorswick	Mrs Wicks	Rivoli	Mr Bridgford
Garnes	Mr A. G. Dickinson	Rydals	Mr Oldfield
Heydown	Miss Carnegie	Walcott	Miss A. S. Pryce
Machars	Miss Tory Edgar	Waldiff	Mrs Shakespeare
Merok	Mr and Mrs McKinney	Ware	Mr H. S. Lloyd
		Woodcock	Mrs McIntyre

In post-war years, amongst the most successful kennels breeding red cockers have been:

Broomleaf	The late Mrs Kay Doxford (now Miss Poppy Becker)
Bryansbrook	Mr and Mrs Bryan Fosbrook
Kavora	Miss Pam Trotman
Lochdene	Mrs Patricia Shaw
Lochranza	Miss Joan Macmillan and Mrs Jean Gillespie
Noslien	Miss Pat Neilson (previously in partnership with her late mother)
Sorbrook	Mrs Jean Smith
Treetops	Mrs Judy de Casembroot

as well as the Sixshot kennels belonging to the author.

The names of the great dogs which spring quickly to mind are Champion Broomleaf Bonny Lad of Shillwater, Show Champion Lochranza Dancing Master, and Show Champion Sixshot Woodywoodpecker, all of whom had a great influence on the breed through their progeny. Mrs de Casembroot's Treetops Turtle Dove born in 1937 is still the only red to have a Championship Show All Breeds Best in Show award to her credit.

In the 1970s Show Champion Kavora Merryborne Sweet Martini, bred by Mrs Irene Martin and owned by Miss Pam Trotman had a wonderful run, winning 19 Challenge Certificates before illness brought her show career to a premature end. Of late years quality at the top has been so high that many dogs have shared top honours. A red dog, Bryansbrook High Society, best of breed at Crufts in 1980, sold by Mr and Mrs Fosbrook to Mr Eugene Phoa in Canada, attained the official No. 2 cocker spot in Canada and No. 4 in the USA.

Some of the Noted Blacks

Dominorum D'Arcy, although 50 per cent particolour bred, sired only three particolours, all of which were Challenge Certificate winners, namely, Dame Fortune of Ware, Apex of Ware, and Charleston Lyric.

There is little doubt that D'Arcy was the key to the present-day blacks. His daughter Dunford Judy mated to Joker of Padson produced the great Bazel Otto. Otto was mated to Felbrigg Hortensia and the litter resulting produced Treetops Treasure Trove, the foundation of the Treetops cockers. In turn Treasure Trove was mated to Woodcock Ringleader and this mating produced Treetops Talkie and Treetops Trivet.

Treetops Talkie mated to Treetops Treasury produced Treetops Terrific. Sixshot Mavis was also mated to Bazel Otto. This mating produced Sixshot Brown Owl, who, when mated to Treetops Terrific, produced Sixshot Black Swan. The above dogs had practically all the say in the pre-war blacks.

In general it took some years for them to catch up with the other colours in quality, although champions were produced by Mrs Gold (Oxshott), Miss Macmillan (Lochranza), Mr and Mrs Hill (Rafborn), Mrs de Casembroot (Treetops), the author's bitch, Sh. Ch. Sixshot Sugar Bird, and Miss Hahn (Misbourne). Later in the 1950s came the Astrawin winning blacks, and by this time it was not possible to say that any colour produced the best specimens. Miss Macmillan's Show Champion Lochranza Strollaway, who won 19 Challenge Certificates, was Reserve Best in Show at Cruft's in 1969, and his then record number of Challenge Certificates for a black was beaten by Show Champion Roanwood Ripple with 25 Challenge Certificates. This number has been surpassed by Sh. Ch. Quettadene Emblem (*see* Pedigree on pages 42–43), but still remains the record number of Challenge Certificates for a black bitch. Ripple unfortunately died in pregnancy whilst still young. In 1984 Mrs May Snary (Platonstown) won the Best in Show award at Belfast Championship Show with Show Champion Platonstown Scooby Doo.

It is surprising how much more heavily coated some of the present blacks are than the other colours, and the practice of some of the newer exhibitors to present their dogs in what older exhibitors would call an over-coated state has been one of the notable changes in recent years. Many of the older exhibitors do not approve.

Pedigree of Sixshot Black Swan

Sixshot Black Swan, I think I can rightly say, was one of the best black dogs ever. His brilliant show career was cut short by the outbreak of war. He came from a line of very famous bitches, and made a great name as a stud dog. Figuring in most of the whole colour pedigrees of today, he was home-bred, and owned by me until his death in 1951, at the age of 12½ years (*see* Pedigree on page 40).

PEDIGREE OF SIXSHOT BLACK SWAN

Black dog, born 18.8.1937. K.C.S.B. 397 VV

Winner of I.C.C. in 1939

Sixshot Black Swan	Sire: Treetops Terrific	Treetops Talkie	Woodcock Ringleader	Rufus of Sauls
				Sunflower of Lightwater
			Treetops Treasure Trove	Bazel Otto
				Felbrigg Hortensia
		Treetops Treasury	Oxshott Barilo	Oxshott Boreas
				Tynker of Oxshott
			Treetops Treasure Trove	Bazel Otto
				Felbrigg Hortensia
	Dam: Sixshot Brown Owl	Bazel Otto	Joker of Padson	Blackcock of Lightwater
				Youlden Firefly
			Dunford Judy	Dominorum D'Arcy
				Ottershaw Beauty
		Sixshot Mavis (later became Treetops Temptress and Dam of Treetops Turtle Dove)	Woodcock Ringleader	Rufus of Sauls
				Sunflower of Lightwater
			Sixshot Ring Ouzel	Woodcock Othello
				Sixshot Bunting

The History of the Black and Tan Cocker

The original colour of the cocker spaniel was either black and tan or liver and tan. In those early days blacks were rare, and it was considered a great achievement when a whole litter of blacks were bred. The late Mr R. Lloyd, father of Mr H. S. Lloyd, owned a black and tan dog named Little Prince, who was, incidentally, the sire of the first champion owned by the 'Of Ware' Kennels, although in those days the suffix 'Of Ware' had not been adopted. For many years the black and tan lost favour with the exhibitor, and very few were seen at the shows, until Mrs Doxford brought out the bitch which was aptly named Broomleaf Black and Tan, a daughter of Champion Broomleaf Bonny Lad of Shillwater, out of the blue roan and tan Butterfly of Broomleaf. From her first appearance in the ring, Black and Tan became the subject of much criticism and caused quite a sensation when she won her first Challenge Certificate at the Richmond Championship Show in 1949. At the time of the Show, Black and Tan was already in whelp to Oxshott Pendarcye, a mating which was expected to produce a black and tan, as Pendarcye carries coloured blood. The litter resulted in six all blacks, which at the time was somewhat disappointing. However, one of the black dogs was retained and named Black Friar of Broomleaf. It was felt he would undoubtedly sire some puppies of his dam's colour, but, alas, his first four bitches failed to produce a black and tan; his fifth bitch was a red by Eros of Padson, and from this mating two black and tans turned up, which was a great joy. His next bitch was Blanchfleur of Broomleaf, a daughter of Blare of Broomleaf. She also produced two of this elusive colour; one dog was retained and named Brainwave of Broomleaf, who did so well at Crufts in 1952, competing against all colours. The day is not far distant when we shall see many of this fascinating colour in the show ring. I feel that to see this colour at its best, they should be in a class of their own. Who knows? In years to come perhaps they will become as popular as the reds, who have made such great headway in recent years.

In 1972 and 1973 a black and tan bitch owned by Mrs I. Robinson, Rivermist Tango Royale, won two Reserve Challenge Certificates, and in 1987 at the Border Union

PEDIGREE OF SH. CH. QUETTADENE EMBLEM

Black dog, born 30.4.1983 K.C.S.B. 0705 BT
Winner of 27 C.C.s, 4 Gundog Groups,
Res. B.I.S. Blackpool Ch. Show 1985,
B.I.S. Gundog Breeds of Scotland Ch.Show.

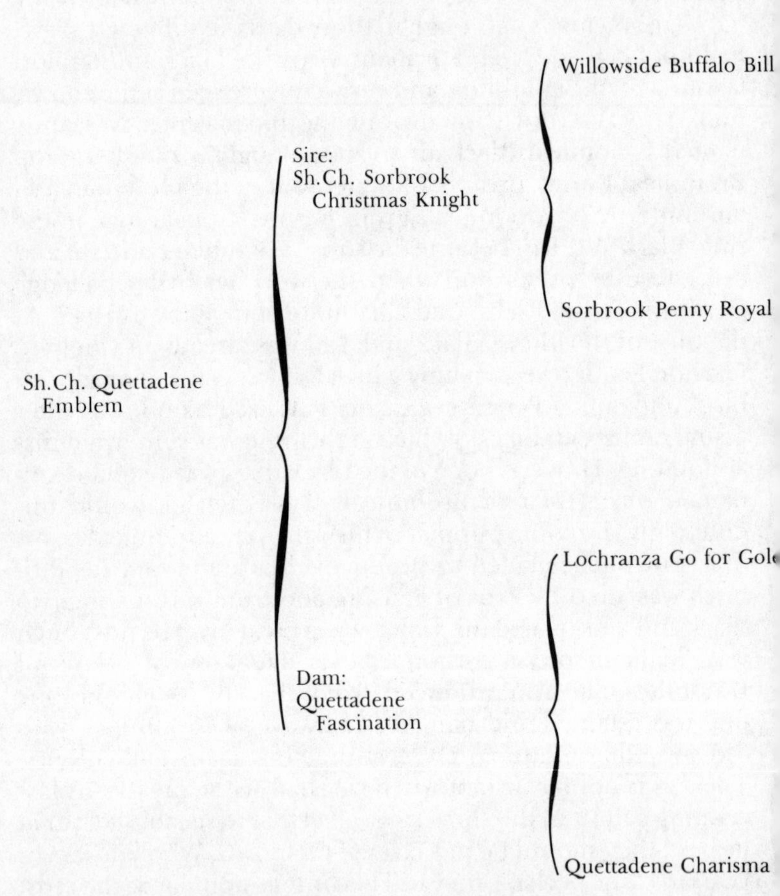

Sorbrook Boomerang	Sh.Ch. Lochdene Sorbrook Sundowner	Sunglint of Sorbrook Butterkist of Sorbrook
	Sorbrook Black Pepper	Astrawin April Night Quettadene Bernadette
Sh.Ch. Burnished Gold of Bryansbrook	Sunglint of Sorbrook	Cornbow Manfred Quettadene Bernadette
	Colinwood Spun Gold	Colinwood Peregrine Golden Shrew of Lochnell
Sh.Ch. Sorbrook Beechnut	Sh.Ch. Janeacre Night Skipper of Helenwood	Sunglint of Sorbrook Janeacre Maid Marion of Lochnell
	Sorbrook Sweet Pepper	Butterprint of Broomleaf Sorbrook Black Pepper
Sorbrook Blackberry	Norw.Ch. Kavora Night Sky	Sh.Ch. Janeacre Night Skipper of Helenwood Kavora January Jane
	Sh.Ch. Sorbrook Holly Berry	Lochranza Quettadene Diplomat Quettadene Bernadette
Lochranza Country Squire	Lochranza Farmers Lad of Merrylake	Sh.Ch. Lochranza Farmers Boy Jossa Tanyita
	Lochranza Sweet Rosalie	Sh.Ch. Janeacre Night Skipper of Helenwood Glowhill Nutmeg
Lochranza Patricia	Sh.Ch. Lochranza Newsprint	Butterprint of Broomleaf Sh.Ch. Lochranza Bittersweet
	Lochranza Santa Maria	Sh.Ch. Lochranza Dancing Master Sh.Ch. Lochranza Peelers Legal Love
Cordura Barbarloo	Sonic Sandmark	Lochranza Quettadene Diplomat Hightrees Bright Dawn
	Hightrees Daisy Chain	Sh.Ch. Quettadenes Mark Hightrees Ring o Roses
Quettadene Remembrance	Quettadene Golden Miller of Glowhill	Sunglint of Sorbrook Quettadene Little Toff
	Cornbow Tantalizer	Sorbrook Boomerang Mint Toes of Cornbow

Championship Show, a black and tan dog owned by Mr K. B. and Mrs B. Taylor, Kendrick Surprise Surprise, won the dog Reserve Challenge Certificate.

It is interesting to note that one of the top stud dogs of the mid-1980s, the black Show Champion Quettadene Emblem, owned by Mrs Penny Lester, sired quite a number of black and tan puppies.

The Standard and its uses

The standard of the cocker laid down by the Kennel Club is indispensable, as it indicates to the beginner what points to breed for, but the best education for the novice is to attend Championship Shows, where one can see good dogs in the flesh and study the points of each one individually. The novice breeder may have a small kennel of useless specimens, but perhaps one is very much better than the others. He becomes impressed with this one dog, the pick of a poor bunch, and if he never sees a better elevates him into a standard. So many

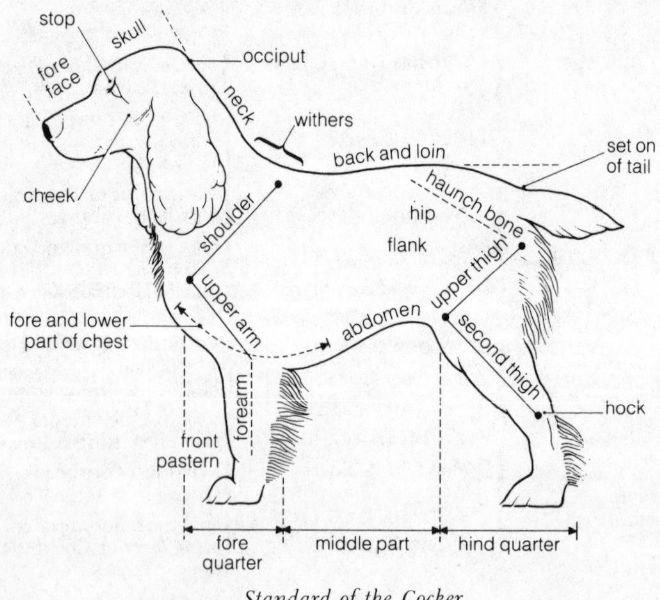

Standard of the Cocker

novice breeders never see beyond the head, but a good head alone will do little towards gaining top honours in the show ring. The novice will do well to study the points closely. If your dog fails badly in one of them he will not go very high in the prize list. Much money and precious time will have been wasted in travelling the country to the various shows. When the novice is making a start in building up his stock he must have in mind the type he aims at. Among show dogs of today there is a wide diversity of type, which is an advantage. Therefore you can win with a cocker provided it complies with the Standard, even though it retains the marked individuality of your own individual strain. You can often sit at the ringside and pick out the progeny of a well-known stud dog, as some have the happy knack of stamping their own particular attributes; it is a great advantage, if the said dog is the type desired. There are different types within the limits of the Standard. We get the masculine short cobby type and the feminine racy type; a dog which has type is not always perfect, but embodies much of the ideal cocker. Type is most difficult to define; you have only to look at the interpretation of the Standard as seen by different judges and if you follow their placings you will see one favours the short cobby masculine cocker, whereas another will go for the feminine racy one. All this will no doubt appear very complicated to the novice, but if he makes a study of judging it will soon become clear.

Standard Points of the Cocker Spaniel

When in 1981, the Kennel Club decided to bring all breed standards into the same format, the chairman of the Breed Standards sub-committee wrote that his committee felt that the purpose of a Standard is not to enable a person who has never seen a specimen of the breed in question to know exactly what that dog looks like. A Standard should be a guide to help the person who has some familiarity with dogs in general and the breed in particular. In its most simple form a Standard is an elementary description of the breed, pointing out the qualities (characteristics) that make the breed unique. It indicates certain areas (sometimes with respect to general canine soundness) where judges should be alert for problems.

From 1 July 1988, Kennel Club Regulations provide that: 'Judges at Kennel Club Licensed shows must judge in accordance with Kennel Club Breed Standards.' (NB: Licensed Shows are Championship, Open, Limited, Sanction, Primary, Matches and Exemption.)

The Standard by itself is an important guide, but in presupposing knowledge by the reader, it leaves the need for a fuller explanation. So, with the kind permission of the Kennel Club, the Standard is reproduced here, with explanatory comments. We are grateful to the Spaniel Club Français for their ready co-operation in allowing us to use diagrams from their excellent publication, *L'English Cocker Spaniel – Standard et Commentaires Illustrés* to illustrate the amplification of points in the Standard.

General Appearance Merry, sturdy, sporting; well balanced; compact, measuring approximately same from withers to ground as from withers to root of tail.

Characteristics Merry nature with ever-wagging tail shows a typical bustling movement, particularly when following scent, fearless of heavy cover.

Temperament Gentle and affectionate, yet full of life and exuberance.

Head and Skull Square muzzle, with distinct stop set midway between tip of nose and occiput. Skull well developed, cleanly chiselled, neither too fine nor too coarse. Cheek bones not prominent. Nose sufficiently wide for acute scenting power.

Eyes Full, but not prominent. Dark brown or brown, never light, but in the case of liver, liver roan, and liver and white, dark hazel to harmonize with coat; with expression of intelligence and gentleness but wide awake, bright and merry; rims tight.

Ears Lobular, set low on a level with eyes. Fine leathers extending to nose tip. Well clothed with long straight silky hair.

Mouth Jaws strong with a perfect, regular and complete scissor bite, i.e. upper teeth closely overlapping lower teeth and set square to the jaws.

Neck Moderate in length, muscular. Set neatly into fine sloping shoulders. Clean throat.
Forequarters Shoulders sloping and fine. Legs well-boned, straight, sufficiently short for concentrated power. Not too short to interfere with tremendous exertions expected from this grand, sporting dog.
Body Strong, compact. Chest well-developed and brisket deep; neither too wide nor too narrow in front. Ribs well sprung. Loin short, wide and firm, level topline gently sloping downwards from end of loin to set on of tail.
Hindquarters Wide, well rounded, very muscular. Legs well-boned, good bend of stifle, short below hock allowing for plenty of drive.
Feet Firm, thickly padded, cat-like.
Tail Set on slightly lower than line of back. Must be merry in action and carried level, never cocked up. Customarily docked but never too short to hide, nor too long to interfere with the incessant merry action when working.
Gait/Movement True through action with great drive covering ground well.
Coat Flat, silky in texture, never wiry or wavy, not too profuse and never curly. Well-feathered forelegs, body and hindlegs above hocks.
Colour Various. In self colours no white allowed except on chest.
Size Height approximately: Dogs 39–41 cm (15½–16 in); Bitches 38–39 cm (15–15½ in). Weight approximately: 28–32 lb (61.6–70.4 kg).
Faults Any departure from the foregoing points should be considered a fault and the seriousness with which the fault should be regarded should be in exact proportion to its degree.
Note Male animals should have two apparently normal testicles fully descended into the scrotum.

General appearance

This details the general attributes necessary to make up the typical cocker spaniel. The 'merry' cocker is the description most generally applied to the breed, and the happy temperament should be a MUST whether the dog fufils his original rôle as a gundog, is a show dog, or a loved and loving family pet. It is as a gundog that he must have a sturdy frame enabling him to work all day in rough cover and to pick up and carry a heavy cock pheasant or hare. His sporting instincts should be shown by his readiness to follow scents when he is out in the fields.

Balance is an all-important feature. Each part must blend with the others, and be in proportion. A very long neck and a very short body will never look right, or a heavy body with light-boned legs. The approximate measurements conform with the appearance of a balanced dog. The aim is a compact, symmetrical dog, measuring roughly the same from the withers to the ground as from the withers to the root of the tail – a big dog in a small frame – with freedom of movement and as close an approximation as possible, in points of conformation, to the Breed Standard.

Typical Cocker Spaniel

Ted Obo

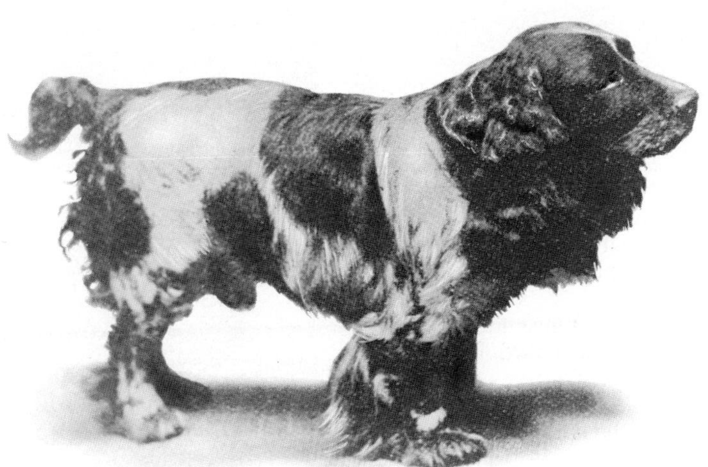

Braeside Bustle

Thomas Fall

Sixshot Black Swan

Thomas Fall

Ch. Broomleaf Bonny Lad of Shillwater

Above: The Sixshots
Bronze Turkey, Goldfinch, Black Grouse, Black Swan and Brown Owl

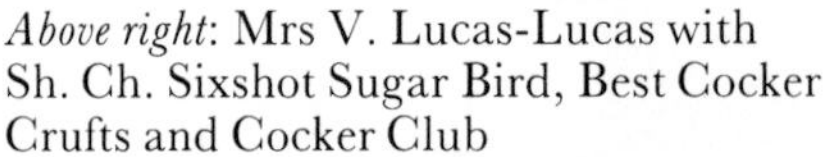

Above right: Mrs V. Lucas-Lucas with Sh. Ch. Sixshot Sugar Bird, Best Cocker Crufts and Cocker Club

Right: Sixshot the Black Cockatoo

Sh. Ch. Sixshot Woodywoodpecker

F. W. Simms

Ch. Oxshott Marxedes

Thomas Fall

The Of Wares

Cavalier Mark Marcus of Akron Countess Chloe Tracey Witch Hyperion

Characteristics

This again stresses the need for an outgoing happy dog. It is a pleasure to see a cocker working and enjoying his work. His tail never stops and it is clear to anyone that his original instincts still remain.

It would be unreasonable to expect any dog in the restricted conditions of a show ring to exhibit the same bubbling enthusiasm, although there are quite a lot which demonstrate their enjoyment with their tails. Nevertheless in the show ring they should move with freedom and with tail action. The clamped tail is untypical and is usually heavily penalised.

Temperament

As the Standard says, this should be gentle and affectionate, without being subdued in any way. The cocker is a dog who loves everybody – and expects everybody to love him.

Head and skull

The head and skull should be balanced, with equal distance between nose and stop, and stop and occiput. The stop should be well defined, but the frontal bones above the eyes should

Typical head and skull, showing good eye and expression

not be over prominent. The muzzle should be square, with good width of nasal bone and good width of nostril–necessary for the scenting power used when working. The skull and forehead should be well developed, without being in any way coarse. The width of the muzzle should be about the same as at the cheek bones.

A 'snipy' or weak muzzle is not desirable.

Eyes

The Standard is quite full and descriptive. It is a common misconception that a cocker spaniel has sad or soulful eyes. In actual fact it should have a sweet expression with very expressive eyes reflecting intelligence, kindliness, brightness, happiness, or on occasions, sadness.

Light coloured eyes are undesirable. So too are slack eye-rims, showing haw.

Correct balance of muzzle and skull

Muzzle longer than skull

Muzzle shorter than skull

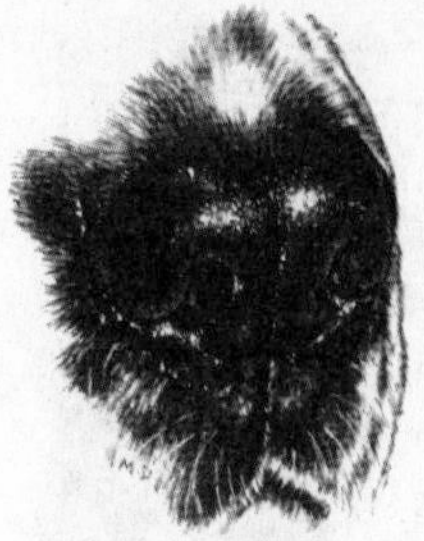

Good width of nostril

Eye too prominent

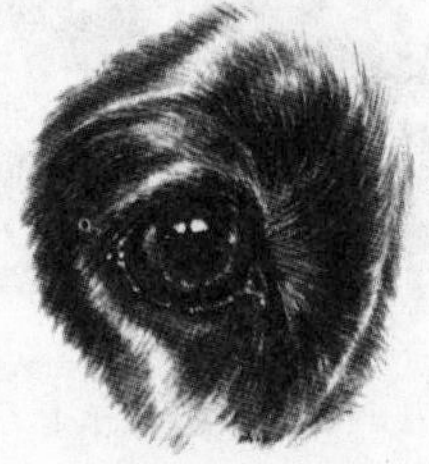

Typical eye and expression

Eye too small

Neck

The moderate length neck should be muscular, giving the dignified head carriage which is so desirable – except when hunting. When working, the cocker needs the strong neck muscles in order to be able to carry a bird or other game well above the ground.

The word 'moderate' again emphasises the need for balance. An overlong neck will result in a lessening in the strength of the muscles, and the ability to carry heavy weights. An overshort neck will usually go along with straight or upright shoulders.

There should be an absence of loose skin in the throat.

Ears

The leather of the ear should reach the tip of the nose when held loosely against the cheeks. A fully mature dog will have quite a length of feathering giving a fringe at the end of the ears, thus making the ears look longer. The ears should be set on low, on a level with the eyes, but when a dog is excited, or interested in something happening a distance away, he may carry his ears high, even though the set-on is correct.

Ears correctly set and well feathered

Ears too high set

Ears too low set

Mouth

The correct bite is regarded as being of great importance by most judges, i.e. the scissor bite (where the upper teeth closely overlap the lower teeth). Undershot mouths (when the lower jaw is longer than the top), or overshot (when the top jaw is longer than the bottom jaw), are inherited faults which it is difficult to breed out.

In a few countries there is a requirement for a full set of 42 teeth, but it is not normal for them to be counted in Great Britain.

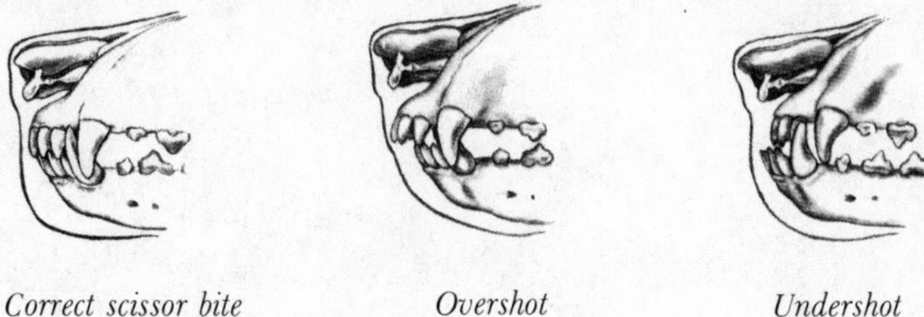

Correct scissor bite *Overshot* *Undershot*

Forequarters

The shoulders are made up of the shoulder-blade (the scapula) and the upper arm (humerus). These should be well laid back, i.e. sloping backwards and forming almost a right angle to one another. With a reasonable length of upper forearm, the front legs are set well under the body. If the angle at which the bones are set is too great, the result is straight shoulders, causing a reduced length of stride, and faulty front movement. It is commonly believed that a straight or upright shoulder is a very difficult fault to breed out.

At the withers, the blades should be fairly close together (i.e. there is an inward slope of the scapula as well as a backward one) – but not too close to interfere with free movement. If

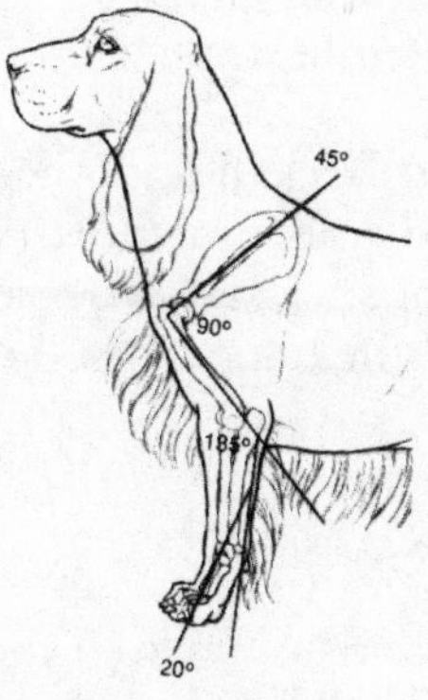

Correct angulation

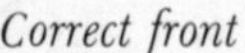

Correct front

Too narrow in front

Too wide in front

they are wide apart, short upright shoulder blades are usually present.

The bone in the front legs should be round, substantial and straight, with firm pasterns. The elbows should not be loose, and the front legs must be set far enough apart to allow a reasonable amount of heart room.

Body

This should be compact and deep with well-sprung ribs, and broad and strong in the loin, with the ribs running well back to the loin. There should be an appearance of concentrated power – the big dog in the small frame. The topline should be firm and level, with a gentle slope from the end of the loin to the root of the tail.

In calling for a short-backed cocker, it should be emphasised that this does not mean a short-ribbed dog. The ribs enclose the engine house of the dog, and they must allow adequate expansion of the lungs. The short coupling refers to the length of the loin.

Hindquarters

The cocker must have substantial, well-muscled hindquarters, with good second thighs. The hindquarters provide the propelling power and drive when the dog is in motion. He must

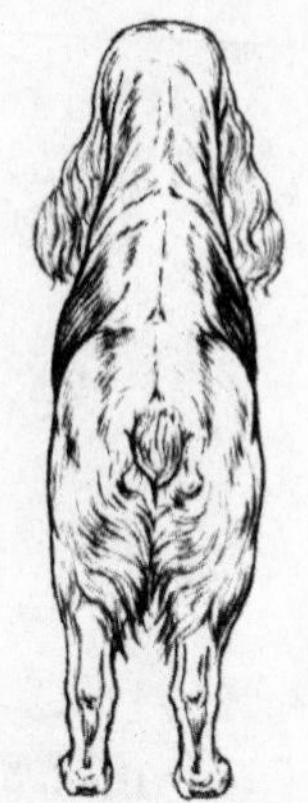

Well-developed body

Too flat in ribs

Good hindquarters

Too wide in hindquarters

Too narrow in hindquarters

Good bend of stifle and short below the hock

Too straight in stifle

Sickle hock

never appear to be pulled forward by his front legs. Viewed from the side, there should be a good width of thigh, and well-bent stifles. The hock should be set on fairly low. The lower legs should be vertical when viewed from the side or the back. A narrow back end is highly undesirable, and coupled as it usually is with straight stifles, will inevitably affect movement and drive.

Feet

These should be firm, round, thickly padded, and never large or spreading, or loose-jointed.

Tail

The tail is a very important part of the cocker – it is the one feature which encourages the description of a 'merry' cocker. It should be constantly in action, wagging joyfully. When working it is lovely to see a dog get onto the scent of game, and this is reflected by the incessant wagging, showing the dog's enjoyment of what he is doing.

The tail should be carried on a level with the back. A high tail carriage spoils the outline of the dog when moving, and a 'tucked' tail is not compatible with the merriness that is so necessary in the breed.

There is nowadays a lot of controversy over docking. Most exhibitors are in favour, but a genuine minority feel that it should not be allowed. In the Breed Standard, docking is now

Correct set-on of tail

Too low tail set

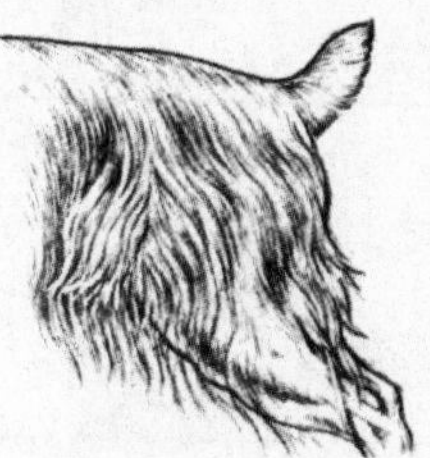

Too high tail set

optional, though it is at present most unusual to see an undocked dog in the show ring. Most people who use their cockers for working, particularly in heavy undergrowth, feel that a long tail would be detrimental to the dog. This is not a problem confined to Great Britain. From late 1988, undocked cockers will not be able to be shown in Norway.

Gait/Movement

A cocker should move with both front and back legs parallel. The legs should be straight and should not turn in or out. There should be a reasonable width between the legs, i.e. not 'two pegs from one hole', or too far apart.

A side view shows the drive or power which is generated by the hindquarters with a good length of stride. There should be a full extension forwards of the front leg, and backwards of the back leg on one stride, and a full extension backwards of the front leg and forwards of the back leg on the next. This should result in the front and hind legs on one side being fully extended, and on the other almost coming together.

This should be distinguished from a shorter, possibly bustling stride of a dog not correctly made at one end.

Movement shows up many faults: pin-toes, out at elbows, weak pasterns, wide fronts, narrow fronts, close behind, cow hocks, sickle hocks, etc. A dog that is correctly made should move correctly.

Topline is another feature which can be judged more easily in movement. Whilst non-level topline is sometimes due to lack of condition, it is usually caused by faulty construction. It should be remembered that a cocker should maintain a level topline on the move – not a sloping topline like his American cousin.

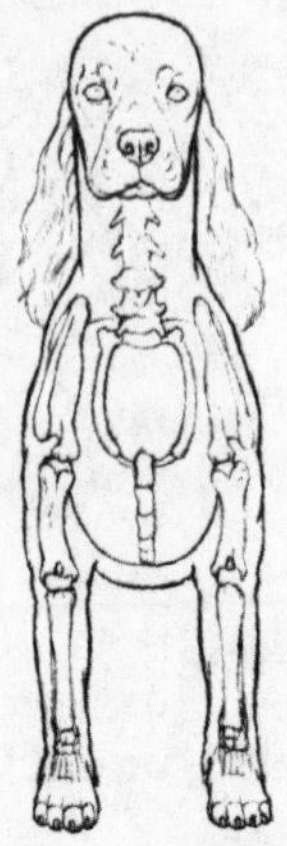

Correct front

Too narrow front

Too wide front

Correct hind action

Too close behind

Cow hocks

Coat

The coat should be flat and silky, not too profuse but with nice feathering on forelegs, body and hindlegs above the hock joint. Regular grooming will enhance the appearance of the coat.

Young puppies quite often grow heavy coats up to six or eight months of age, and owners despair of ever getting them looking right. Do not be too alarmed, or in too much of a hurry. The puppy coat will come out easily at between 6 and 8 months. If you cut it before it is ready to be plucked, you are asking for trouble. If you wait, you will usually have a good coat for life.

Presentation of the coat is a subject in itself, and only experience allows you to become an expert. If you are new to showing and intend to show, do not have your dog clipped or trimmed at a pet shop. Ask a local exhibitor, or your breed club Secretary, where to go to get him 'show-trimmed'.

Colour

The Standard says 'Various. In self colours no white allowed except on the chest.' The original Standard said that the white on the chest of a solid coloured cocker was 'permissible but undesirable' – but it has never been a disqualification.

It is a misconception that evenness of colour in particolours is essential, although obviously it is visually more attractive. The same difficulty arises with black patches on the shoulder or loin which can cause a dog to look upright in shoulder or longer in back than he actually is, or a wide blaze making a head look heavy. These can create optical illusions, but a good judge, judging to the Standard would not let this affect his decisions.

Size

The height and weight given in the Standard is, and always has been, approximate. The overall measurement, from 15 in to 15½ in for bitches and from 15½ in to 16 in for dogs is meant to describe the ideal height, and the weight of 28–32 lb covers both sexes. Cockers are never measured in the ring, as are some breeds.

For many years weight but not size was mentioned in the Standard, and books on the cocker spaniel gave different ideal sizes over the years. It would be an interesting experiment to measure present-day winning exhibits to see how closely they approximate to the Standard height.

Faults

The Standard says that any departure from the Standard is to be regarded as a fault. The faults mentioned specifically in the earlier Standard were coarse skull, light or fine bone, straight or upright shoulders, open feet, poor movement, weak hocks, high tail carriage, lack of stop, light eyes and curly coat. It also stressed that character and temperament varying from the Standard, e.g. aggressive, shy, or uncertain, was to be considered as a fault.

Finally, lack of two apparently normal testicles fully descended, is also a fault. In most countries, cryptorchidism (i.e. lack of one or both testicles) is a disqualifying fault, and in many places a veterinary certificate that the sire is entire is required on importation.

3
Breeding

If there were any underlying principles which definitely produced winners, dog breeding would become simple indeed – too simple. It would lose its joy and fascination, and also its value. Everyone would be breeding winners, therefore winning dogs would become two a penny. Needless to say this is not the case, even nowadays when we have so many good stud dogs to choose from. If one succeeds in breeding a 'top notcher', by this I mean a Challenge Certificate winner, it is a great achievement. There are probably hundreds of winners bred yearly but few are good enough to go on winning when they are out of the junior classes, although breeders of past years have accomplished wonders in the development of the modern cocker. There are certain principles founded on the experience of modern breeders which are well worth studying. Most breeders who have the love of the cocker at heart are only too pleased to give a word of advice to the novice, which should help him to make a right start. As I shall mention later in this chapter, your fundamental stock is most important. Always seek information about the faults of the ancestors of your brood bitch when you are choosing your stud dog; avoid using a dog with any of these faults. If you study pedigrees you can soon form a fairly clear idea of how today's winners were produced. In the period between 1930 and the early 1950s, it will be seen that in blacks Dominorum D'Arcy played a big part, as did Bazel Otto, Treetops Talkie, Treetops Terrific, Sixshot Black Swan, Treetops Foxbar and Champion Lochranza Latchkey. In reds Rufus of Sauls and his son Woodcock Ringleader figured in most pedigrees and Robinhurst of Ware, imported from America by Mr H. S. Lloyd did a lot to improve the reds of his day. Then we find the Byfleets and Lodestar of Sorrelsun (who was sired by the blue

Luckystar of Ware). Champion Golden Rod of Ide sired many winners as did Blare of Broomleaf and his illustrious son, Champion Broomleaf Bonny Lad of Shillwater. Sixshot Willy Wagtail and his son Sixshot Woodywoodpecker were also predominant sires.

In particolours there was the great Invader of Ware who probably did more for his colour than any dog in history. Falconers Mark of Ware was the sire of Champion Oxshott Marxedes, himself a great producer. The great and famous Tracey Witch of Ware, twice Best in Show at Crufts, was by Falconers Padlock of Ware, and Sir Galahad of Ware, who sired Champion Colinwood Cowboy, the first of many champions produced at Colinwood, is to be found on both sides of the pedigrees of practically all the post–war particolour Challenge Certificate winners.

Breeding as a Hobby

If you intend to start a cocker kennel as a hobby, first of all be sure that you are doing it for the right reasons, i.e. that you love the breed and you are interested in producing good-quality stock, with fine temperaments, with as far as possible no history of defects in antecedents, reared well and in perfect health. There are too many commercial kennels without these priorities, and all conscientious breeders deplore the damage done to the breed by these 'puppy farmers'.

With a bit of luck you may break even though I would think that most small-scale breeders, if they are exhibitors as well, will find the costs incurred in housing, feeding, and showing usually exceed the returns from puppy sales. But once you start showing and win your first prize, you will probably be hooked. The first thing to do is to go to a few shows, see what the winners are like and make your mind up about what you want, e.g. dog or bitch; red, black or particolour.

In the years after the war a lot of people tended to breed just to produce pet puppies for sale, but with so much national criticism of indiscriminate production of surplus puppies, few people now see this as an ideal situation, and most want puppies from sound, healthy show stock. If you decide you want to breed, go to a reputable breeder. If you do not know where to find one, write to the secretary of your nearest breed club who will give you suitable names. The names and addresses of the secretaries of all the breed clubs are shown in Appendix A, pages 165–167.

When the time comes for mating, take your bitch to a sound dog. If you are going to keep a puppy, choose it at about eight weeks. After that it will go through different growing phases, but will have nearly reached adulthood by the time it is six to eight months old. Aim to sell the rest of the litter at the age of eight weeks. The longer you keep them after that age, the less profit you will make. You may find yourself out of pocket.

You will have to register or record the litter with the Kennel Club if you are to sell them as pedigree puppies, and you will have to provide the buyer with:

a) A pedigree
b) A Certificate of Registration or Recording at the Kennel Club
c) For the puppy's sake, it is always wise to provide a diet sheet too, so that no drastic changes in diet are made in its new home.

Whilst a male can be a delightful pet, a good worker and an excellent show dog, do not imagine that there will be a great call to use him as a stud dog and, unless he proves to be a regular top winner, it will cost you far more to advertise him at stud than you will receive in stud fees. If you are keen on breeding, then the importance of the selection of the brood bitch cannot be overstressed.

A great number of novice breeders, intending to take up dog breeding, have the mistaken idea that any sort of bitch mated to a famous stud dog will produce a champion. I have so often heard, 'She is not a good specimen, but I intend to mate her to a good dog and get something to show and win with.' If their belief is put into practice they will no doubt be heading for disaster; in my opinion it is equally important to select a first–rate brood bitch as it is a good stud dog, and if one is lucky enough to find a brood bitch which can turn out consistent winners she is worth her weight in gold. It is the secret of sucessful dog breeding.

Assuming your have your puppies, and they are now eight weeks old, perhaps you could get some experienced person to advise you which to keep. Do not attempt to run on too many, in the hope that they will all turn out winners, as your kennel will soon get filled with fully grown nondescript cockers, which will be difficult to find homes for, unless you are prepared to let them go for a few pounds, and they will have already cost you very much more to bring up. Therefore your bank balance will suffer. I find that when people are buying a pet they prefer a puppy under six months, and are usually willing to pay much more for it at that age. It is a mistaken idea to suppose you will get more for them when they are grown up, unless of course you have a show specimen, which is quite a different proposition. A few promising puppies may be run on for four or five months when your experienced friends will probably again review them for you. There are many disappointments in dog breeding, and you may find that after all your puppies are not up to show standard and will have to be sold as pets. But do not despair. In your next litter you may breed the very puppy you have been dreaming of, and you will be well rewarded for all your previous troubles and disappointments.

Nevertheless, the beginner with little practical knowledge and no comprehension of dogs must not expect to make a lot of money for several years after he has started his kennel. He cannot hope to compete with breeders who have spent a lifetime at it, so I should say that provided your dogs are showing a small profit and have not become a drain on your pocket you are doing very well.

Inbreeding and Line Breeding

The relationship of ancestors is an important factor in dog breeding, plainly due to the consideration that related animals are more alike than unrelated ones. Therefore the nearer alike two parents are, the greater the possibility that their children will possess most of their good points. The aim is to breed a cocker with all the good qualities of the parents, and if possible to make an improvement. If inbreeding is resorted to, which is the mating of stock closely related, such as sire and daughter, dam and son, or brother and sister, both dogs should be free from any physical defect. Mental soundness is of the greatest importance and can be bred for as much as any physical feature. Do not attempt to breed from a nervous bitch, however beautiful she may be; the temptation will be great, but it is not worth the risk. The nervous trait is almost certain to come out, if not in the first generation it will crop up again later, and you will finish up by having a kennel full of nervous cockers. If they are to be shown, dog-showing will become a nightmare to you and your dogs. Most experienced breeders favour line breeding, and if you study the pedigree of the majority of famous winners you will find they have been bred this way. Linebreeding is the mating of less closely related stock than inbreeding. To line breed successfully one should have a thorough knowledge of the breed. For instance, supposing a strain does not excel in heads and a mating is being contemplated with a dog who has a good head, his ancestors for three generations back should be considered to see if they have any failing in this feature. Throwing back and unwanted faults can crop up when least expected. Consequently the pedigree on both sides should be studied and the family characteristics gone into. You cannot go on inbreeding or line breeding for too long, as you are likely to produce nervous, highly strung cockers. When you have established your strain you will need to bring in an outcross – which means the mating of unrelated stock. This is extremely valuable in breeding out some weakness that may have crept in, or to correct some fault which is becoming prevalent, probably the result of inbreeding for too long. So many breeders are inclined to neglect the female side and will breed from a bitch so much below standard and the breeding of a good cocker becomes more difficult. The dam's influence will be quite equal to that of the sire's; to mate a poor quality bitch to a first-rate dog is no reason why the progeny should inherit all the good points of the stud dog. Some of them may, but they are also just as likely to inherit the bad points of the dam. Faults are much more easily transmitted than are the good qualities; therefore too much attention cannot be paid to the defects of your breeding stock if you wish to make headway in the show ring.

As an illustration, let us imagine we are founding a strain. As we have said before, a strain is something that is established; we must inbreed as a means to the end. Strain may be termed an element, not only so far as physical attributes are concerned but one also able to transmit characteristics with some degree of regularity. Should heads be the prime consideration in our supposed strain, other points should not be subjugated; but if your breeding stock fails to reach the first objective you must not breed from them again. Naturally it should be determined whether or not the point we seek appears strongly enough in the pedigree. Mathematically we have one-half, one-quarter, and one-eighth, going back through the pedigree. This divided in half expresses the possibilities of both sire and dam, so far as potency is concerned. If the individuals have been selected to the same standard each controls 50 per cent of the offspring, backed by these individual ancestors: sire to daughter gives us 75 per cent of the sire's blood – a daughter from this mating bred back to the original sire gives us 87½ per cent of the sire's blood in the offspring. Son to mother produces the same resultant fraction, giving the preponderance in the dam's blood. Mating the off-spring back to the original stock will show where the prepotency of each character lies. If a son mated to his mother sires puppies resembling her, her prepotency is established, although the young son may resemble his father. The same applies to the mating of father and daughter. By mating a dog with 75 per cent of his father's blood to a bitch with the same amount of her mother's blood we should produce puppies resembling to a large degree the original pair. By continuing with these matings we produce a family of unvarying type. Thus we are breeding by the law of mathematics.

Inbreeding without discrimination will spell disaster. The novice should be well acquainted with his subject before attempting to inbreed. Then we have the outcross, a matter of supreme delicacy. Some lines of blood suit other lines of blood; there are others that will not mix in at all satisfactorily, so one must first take into consideration blood-lines of the past, and if a certain outcross suited a certain blood-line years ago it is possible that a similar outcross will suit it again today. If you wish to make a success of breeding, all this is well worth studying. I have seen dire results from outcrossing when the blood-lines have not suited, but as I have said earlier you cannot go on inbreeding for too long; you must bring in an outcross occasionally, as inbreeding may retain and accentuate the show type but in the end deterioration of the breed is certain to come.

The Stud Dog and the Visiting Bitch

It is unwise for the novice breeder to commence with a stud dog. Wait until you are well known in the show ring before attempting to place a dog at public stud. Advertising is very expensive and the dog will not make enough to pay his bills. A successful stud dog must come from a line of good bitches, so you should become established in your bitch line before attempting to breed a dog for stud. The bitch line behind him is of the greatest importance, therefore his dam, and also her ancestors, will have a great influence on the quality of the puppies he will sire. Past history of the breed will prove this, so if you have to take your bitch to another breeder to be mated choose a suitable stud dog, and if possible choose one largely on the merits and breeding of his dam. To become a successful breeder you must look further than the dog – although the sire plays a very important part you cannot expect him to do it all. It is no use flying off to the latest sensational sire with a poor sort of bitch expecting to breed a champion. Your aim should be to keep improving your stock, but it will need endless patience; it cannot be done in a hurry. Make a point of getting good foundation stock. If you make a wrong start your progress will be slow; it is better to start with one good bitch than half a dozen poor specimens. You sometimes hear of a beginner breeding a champion in his first litter, but usually if you probe into this you will find he started with a good bitch. The better your bitches, the higher the grade of puppies you will breed, and the greater your chances are of breeding a first-prize winner. The stud dog must be in perfect health and condition. He will need to be fed liberally, with good raw beef, eggs, milk, or any of the vitality-giving foods, but should never be allowed to get over-fat. He will also need plenty of good, regular exercise. A popular stud dog is always very sought after, but owners who study the welfare of their dog will strictly limit the number of bitches they allow to visit him. If a stud dog is well looked after and not overworked he will go on for many years, siring big, strong litters, but if a dog is overdone when he is young he will be useless in a few years. So if you have a dog and you value him it will pay you in the long run not to overtax his strength by having too many bitches.

If you have no stud dog of your own when you contemplate breeding from your bitch, you will want to know which dog to choose. Nowadays there are very few adverts in the two weekly dog papers for cocker spaniels at stud. Both the Cocker Spaniel Club and the London Cocker Spaniel Society produce annuals with adverts and photographs from most of the leading kennels, and for those in Scotland, the Cocker Spaniel Club of Scotland also produces a similar booklet. These are all distributed to members and details of how to become a member can be obtained from the respective secretaries. (See names and addresses of secretaries in Appendix A, pages 165–167.)

Some years ago the railways were used a lot for transporting visiting bitches, but although a few owners still use these facilities, it is more usual nowadays for the bitch to be taken to the stud dog by car. It is of the greatest importance that the mating should be done on the correct day when the bitch is most receptive. This is usually between the tenth and twelfth day. At this stage the colour of the discharge changes from red to pink, and the bitch's tail will turn vigorously sideways if she is tickled at the root of the tail. If you choose a day to suit your convenience rather than the best day for the bitch, do not be surprised if she produces no puppies.

If the bitch is to be sent by rail, use a roomy travelling-box with plenty of ventilation. Do not despatch her until the ninth day of her season. That will be quite soon enough. She may be your dearest little pet but the owner of the stud dog will not want to keep her longer than is necessary, as she will have to be locked up very securely in a kennel alone, which she will no doubt object to. She will probably bark day and night, which will not be good for her, nor will it be for the nerves of anyone within hearing. Always remember to pay return carriage your end; this will save the owner of the stud dog a lot of trouble. When sending your bitch by rail for a long distance it is better to send by night, when she will probably sleep through the journey. Before despatching, enquiries should be made as to the route by which she will travel and the time of arrival at her destination, in order that the person to whom she is being sent can be on the look-out for her. It is advisable for the sender to instruct the recipient to telephone should your bitch fail to arrive at the given time.

I find the railways very considerate on the whole with all livestock, and do their utmost to see they arrive at their destinations as soon as they can.

When a travelling-box is used make sure that it has sufficient ventilation so that the dog will not suffer in hot weather. Painted on the box in bold letters should be VALUABLE LIVE DOG. A strongly made box is a most useful adjunct to a kennel and can be used for other purposes on many occasions, such as travelling by car, though nowadays the purpose-made collapsible wire crates are more commonly used. If you have a sick dog which is in need of constant attention night and day, and it is more convenient to have it indoors, either of these types of container is invaluable as an indoor kennel. It must be remembered that a travelling-box should be of such a height that the dog can stand upright without any difficulty.

All stud fees are payable in advance, or at the time of mating. Most owners allow a return service if the bitch should not prove in whelp to the first mating, but it is not legally enforceable as the fee paid is for the service given, with no guarantee that a litter will result from the mating. If a return service is given, the owner of the stud dog is within his rights to insist that the second service be to the same bitch at the next season. It is usual for owners of visiting bitches to be allowed to see the animals 'tied' during the mating.

When you mate a young dog for the first time start if possible with an experienced brood bitch. You should not attempt to use him before the age of ten months, and if he does not appear keen wait for another month before trying again. Do not force him. Some dogs are later maturing in this way than others. From the start let him know the bitch will be held for him. This will give him confidence; so many bitches will snap at a dog when being mated and this is inclined to put some young dogs off, particularly if they get badly bitten.

The dog will become locked or tied to the bitch during mating, so that he cannot get free for approximately ten to thirty minutes, or even longer. Without this tie fertilization is very doubtful, although on rare occasions you hear of puppies being born when there has been no tie. Once the mating is accomplished it must be remembered to keep a strict eye on your bitch for a week or so as she will probably be very eager to accept further attentions from any dog that might come her way. During this period the chosen dog can repeat the mating if you think it is advisable, although there is no necessity for two matings if the first one is satisfactory. When the dog has mated the bitch, and the tie is effected, the bitch should be held by the collar, so that she is unable to drag the dog about and perhaps injure him by causing a rupture.

When can you tell if your bitch is in whelp? It is difficult to say with certainty; some show earlier than others, but you should know five weeks after the mating has taken place. One of the first indications of conception is that the bitch may eat indifferently; on the other hand, she may become very hungry, or perhaps vomit her food and become lazy. At the sixth week there is usually a rounding of the flanks; at this stage the bitch should be fed three times daily instead of the one big meal. I shall deal with this matter in another chapter.

The Brood Bitch

If you are hoping to breed puppies of sufficiently high standard to enter the show ring the importance of the choice of your brood bitch cannot be overstressed. Only the best is good enough if you aim to breed show stock. It is quite impossible for us all to be in a position to pay a big price for a show bitch, so the next best thing is to get one with no glaring faults, and of superb breeding. Many well-known breeders are able to supply a bitch of this sort, but she is not likely to be cheap. The bitch lines count for a lot. She should be well bred on both sides of her pedigree. Her immediate forebears should be good; do not rely on dogs two or three generations back to produce your winners – if you do you will no doubt be disappointed. It does happen sometimes, but the chance is almost negligible. If you are successful in finding a bitch fulfilling all the requirements of the perfect brood she will be of untold value and should never be parted with. Your objective should be to produce puppies of better quality than the dam.

It is wise not to mate your bitch until the second heat, unless of course she does not come into season until 12 months of age, which is often the case. It is a mistake to mate a bitch too young, a litter will be developing and born before she herself has finished growing. This would be a great strain on her, although many are of the opinion that a bitch in the wild state would breed as soon as nature permitted. This may be so, but dogs have become domesticated and are very different from the dogs of long ago, when they were in their wild, natural state.

Having settled on your brood bitch, now is the time to find your stud dog. Use a dog which is producing winners. There are many famous stud dogs available. In making your choice remember that the bitch line behind him is of great importance. Do not use a dog whose female ancestry is unknown; he may be a chance bred one and will make a very poor sire. Then your puppies would be suitable only for the pet market, and valuable time would have been wasted. Do not choose a stud dog of an entirely different type from your bitch. You will get better results from a dog of similar appearance, provided he is good enough.

Celibacy

Celibacy is unnatural. It is good for all bitches to have a least one litter in their lives, and – who knows? – after you have had the pleasure of breeding one litter you may want to become a regular breeder. Many famous exhibitors have begun this way. If your bitch does unfortunately produce a puppy with defects that appear to be hereditary, do not breed from her again. It is important for the breed that we keep it as healthy as we can.

The Bitch in Season

Sexual behaviour is seasonable in most animals, but when a bitch reaches the age of about eight months (and in certain cases younger or later) oestrum will occur; in other words, the bitch will be 'in season'. The condition is recognized by the swelling of the organs. At first there will be a clear mucous discharge, followed by a red discharge which usually continues for ten or twelve days. In some cases it will clear up earlier, in others it will go on longer. This is followed by a heavy white discharge which will go on for another few days. In normal cases the heat lasts from three to four weeks. During the 'in season' period a bitch will change her habits considerably. She will become very skittish and perhaps may become faddy with her food. Most people do not show 'in season' bitches out of consideration for dog-owners, but in any case her movement may be affected. Generally speaking, however, you should watch for your bitch puppy coming in season at about the age of eight months, although it may not occur until the age of ten or twelve months or even later – I have known bitches not to come in until eighteen months of age. In very rare instances a bitch does not come in season at all; in a case of this sort you should see your veterinary surgeon.

Another very trying thing for a breeder: a bitch will sometimes have what is called a false heat, coming in season long before she is due. This condition is difficult to recognize from a true heat. The bitch will even stand to be mated, but does not prove in whelp, and just when she is due for her puppies she will come in season again. This time she may be mated with every success. Often bitches will show colour for a week or even longer after mating – it may be they have been mated too early. If it does not continue for too long it may be disregarded.

After its first appearance the heat should recur about every six months, but there again you cannot always be certain to a month or so. When the bitch has been mated it often recurs when her puppies are four months old, or six months after the previous heat. Until all signs of season have completely disappeared the bitch must be most carefully protected or she is almost certain to get out and mate herself, to perhaps an un-

TABLE SHOWING WHEN A BITCH IS DUE TO WHELP

Served January	Due to Whelp March	Served February	Due to Whelp April	Served March	Due to Whelp May	Served April	Due To Whelp June	Served May	Due to Whelp July	Served June	Due to Whelp August	Served July	Due to Whelp September	Served August	Due to Whelp October	Served September	Due to Whelp November	Served October	Due to Whelp December	Served November	Due to Whelp January	Served December	Due to Whelp February
1	5	1	5	1	3	1	3	1	3	1	3	1	2	1	3	1	3	1	3	1	3	1	2
2	6	2	6	2	4	2	4	2	4	2	4	2	3	2	4	2	4	2	4	2	4	2	3
3	7	3	7	3	5	3	5	3	5	3	5	3	4	3	5	3	5	3	5	3	5	3	4
4	8	4	8	4	6	4	6	4	6	4	6	4	5	4	6	4	6	4	6	4	6	4	5
5	9	5	9	5	7	5	7	5	7	5	7	5	6	5	7	5	7	5	7	5	7	5	6
6	10	6	10	6	8	6	8	6	8	6	8	6	7	6	8	6	8	6	8	6	8	6	7
7	11	7	11	7	9	7	9	7	9	7	9	7	8	7	9	7	9	7	9	7	9	7	8
8	12	8	12	8	10	8	10	8	10	8	10	8	9	8	10	8	10	8	10	8	10	8	9
9	13	9	13	9	11	9	11	9	11	9	11	9	10	9	11	9	11	9	11	9	11	9	10
10	14	10	14	10	12	10	12	10	12	10	12	10	11	10	12	10	12	10	12	10	12	10	11
11	15	11	15	11	13	11	13	11	13	11	13	11	12	11	13	11	13	11	13	11	13	11	12
12	16	12	16	12	14	12	14	12	14	12	14	12	13	12	14	12	14	12	14	12	14	12	13
13	17	13	17	13	15	13	15	13	15	13	15	13	14	13	15	13	15	13	15	13	15	13	14
14	18	14	18	14	16	14	16	14	16	14	16	14	15	14	16	14	16	14	16	14	16	14	15
15	19	15	19	15	17	15	17	15	17	15	17	15	16	15	17	15	17	15	17	15	17	15	16
16	20	16	20	16	18	16	18	16	18	16	18	16	17	16	18	16	18	16	18	16	18	16	17
17	21	17	21	17	19	17	19	17	19	17	19	17	18	17	19	17	19	17	19	17	19	17	18
18	22	18	22	18	20	18	20	18	20	18	20	18	19	18	20	18	20	18	20	18	20	18	19
19	23	19	23	19	21	19	21	19	21	19	21	19	20	19	21	19	21	19	21	19	21	19	20
20	24	20	24	20	22	20	22	20	22	20	22	20	21	20	22	20	22	20	22	20	22	20	21
21	25	21	25	21	23	21	23	21	23	21	23	21	22	21	23	21	23	21	23	21	23	21	22
22	26	22	26	22	24	22	24	22	24	22	24	22	23	22	24	22	24	22	24	22	24	22	23
23	27	23	27	23	25	23	25	23	25	23	25	23	24	23	25	23	25	23	25	23	25	23	24
24	28	24	28	24	26	24	26	24	26	24	26	24	25	24	26	24	26	24	26	24	26	24	25
25	29	25	29	25	27	25	27	25	27	25	27	25	26	25	27	25	27	25	27	25	27	25	26
26	30	26	30	26	28	26	28	26	28	26	28	26	27	26	28	26	28	26	28	26	28	26	27
27	31		May	27	29	27	29	27	29	27	29	27	28	27	29	27	29	27	29	27	29	27	28
	Apr.	27	1	28	30	28	30	28	30	28	30	28	29	28	30	28	30	28	30	28	30		Mar.
28	1	28	2	29	31		July	29	31	29	31	29	30	29	31		Dec.	29	31	29	31	28	1
29	2	29	3		June	29	1		Aug.		Sep.		Oct.		Nov.	29	1		Jan.		Feb.	29	2
30	3			30	1	30	2	30	1	30	1	30	1	30	1	30	2	30	1	30	1	30	3
31	4			31	2			31	2			31	2	31	2			31	2			31	4

certain character; she will not mind if he is a champion cocker or the lowest scruffy mongrel. Some bitches will go to any extreme in order to get out and will travel for miles followed by a retinue of dogs, whilst others are quite indifferent about the whole thing.

The greatest menace of all are the crossbred street dogs. They will scent and trail a bitch for miles; therefore never let her off the lead when being exercised. It is surprising how a dog can suddenly appear from nowhere, even in the midst of the country when you think it is quite safe to let your bitch have a lovely scamper over the moors. If your bitch has been mated, and her season is over, let her have as much natural freedom as possible right up to the time she is due to whelp. Both she and her puppies will be all the better for it. Failure to take care of one's bitch when in season, and failure to control a dog when there is obviously a bitch about in that condition, is one of the worst forms of neglect.

The Bitch in Whelp

A bitch in whelp should have every care and attention. The success of her litter will depend largely on the way she has been looked after during pregnancy. She will need plenty of nourishing food, although it is imperative to avoid excessive fatness as this is likely to cause difficulty at whelping time. You cannot do better than to give her a liberal supply of raw beef, or horseflesh; about three-quarters of a pound to a pound daily should be sufficient. This could be divided, and given with some rusked brown bread or biscuit morning and evening. In addition, an egg beaten with milk is good, and a teaspooful of cod liver oil. Also, calcium should be added to her food intake. There are many forms of calcium with added vitamins and trace elements available from pet shops or veterinary surgeons, but it is necessary to realize that dosage instructions are usually given for 'medium-sized' dogs. Remember that this can include the lightly boned miniature poodle, whilst you are looking for a really sturdy dog. Do not underdose, rather tend to overdose a little. One cannot overstate the importance of the care and feeding of the bitch in whelp, and of the puppies if the litter is to reach its full potential. Some people believe that a good teaspoonful of milk of magnesia every morning will be beneficial as, apart from being a mild laxative, it will reduce the risk of acid milk, which causes the death of so many puppies.

A bitch will need exercise right up to the last, or as long as she can take it without discomfort, but do not overdo her. If you are conveniently situated, let her have as much natural freedom as possible.

Bitches in whelp should be free from worms, particularly because they may be passed on to the unborn puppies through the blood-stream. It is wise to worm her a fortnight after mating if you see any sign of worms.

The bitch should be given a box for whelping in, large enough for her to stretch herself out. It is wise to have a ledge all round the inside, about two-and-a-half inches wide and three inches from the floor. This will prevent the bitch crushing the puppies on the side of the box, and many lives will be saved this way if your bitch is clumsy. It is wise to prepare the bed where she is to have her puppies some time before. If you move her just as she is due to whelp you will be asking for trouble. Do not attempt it; she will probably not settle and as the puppies are born she will try to carry them back to her old bed and you may lose the lot in consequence. Whatever bedding you put into the box before whelping will possibly be scratched out, so it is best to give very little of any kind. Many people line the box with newspapers during the whelping.

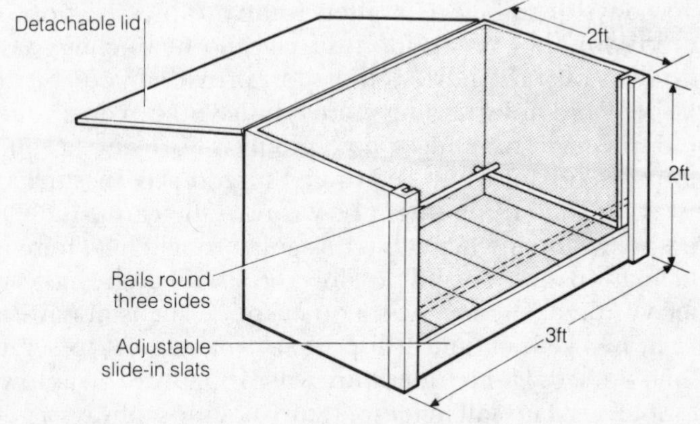

Top layers can be removed during whelping, or more layers added, and the whole lot easily taken away whilst the bitch is out relieving herself after she has finished whelping.

Avoid a loose blanket or anything of that sort. It could easily get bunched up and suffocate the puppies. After the puppies are born it is a good idea to put a piece of plywood into the bottom of the box, covered with a piece of fleecy blanketing fitted like a pillow case, so that it cannot be scratched up by the bitch. Providing something other than newspapers seems to give the puppies a good footing, and they are more easily able to get a grip with their paws when sucking.

There are now many materials available similar to those in hospital use for incontinent patients and, being very warm as well, they have become a boon at whelping time. They can easily be removed for washing, are machine washable, and can be tumble dried very quickly. Most bitches do not try to scratch this type of bedding up, but if they do, then a light backing of cotton or nylon sheeting to form a 'pillow case' for the plywood can be used. This type of bedding seems to help puppies to get on their feet very much more quickly than if they are on the floor of a box with a plain wooden surface.

It is always wise to advise your veterinary surgeon when you have a bitch due to whelp. He is then forewarned and will not delay in coming to help if needed.

The full period of gestation is 63 days from the time of mating, although it is a common thing for the puppies to be born a few days early; but there is no need to worry, within the limits of a few days or so before or after. If the puppies are born six days too soon they very seldom survive. Some bitches go one or two days over the normal time, but provided your bitch is fit and well and not straining there is little you can do about it. Should she begin straining and no puppy is born after a couple of hours, send for your veterinary surgeon as in such circumstances something might be wrong. One can usually tell within a few hours when a bitch is going to whelp. There is a disinclination for food and possibly the last meal she has eaten will be vomited; she will seek a quiet spot if she is not already alone in her kennel, and will probably pant, start to scratch and make a bed. Her temperature will probably drop as low as 98°F (36.5°C). This fall in temperature is almost always a good guide as to when whelping will begin – usually within 24 hours. Use a 'stubby' thermometer, pressed against the anal wall, and leave for about a minute and a half. Cockers in general are easy whelpers and no difficulties should be expected. Should anything appear to be abnormal, veterinary assistance should be sought. The puppies are usually born at night and, particularly when it is a first litter, it is as well to be with the bitch at least until the first puppy arrives. Some bitches become worried and your presence helps to soothe their nerves, and many, particularly house pets, are comforted by their owner's presence. There are some who prefer to be left alone, but even there you will want to know that no complications have set in; frequent checks should be made. Most breeders today prefer to have their bitches whelp in the house, in the kitchen or utility room, where a watchful eye can be kept in comparative comfort for the bitch and owner.

The bitch is usually capable of doing everything for herself, but if she fails to sever the umbilical cords of the puppies it is advisable to tie a thread ligature tightly around the navel cord about an inch from the puppy's body, and sever the cord with scissors sterilized before use. Care should be taken not to pull the cord *away* from the puppy's tummy. Always pull *towards* it, to avoid causing an umbilical hernia.

The interval between the delivery of puppies can vary considerably, but if more than two hours elapses, especially if the bitch is straining with no result, you should speak to your veterinary surgeon. Often the last puppy in the litter is born some time after the others, the bitch being busy attending to her little family at this stage, not continually straining. There should be no need for worry. When the litter is born, the bitch should be encouraged to settle down quietly, if possible lying flat out on her side rather than curling in a ball round the babies, as this will prevent the puppies reaching the milk bar easily. Lying flat out exposes the teats to all the puppies.

For the first 24 hours or so the bitch will not require solid food, but plenty of milk. Better still, give her a milk food such as Bengers or Ostermilk, with maybe a cereal such as Farex added. The bitch's temperature may be slightly raised for 24 hours or so, hence the liquid diet. Also, it must be remembered that each puppy born is followed by an afterbirth, a dark, nasty, greenish-looking mass which is eaten by the bitch. It is quite right and proper for her to consume it, therefore do not interfere with her at all. This is nature's way of providing nourishment for the exhausted mother. Do not disturb her by cleaning out her bed immediately after the whelping – a little job like this can wait until the mother has had a well-earned sleep. After some hours she will come out to relieve herself. You can clean up her box and also sponge her down with a very weak solution of disinfectant, drying her well, and if she is a good mother she will be very eager to get back to her family. Do not worry the bitch by frequently disturbing her. She will normally do all that is necessary for the puppies by herself. It is, however, important to see that they are all feeding, and that the smaller ones are not being pushed out by their bigger litter mates. After a day or so, it is useful to record weights every day or so to see that each is growing satisfactorily. In a large litter, if any puppies are not making steady progress, it may be necessary to supplement the feeding for these. 'Welpi', a proprietory make of puppy powder, is readily available from veterinary surgeons or pet shops. It is very reliable and is reputed to be the nearest thing to bitches' milk.

After the first few days the bitch will need plenty of good food, and to be let out of her kennel for short outings, two or three times daily. It is wise to leave the pups untouched for the first 24 hours; this will be time enough to discover their sexes, although one is always so curious, and no matter how many litters one has bred there is always the thrill: maybe in this litter there will be a certificate winner.

The first milk given by the bitch is called colostrum and its composition gradually changes until it becomes milk proper. The colostrum is a mild laxative, and one of its purposes is to eliminate the impurities which will possibly have accumulated in the puppies during the period of gestation. It is reasonable to assume that the change in the composition of the milk would be completed within about 24 hours.

The feeding of the puppies can be left entirely to the mother for the first three weeks after whelping, and it is obvious that the feeding of the dam during this period is of great importance if the puppies are to do well.

Puppies are easily fatally chilled if they stay away from their mother or are unable to find their way back. Heat is therefore essential to them and many breeders now use the infra-red lamps (either the red/orange lamps or dull-emitter type) to ensure an even, constant, heat in the box of about 70 °F (21 °C), at least during the first week or so. This is obviously important for winter puppies and for those in kennels, more so. Another modern means of heating is the use of an electrically heated pad which is inserted underneath the bedding. Do be certain whatever type of heating is used, especially in kennels, that the installation is absolutely safe.

In normal circumstances a cocker is a hardy dog, needing heat only when the weather is really cold, but puppies fall into a different category.

Anyone interested in breeding from their bitch would be extremely well advised to read *The Popular Guide to Puppy Rearing* by Olwen Gwynne-Jones, published by the Popular Dogs Publishing Co. Ltd. Although the author is a Shetland Sheepdog breeder, all she writes is equally applicable to cocker spaniels, and the book is an invaluable aid, written by a lady with practical experience and a commonsense approach.

Perhaps it is hardly necessary to warn the owner, or whoever might be in charge, not to allow visitors or another dog to approach the mother and her young family for several weeks. If she is a good mother she will resent this and it is unfair to cause her worry. She needs peace and quiet to cope with rearing her young family.

False Pregnancy

A false pregnancy is not uncommon and it is not possible to predict when it is likely to occur. After being properly mated, though not in whelp some bitches assume an appearance of pregnancy and behave in every way as if they were going to have a litter. When the time is due for the puppies to arrive, nothing but a little discharge comes away and the bitch gradually gets back to her normal size. There will be milk; if a large amount some of it will need removing but not in sufficient quantity to leave the glands empty, otherwise the flow is stimulated. The treatment for this condition is the administration of sex hormone, which can be supplied only by your veterinary surgeon. Maiden bitches with strong leanings towards maternity are also known to have a false pregnancy during the weeks following a season, apart from any question of mating. They will also develop a secretion of milk in the glands, and the abdomen will become enlarged and give a general picture of pregnancy. This is an effort of nature in accordance with what should have taken place had the bitch been mated and was to have a litter. In a case of this sort it is not advisable to leave her in one of your rooms alone between the seventh and ninth week, as she is liable to tear up cushions and scratch all the stuffing out of chairs, but if you are unlucky enough to experience this do not be too hard on the bitch, she is just trying to make a bed – it is nature's way, not destructiveness.

The Foster-mother

One seldom loses a bitch when she is giving birth to her puppies, but should such an unfortunate thing happen one has to decide whether to put the puppies down or bring them up by hand. You may be lucky enough to get a foster-mother. There are one or two Kennels who hire bitches out for this purpose – you will often see them advertised in the dog papers – or perhaps your local vet can help you. He may know of a bitch with an unwanted litter, and the owner might be pleased for the bitch to bring up your puppies, particularly if you gave one in return for her services. You must be quite certain that the bitch used as a foster-mother is perfectly healthy, has a good supply of milk and is not bad-tempered. Also, her time of whelping should be more or less the same day as that of the bitch whose puppies she is to rear. The composition of the bitch's milk changes daily, and will be too strong for newly-born puppies unless the time of whelping of the two bitches was about the same . Before introducing the puppies to the foster-mother they should be well rubbed over with the foster-mother's milk; if she licks them and allows them to suck, you know all is well.

Head study of Sh. Ch. Sixshot Woodywoodpecker

Sh. Ch. Sixshot Otto the Owl

F. W. Simms

Ch. Colinwood Silver Lariot

Ch. Lucklena Musical Maid

Ch. Craigleith Cinderella

Thomas Fall

Sh. Ch. Crosbeian Thornfalcon Flamenco

Sh. Ch. Sixshot Dan the Duck

Thomas Fall

Sh. Ch. Courtdale Flag Lieutenant

To bring puppies up by hand is a thankless job, and needs a lot of thinking about. They will need to be kept warm and constantly fed, which means getting up two or three times during the night. And after all your work you may lose them. It was usual in the past to use a fountain-pen filler, and later a small feeding bottle. However, it is now possible to get a human premature baby feeding bottle, with a small teat and a larger valve, which enables the milk to be more easily transmitted to the puppy. The one most used by cocker breeders is the Belcroy Baby Feeder, manufactured by Messrs. John Bell & Croydon Ltd, Dispensing Chemists, Wigmore Street, London W1, and is available from them, as are replacement teats and valves. Your chemist may also be able to place an order. One purchased before the litter is due is a good investment as, if not necessary for this litter, it is always available in future if needed.

Ideas on what to feed to the puppies being hand-reared differs between breeders, but 'Welpi', mentioned previously, is most suitable. If this is not available, a mixture of Evaporated condensed milk and water in equal parts, fed at blood-heat, is also good to begin with. A *gradual* change over to one of the proprietory puppy feeds can then take place. By the time they are three weeks old they should be able to start lapping; also a tiny morsel of scraped lean beef (preferably scraped with the ball of a spoon from a slice of lean braising steak) may be given.

A litter reared by hand, even though it is most tiring and time-consuming, can be very self-satisfying when successful.

Docking

There is a great deal of controversy nowadays about tail-docking, and some veterinary surgeons will not perform this operation. Check beforehand so that you can make the necessary arrangements if your own veterinary surgeon will not do it. Contact local bona-fide breeders for their advice if you are a novice and have no experience of this.

Most breeders dock their puppies' tails themselves at about 4–5 days of age. This operation must be performed with docking scissors or a pair of sharp scissors well-sterilized before use. Most breeders recommend taking three-fifths of the tail off. After the required amount has been removed, the end of the tail should be dabbed with permanganate of potash crystals to prevent any bleeding; some breeders use a silver nitrate stick instead of this, but the object is the same, to prevent any loss of blood.

At the same time as the docking of the tails the dew-claws should be removed. They are small semi-circular nails which grow on the inside of the front legs just above the feet and very occasionally on the hind legs. It is wise to remove them as, apart from looking neater when the dog grows older, they often grow round into the leg, causing considerable pain; or, if working in the field, they will probably get torn when going through thick cover or bramble. Rounded operating scissors are best for removing them, or a pair of curved nail scissors are equally successful. It is kinder to take the mother right away whilst this operation is in progress. If correctly done, very little pain is caused as at this age the tail is only cartilage, and you will find the puppies feeding from the mother immediately she is put back to them, a few minutes after the operation.

If you are quite a novice, and have had no experience of docking and removing dew-claws, it would be as well to get your veterinary surgeon or an experienced breeder to dock your first litter. You will then see how it is done, and should be able to do your following litters without any help.

Weaning

As I have said previously, until the age of three weeks the puppies can be left to the dam, assuming she has a good supply of milk and is liberally fed. During the first few days after whelping the bitch should be fed on milky foods, such as groats made with milk, an egg beaten up, or any of the patent milk foods. On the third day steamed fish or chicken may be given. If all is well with the mother, and she is nursing a big litter, you will find her very hungry so she should be fed four times a day. After the fourth day the bitch can go back to her normal diet, and should be given raw beef, well-boiled tripe, fish, eggs, brown bread, etc. All the time she is feeding her pups she will need extra food. Changes in food can be made; she will also need milk foods, porridge made with milk, Slippery Elm food, or any of the innumerable milk foods available that are very helpful in stimulating lactation.

The eyes of the puppies should open between the ninth and twelfth days, and at this stage the puppies will be crawling about, although they will not have their full power of vision until about three weeks.

The time at which weaning is commenced is usually influenced by the size of the litter. If it is a small litter of two or three puppies, commencement of weaning can safely be left until about three-and-a-half to four weeks of age, but if a large litter of seven or more, then two-and-a-half to three weeks is much kinder to the bitch, though naturally very small quantities must be given to puppies at this tender age.

Some bitches tend to vomit partly digested food for the puppies to eat. This is a natural thing; it is nature's way of providing the pups with half-digested food until they are at an age when they can digest their own. I have heard of several novice breeders thinking there was something wrong and sending for their veterinary surgeons post haste. You must be careful at this stage not to allow the mother large pieces of meat. I once had a puppy choke in this way, so immediately I know weaning is in progress I feed the dam on foods that cannot harm the puppies when vomited. If the bitch brings up too much of her food to the puppies it is wise to keep her away from them for a couple of hours after she has had her meal; it will give her time to absorb some for herself, otherwise she will get into a very low state – you could give her a little extra food at this time.

Now is the time to give the puppies their first lesson in lapping. Most puppies will take milk at blood heat, slightly sweetened with either glucose or sugar. Begin by dipping their noses once or twice into the dish – a very shallow one is needed when they are so young. Goat's milk is excellent but for town dwellers somewhat difficult to obtain. Any of the baby foods are very useful. It is wise to feed the puppies separately, then you know each one has had his share, as some eat more quickly than others. Start with two meals a day of about a dessertspoonful at each meal, after three days a small amount (about half a teaspoonful) of lean, scraped raw beef may be given as a third meal. After a week, a fourth meal of scraped raw beef may be given, making four feeds daily, alternating between a milk feed and a meat feed in turn. As the puppies grow, the meals must be increased in size very gradually so as not to upset the digestion – puppies' digestions are very easily upset. By the time they are five to six weeks of age, the milk food should be made a bit more substantial by the addition of a cereal such as Farex, Farlene, etc. – any of the human baby cereals are suitable. At seven weeks of age the raw meat can be finely chopped or minced, and a gradual introduction of tinned puppy meat (e.g. Chum Puppy) may be made instead of raw meat, especially if the puppies are destined for the future to become pets or companions, where they will nowadays more often than not be fed on the convenient 'tinned' food. This will avoid a sudden change of diet. By the time the puppies are about eight weeks old, they should have been introduced to the small 'puppy' grade of biscuit meal or soaked brown bread, mixed with the meat meals; and of course the introduction of calcium to create strong bone and teeth, combined with vitamins and trace elements should be made very gradually from about five weeks of age, increasing as they grow. Always give a diet sheet, detailing what the puppy has been given, how often, etc., to any new owner.

About five weeks after birth the mother should be allowed to leave the puppies for a few hours daily. It is now time they got used to being without her. I find a very good thing is to provide a bench or a low platform where the dam can get away from the too persistent attentions of her little family, as by this time their teeth and claws are sharp.

Usually the dam has ceased to secrete milk when the puppies reach the age of eight weeks and the weaning is complete. The mother having done her duty to her family, rearing is now in the hands of the breeder. When puppies reach the age of three months you can start cutting their meals down and at the age of four months three meals daily should be sufficient, provided the meals given have adequate nourishment.

In regard to the various foods for a growing puppy, give

plenty of good raw meat, milk, boiled fish and rice. A hard biscuit or a big bone with the bits of lean meat left on, will be very helpful to their teeth. Cod liver oil is very good for them; a teaspoonful can be put in one meal a day. Although they will need plenty of good food never overload them, or you will upset their digestion. Great care must be paid to the cleanliness of food bowls or dishes, and freshness of food is most important. On no account should left-over food be given the next day, particularly soaked dog biscuit, which becomes sour if not used almost at once. At seven to nine months puppies in most cases are fully grown, but they are not fully developed until twelve to eighteen months, sometimes even later than that. According to the law, they cease to be puppies at the age of six months and then require dog licences, but according to the Kennel Club they are puppies up to the age of twelve months and can be shown in puppy classes until that time.

A few more remarks may be appropriate here. You cannot be too particular about the cleanliness of the bedding and of the puppies themselves. Start to groom at an early age with a soft brush. As mentioned earlier, always see that the feeding utensils are scrupulously clean. Puppies will not thrive amid dirt. Also see that they are free from insects, especially lice, as they cause great discomfort, and if heavily infested the puppy will soon become in poor condition. I do not believe in frequently dosing with medicine, a procedure to which some dogs seem to be subjected by their owners. If puppies are thoroughly and efficiently wormed during puppyhood, and thereafter are properly fed with good nourishing wholesome food and exercised regularly, they should ordinarily require no medicine.

4

General Care of your Cocker Spaniel

Feeding

A dog's natural food is raw meat, and this should be treated as the most important item in his diet. The dog by nature is carnivorous, or meat-eating, and in his wild state hunts and kills his own food, pulls it apart and devours it. The gastric juices in a dog's stomach are very strong and are capable of dissolving almost anything, including bones. Possessed as he is of these strong digestive powers he should be allowed to use them. Although dogs will eat farinaceous or starchy foods, they are not sufficient to keep the dog in good health and hard condition. If biscuit meal is given as a full meal I recommend it is scalded first with a good stock made from bones. Apart from the addition providing extra nourishment, hound meal or such-like swell with moisture; therefore, if a dog is given a large quantity it will expand in his inside and give him bad indigestion. Assuming that all cockers are like my own, he would wolf it down without stopping to think of the consequences. A healthy cocker is by nature greedy – in other words, he loves his food.

Adult dogs should be given two meals daily, the principal one consisting either of raw or lightly cooked meat, and the small one of good dog biscuit. In the last few years there has been tremendous growth in the pet-food industry and there are many varieties of tinned meat, all-in-one foods and biscuits and biscuit meals available. For many one-dog owners, these often form the basic diet of their pets, although in larger kennels it may not be as economical as other methods. Whatever the feeding pattern, care should be taken to ensure that there is a proper balance between the protein and carbohydrate intake of the dog. If he is not fed quality food, you cannot expect him to be as fit as he should be. If one of the dry, complete, feeds is used, it is essential that clean drinking water is always available as this is necessary for the dog to digest the dry feed. Also, a daily drink of milk is very good for all dogs, and almost essential for puppies. I usually give my dogs a large raw bone to gnaw once a day after their big meal; apart from assisting dentition, it promotes the flow of saliva, which in turn helps to digest the food. As to the quantity of food given, it is difficult to make a hard and fast rule. Some dogs need more than others; also stud dogs and bitches in whelp will need to be liberally fed. Ideally, a cocker should have a good half-pound of raw meat daily, exclusive of his biscuit meal. If you find your dog getting too fat, decrease the biscuit meal but not the meat; lean meat is not fattening and will help to keep him in condition. With a large kennel of dogs the food bill must be kept down if you are to make your dogs pay their way. You must get good nourishing food as cheaply as possible. Bullocks' heads are a good investment, but they will want really well boiling, until the meat falls off the bones. If you then cut up the meat and drop it back into the boilings with a little rice or oatmeal, and perhaps a few carrots, boil together until thoroughly cooked, then leave until the following day, you will find the whole mixture will turn out in a solid jelly which you can cut up in squares, and the dogs will love it. Every bit can be used this way; it is most economical, apart from being nutritious. It is surprising the amount of meat you will find on a bullock's head.[1] Many people give green tripe (the unbleached tripe) to their dogs as it is comparatively inexpensive, and the dogs love it. Though not available from butchers, there are many pet shops which sell it (usually frozen which must, of course, be thawed fully before feeding) and there are also firms specializing in dog meats of all kinds, many of whom advertise in the weekly dog papers.

If you want to put an extra bit of weight on your dog,

[1] Bullocks' heads have become rather expensive and not always easy to get, but they are certainly good food and worth buying when you can find them.

herrings are excellent for this; if very well boiled they can be mashed up, bones and all, and brown bread or hound meal added to soak up the boilings. The use of a pressure cooker is a great help as it speeds up the cooking, and will also make sure that the bones are well softened if left to cook for longer than usual. This will quickly put body on your dog if given on alternate days, and if he is a good doer. I find dogs appreciate a bit of good cooking.

Sheep's paunches, if available, are another useful thing to add to the kennel larder. They should be cheap, are very nourishing and the dogs love them. They also need boiling well. I always give a meal of paunch to a visiting bitch on arrival, if we have it, and I have never known one to leave it, a fact which speaks for itself.

If you cannot get cow beef, horse flesh is very good but unless bought as fit for human consumption it is wise to cook it thoroughly before use; it might have come from an animal which died of disease and would upset your dog's inside. Never feed frozen meat – it should always be allowed to thaw out before use – as this will also upset your dog. Rabbits are very good for tempting the appetite of a sick dog, care being taken to give no bones. The same applies to game or poulty bones; these can be very dangerous because if bitten up and swallowed they are liable to splinter and perforate the intestines.

Do not overfeed your dog. A healthy dog will clear up all that is given to him and ask for more, but be firm and give him just his ration. Do not give him all the tit-bits from the dinner table; collect the scraps and make one dish of them by adding broken biscuit or brown bread and good gravy. The ultimate result of overfeeding will ruin his health and his figure; he will become a fat, lazy dog, spending his life eating and sleeping. Too much sloppy food upsets a dog's inside, and deprives his digestive organs of their exercise.

The important part played by vitamins in a well-balanced diet is a comparatively recent discovery, yet judging by what dogs eat they appear to have always known that foods rich in vitamins were essential for their well-being. In the springtime it is quite a common thing to see dogs rush for the fresh green grass, which is so rich in vitamins; they can also get vitamin D through the action of the sun on their coats. Anyone who has kept a dog will have noticed how impatient he is to be out in the spring sun after the dark days of winter. When dogs lick themselves it is not only for toilet purposes – they are transferring the vitamin crop which has accumulated in their coats.

Some dogs like all kinds of fruit and it is really very good for them, an obvious fact when you stop to consider the proportion of essential vitamins it contains. Apples appear to stimulate the digestion and keep the teeth clean and wholesome. When they are plentiful it is a good idea to give your dog an apple to play with instead of a ball.

Grooming

Every dog should be well groomed daily. Apart from stimulating and cleansing the coat and skin it will keep him free from parasites such as fleas and lice – a well-groomed dog seldom gets infested with these pests. It also keeps him free from odours and dandruff and will remove dead hair. The brush is the symbol of canine hygiene so use it regularly. Use it not once a week but every day if only for a few minutes; it will work wonders with your dog's appearance. Use vigorous motion, brush all parts, and do not forget to brush the ears gently inside and out and the leg featherings. I like the dandy best, the same sort that is used on horses but smaller. Start at the head and work downwards to the tail.

Then comes combing. There are numerous different types of combs; the best to use for a cocker is the steel No. 76. You will find this very useful for the body coat and with the help of the brush it will remove most of the unwanted hair. You will need to use the comb very sparingly on the ears; it might thin out the ear featherings too much if used drastically. Finally, finish off with a chamois leather or hand glove; if this is done daily the coat will be in lovely bloom. Special attention should be paid to the inside of the ears. If they are cleaned out regularly with a piece of cotton wool, and a little boracic powder dropped in, they seldom give trouble.

The majority of dogs look forward to their daily brush. I

find my own cockers each morning after they have had their breakfast lined up waiting to be groomed, and they become quite impatient until it is their turn to be lifted on to the table.

How often should dogs be bathed? Most people wash dogs too frequently; an occasional bath is all that is necessary. It requires a week for a dog to get the natural oil back into his coat. The daily brushing will do as much good as a bath. In the summer months ticks are often picked up by dogs living in the country and coming in contact with sheep, or playing on ground where sheep have been grazing. They will sometimes become infested with these revolting insects. They are greyish in colour and about the size of a small pea. You usually first notice them when they have feasted themselves with blood and their bodies are to be seen standing away from the skin. They generally attack the head and ears. They fix themselves firmly in with suckers and the only way to remove them is to place a little paraffin or methylated spirit on the insects which will sometimes cause them to release their grip. Leave on for several minutes before attempting to pull out, taking great care not to break off the head as if left behind it will cause a sore. After removal it is wise to apply a little antiseptic ointment to the affected area.

Another insect to beware of is the harvest bug, found at harvest time as their name denotes. This is a small red insect, looking like sand. It usually attacks a dog on the head and legs but can quickly be got rid of by any of the parasite powders.

The greatest menace of all in the summertime is the common grass seed. This is contacted on any waste ground or common land throughout this island. By mid-July the stalks have ripened and become brittle; then the seed heads can easily break up, each floret forming a small arrow which gets entangled in the hair, chiefly on the feet, with the base pointing towards the flesh. The seeds are so shaped that with the dog's movement they get drawn tighter to the skin, eventually causing a small hole to be rubbed between the toes or pads. The seeds should be removed as soon as they are discovered, and if a wound has already been started this should be treated with an antiseptic lotion. If the seed is left in, it is surprising how quickly it will disappear into the foot and seriously lame your dog. I have known a grass seed to penetrate the foot between the toes, and it was not possible to extract it until it had reached the elbow. If you have the misfortune to get a seed really buried in your dog's foot it is advisable to get your veterinary surgeon to deal with it at once. Always remember that you must withdraw the seed from the front of the wound and not from the back; if drawn from the back you are liable to leave small particles behind, which will soon cause a festering sore. During the summer months it is always wise to brush and comb your dog after a country walk; by doing so you may save your dog much pain and yourself much worry.

Should the dog become badly infested with fleas or lice powder him thoroughly with insect powder. They are many dependable kinds to be had, but be careful of the eyes as certain preparations can be very harmful if they accidentally get into them. A wise plan is to fill the eye with a liberal amount of a mild eye ointment before commencing the powdering. As soon as the dog has shaken himself this can be removed. As previously mentioned, no regularly groomed, well-kept dog should harbour livestock in his coat, so whatever else happens see to it that he is well-groomed and thoroughly looked over daily; the little time thus spent will repay you well. Dogs usually change their coats twice a year, in spring and autumn, but should they be in a run-down condition, or if bitches have been nursing puppies, they will lose their coats again. Feed on good raw beef, give plenty of exercise and again make sure your dog is regularly groomed. The accumulation of dirt and dust, as well as dandruff thrown off by the skin, is contrary to the maintenance of good health. Dogs are liable to pick up all sorts of germs and parasites on their coats, especially on the feet and lower parts of the body. Therefore a dog's toilet should be as regular and equally as important as that of his master. I have so often heard owners say, 'Go outside, you smelly dog', whereas if the poor little animal had been well cared for there would have been no need for such a remark. I am sorry to say that many people who own pets are under the impression that they require no attention to their personal cleanliness. Needless to say, this is a wrong idea; most dogs appreciate a daily brush and are so much better for it. Resentment is often due to the fact that the coat has been allowed to become matted, and a lot of rough handling and tugging is needed to get it in order again.

Elizabethan Collar

An Elizabethan collar is a most useful asset to any kennel. If you wish to prevent a dog from rubbing his eyes with his paws or, in the case of skin disease or any injured part, to stop him from licking or biting himself, I have found the collar I will describe indispensable. It is very simple to make. You will need some stiff cardboard or linoleum. Cut from this a circular piece about eighteen inches in diameter. Having done this, cut a hole in the centre big enough to fit comfortably round the dog's neck. Then remove a V-shaped piece, the top of the V being on the outer circumference. Fit it round the dog's neck and lace the two ends together with tape or string; for this purpose holes should be punched along the edges. The wide end of the collar should be well free from the side of the face. When it is being worn it should be the shape of a saucer.

Exercise

To keep a dog in really good health and hard condition it is essential he should be regularly exercised. Besides keeping the muscles of the body in tone exercise acts as a stimulant and tonic to the circulation and internal organs. In my opinion exercise is almost as important as good food, and should you intend to show your dog, condition is one of the most important things in the show ring. Getting your dog into physical condition is something that cannot be done overnight; he will need weeks of hard, regular exercise, plus good food.

The fit dog has plenty of spirit, is keen and alert, full of the joy of living, and takes an interest in everything that is going on around him. The dog out of condition does not hold himself erect, he is listless, his coat is dull and lifeless, he is not interested in his surroundings, and in general he makes a very poor impression. He may have a large run or garden but that is not sufficient, and will not be the same as a scamper over the common, in the park or across country, with a thousand new smells. He is constantly sniffing adventure, laps at every stream and looks upon every field as a new world to be explored – perhaps a few rabbits, a woodcock, or a pheasant to put up. There is great value in the mental change of all this delightful excitement. Dogs, like human beings, need a change to keep fit. His mind needs feeding as well as his body, and loneliness is irksome to him. To turn a dog into the garden for an hour is useless; he will simply hang about the gate waiting to be asked in, and if as fond of his food as most cockers he will be worried in case he is losing some tasty morsel in the kitchen. Such strenuous exercise as following behind a horse or a bicycle should not be allowed; it can be very injurious, particularly if the dog is not in hard condition. During very hot weather, it is preferable, if possible, to give exercise in the early morning or in the cool of the evening. Dogs should not be deprived of their exercise because of inclement weather. Taking a dog out in the rain will do no harm provided he is fit and is well rubbed down on his return home. Be sure his coat is dry down to the skin – the dog may be dry outwardly but probably near the skin the hair is still damp. This is the thing that will bring on chills quicker than anything, particularly if he is not used to getting wet. I find a very useful thing for wet days is to keep a bath filled with sawdust. Immediately you return from your walk the dog should be put into this bath and thoroughly rubbed all over. The sawdust will quickly absorb the damp and at the same time will remove the mud. Take care that the dust does not get into the dog's eyes. After you have rubbed him down turn him into a kennel filled with straw, and it will be a joy to see how fresh and clean he will be when you let him out later on. Should you live near the sea, a daily swim will do no harm in warm weather, and most dogs really enjoy one, but do not allow it if you have a show in view as the salt water will remove all the show bloom you have put on. An ordinary healthy dog can do with as much exercise as you can give him within reason. If you are too busy to go for your usual walk the dog will get a good deal of exercise in a short time if a ball is thrown for him to retrieve.

Trimming

When you decide to show your dog you will need to start getting the coat in order some weeks before the show. Begin by giving the dog a bath in a good shampoo. The next thing is to remove all the dead coat; this should be done with finger and thumb, pulling in the direction of the lay of the coat. Your task will be made easier when trimming if you rub your fingers with chalk, or if you wear a thin rubber glove during the operation. This will enable you to get a grip on the unwanted hair. On no account resort to cutting except for the feet and tail, and the throat which is often done with thinning scissors. There is unfortunately a growing tendency to use scissors or clippers on other parts, but when the hair grows again it is very difficult to control.

When you remove the old coat, start at the head and remove all the unwanted hair evenly – do not pluck out bits here and there and make him look moth-eaten. Take out all the long hair from behind the ears, proceed to do the neck and shoulders in the same way and the surplus body coat; also trim under the tail well. A lot of groundwork can be done with a No. 76 steel comb; constant combing and removal of dead hair will be a big help towards keeping the dog in show trim.

There is quite an art in preparing a cocker for the show ring if you mean to exhibit him really well, and it will need years of practice. I advise any novice who means to take up showing seriously to gain experience from an expert; so much depends on the trimming. A well-turned-out dog will look the part. You must not only know the way to trim; you must also know just where to take it off. You should accentuate best points and try to minimize bad ones. When the trimming has been completed, regular grooming will be necessary if you wish to maintain the smart appearance needed for a show dog.

Bathing and Shampooing Your Dog

Although it is not wise to be unendingly bathing your dog, as I have said in a previous chapter, because too much bathing will remove the natural oil from the skin; on the other hand, it is reasonable to assume that the house-dog will need to be washed periodically for his own sake and that of everyone else concerned. A dog emanates body odours, particularly as it gets older, and unless kept clean can be most unpleasant. Whereas in a large kennels a large sink, set at an appropriate height, and sufficiently deep and large for bathing dogs may be available, in most smaller kennels and houses it is more usual nowadays to wash the dog in the bath (or the kitchen sink), using a spray or shower-head sprayer. This means the water can be pre-determined for heat, not too hot nor too cold; when the dog has been thoroughly wetted, the shampoo should be well rubbed in, taking care to avoid the eyes. It is also a good plan to plug the ears with cotton wool, to avoid getting water into the deep ear passages, which can cause much irritation for the dog. *Remember to remove them later*. After shampooing well, rinse all traces of shampoo from the coat, and make sure that the coat is thoroughly clean. For shampooing, many people now use a cream rinse to follow, but make sure that the instructions are adhered to for this.

There are various recommended methods of drying a dog, and one is by using a chamois leather wrung out in warm water. This will soak up a lot of the surplus water from the dog, before using a hot towel to finish off. Another method is to fasten a towel tightly round the body, having combed the body-coat flat, by pinning it under the chin and under the body. While the body is thus starting to dry, use a hair dryer to blow the featherings, combing as you go along. There are many types of hair-dryers on the market, from simple ladies' hair-dryers, to the larger stand-dryers sold by proprietary manufacturers at the larger dog shows and advertised in the weekly dog press. Whichever means of hot air you use (even if only from a fan-heater) make sure it is not too hot for the dog, just comfortably warm. When the leg featherings, trouser featherings and ears are dry, then the towel can be removed from the body, and with the heat directed down on to the body, the whole of the body coat and tummy featherings can be finished off.

During the very cold weather a spirituous dry shampoo, available at most pet shops, may be used. Also available nowadays is an aerosol-type spray dry-cleaner (as used for human hair, available at chemist's shops). A method often used as a cleaning preparation is ordinary talcum powder; rubbed well in, then thoroughly brushed out, and finished off with a dry, soft, clean chamois leather, will give the dog a clean, fresh, sweet-smelling finish.

Should your dog be scratching himself, and you are sure the cause is not 'livestock', there are many remedies available from veterinary surgeons or pet shops.

Do not let a dog go out and lie about on a cold day just after a bath. When he is thoroughly dry he should be encouraged to lie in his box or basket, which should be in a place selected because of freedom from draughts. It is not wise to bath an old or delicate dog during cold weather. Just like human beings, some are tough and can stand almost anything, whereas others are very susceptible to chills. A bitch in season should definitely not be bathed and you should make sure she is quite normal before attempting to do so.

Housing

There are many types of kennel in use; pattern is a matter of choice, but the health of the inmates depends considerably on the building in which they are housed. Stables and loose boxes make ideal kennels if each dog is given a warm sleeping box raised on short legs, or a bench, as stable flooring is mostly stone or concrete and very cold. Dogs, like human beings, need a comfortable bed. I have heard many breeders say that dogs should not be molly-coddled. I am all for making my dogs comfortable and you will find, if given a fresh straw bed, kennel dogs will be contented. The straw should be renewed at least once a week. Old carpets and sacks, which harbour insects, dust and damp, are very objectionable. Hay is also poor bedding as it becomes foul and sodden. No artificial heat is necessary for strong, healthy dogs. Any cocker can live in comfort in an outside kennel of the right type; it is the fireside dog that is more liable to catch cold. Timber kennels are very successful, being comparatively cheap to build, but these should be lined with boarding or plywood. It is also a good idea to line the doors with sheet tin or zinc, as dogs like to bite out if they can and will very quickly ruin a kennel door, and the splinters of wood which they may swallow can be very harmful. Kennels should be light and free from draughts. Plenty of fresh air is necessary to keep dogs fit. Windows should be made to open but they must be placed as high as possible, so that there is no likelihood of the dogs jumping out. If there are at least two windows, one at each end of the kennel, they can be opened together, which will allow a current of air to pass through and take away any doggy smells.

One of the most popular types of kennel is a range where several dogs can be kept under one roof, with a passage way under cover where one can move about in wet weather. Size depends on the number of dogs to be kept. Such a kennel will need an open-air run as large as space will permit. It is wise to place a bench or two in the run where dogs can lie out of the damp if they are inclined to sleep. If it is possible to construct your run so that it encloses a tree the dogs will appreciate this in the hot, glaring sun of summer. I have a weeping willow in my run, which I purposely had planted for the dogs, and they just love it on very hot days, when they can relax in the cool. These trees are very quick growing, and if you are just beginning to construct your kennels it is really worthwhile planting one; apart from being decorative, the dogs will thank you for it in summer days.

A constant supply of pure, fresh drinking water is a recognized necessity for a healthy dog. It must never be neglected. It is wise to change this two or three times a day during hot weather. The drinking vessels, as also the feeding dishes, should be kept scrupulously clean.

I strongly advise that the kennel kitchen is situated away from the other buildings, to save all risk of fire. It should be erected well away from any hen runs – the scattered food will attract rats. The kitchen can be a small building of corrugated iron sheets, with a boiler and a table for cutting up the meat. I find a good farm boiler or sawyer stove very useful, although some people prefer a pressure cooker. The floor should be of concrete, in order that it can be easily washed down. Kennels should always be kept spotless; no dust, dirt or rejected food should be allowed to remain.

When the dogs are let out for their early morning run all soiled bedding and sawdust should be removed and replaced with fresh; sawdust is wholesome and best for all kennel floors. This can be obtained from any saw-mill, but be sure it is fine and not filled with splinters. A thick layer should be spread over the floor of all kennels, particularly if they are concrete floors, as it is warm and absorbent. It is useful to have a small incinerator tucked away in some corner, where droppings, old bedding and sawdust can be burnt. Once every week the kennels should be thoroughly turned out and scrubbed through with a good disinfectant. It is advisable to do this in the morning, so that the kennels have time to dry thoroughly before the dogs are put into them at night. Runs also need regular cleaning and any droppings should be picked up. Should you have a kennel where there has been any infectious disease it must be thoroughly scrubbed with a strong disinfectant, not forgetting the walls and ceilings. When thoroughly dry, seal every crack and crevice to make it airtight, then place in an old tin or bucket two pounds of powdered sulphur – and this should be sufficient for a kennel about twenty feet square; proportionate quantities for larger or smaller kennels – pour a couple of tablespoonsful of methylated spirits over the sulphur and ignite it. Close the door quickly, seal any cracks at the edges, then leave for at least twenty-four hours. Another good way of eradicating germs is to run a blow-lamp over the woodwork, this method will dispose of all forms of infection. When the kennels are thoroughly disinfected or fumigated it is wise to open the door and windows and leave them open to the weather for two or three months before introducing another dog.

Do not forget to disinfect your brushes, combs, collars, leads and everything connected with the dogs and kennel. They are all germ traps.

Buying a Puppy

There is a marked increase in the desire to own a cocker spaniel as a pet. As you go through the suburban districts of London almost every second dog you see is a cocker. This goes to show their popularity and adaptability. They are equally happy in town or country, if given their daily walk. In every town there are parks or commons where dogs can be exercised and have a good scamper off the lead. When you decide to buy your puppy too much importance cannot be attached to selecting a healthy specimen. Make sure of getting one that will bring no regrets; you are buying a pet and you want to enjoy it, so do not be tempted to buy a weed because it is half the price of the others. You will be taking on trouble and in the end it will cost you more in vet's bills than you paid for it. A healthy puppy will repay you time and time again. If it is to become only a companion a typical specimen is all that is necessary, but even so it is wise to choose one from a really good strain, as everyone likes to feel the dog he cherishes is a good-looking one and a badly bred puppy so often grows into an ugly duckling. This is such a disappointment to his owner, as even if it is not intended for show he likes it to look attractive and to feel proud of it when they go walking together. The safest person from whom to buy a puppy is the breeder. In my opinion a bitch will make the best companion. She will need a little extra care, about twice a year for three weeks when she is in season, but she will be no trouble provided you do not keep a dog. I should not advise a bitch if you already have a dog; this would be asking for trouble.

If you are interested in showing and feel you would like to try your luck in the show ring I would advise you to put yourself in the hands of a reliable breeder and buy the best you can afford, but faultless puppies are very difficult to come by and usually a breeder will want to keep his very best puppies to show himself. Before getting your puppy, if you have had no experience of this kind of thing and are at a loss to know how to make a start, there are many open and championship shows during the year which one can attend to gain knowledge, and there you can decide on the colour and type you prefer. To find out about shows in your area, contact by letter or telephone the secretary of your nearest breed club (see list in Appendix A, pages 165–167). Exhibitors are usually very helpful to newcomers, so get to know a breeder who will, I am sure, be only too glad to help you and will no doubt make arrangements for you to visit his kennels with a view to selecting a suitable puppy. It would be possible for you to see the parents and grandparents whilst you are there; this would give you an idea of how your puppy is likely to appear when fully grown. If you are unable to get to any shows, you will probably be able to find what you are looking for advertised in the dog papers, although the local breed club secretary would probably be able to put you in touch with reputable breeders. Genuine breeders are always delighted to welcome visitors at their kennels, provided an appointment is made. Dealing by letter is not always satisfactory unless you actually know the people you are doing business with. Some advertisers will describe very mediocre specimens as certain champions; no one is going to sell a dog which looks like being a champion unless he gets a fabulous price for it, so do not attach any importance to these glowing advertisements. Also, before making your final decision to purchase have a copy of the pedigree sent to you, and if you are in doubt as to whether it is correct the Kennel Club will verify it for you. When the puppy arrives, if you are not too happy about its health have it examined by your veterinary surgeon. This can be done for quite a reasonable fee. If, after examination, you find it is not in good health communicate immediately with the sender and arrange to return it to him. It seems hard luck for the poor little puppy but it is the only thing to do.

If the puppy comes up to expectations and you keep it, the next thing to do is to register it at the Kennel Club. This, of course, is not essential, but if you intend to use it for breeding or showing at any time it will need to be registered. If the puppy has already been registered the new owner must get it transferred into his or her name. Transfers must also be registered at the Kennel Club.

For the first couple of days after arrival the puppy will possibly feel very strange and he will be a bit suspicious and unresponsive. If he has come from a kennel he will miss his companions and will be very homesick and may cry a lot at night, but if he is given a good meal, treated kindly and made comfortable, he will soon settle down, particularly if he knows friends are not far away. An old stocking, stuffed with a cosy filling, for the puppy to cuddle up to may be helpful. Another method of settling a new puppy into a strange place at night is to place a clock, well wrapped up in an old towel, into his bed. The ticking of the clock is supposed to simulate the hearbeat of another puppy, and comforts the puppy as a litter mate would.

Selling a Puppy

When you have puppies for sale, after the puppies have reached seven or eight weeks, decide as soon as possible which you intend to run on for show or breeding and let the remainder go as soon as practicable. The longer you keep them, the more they will cost you; therefore it will pay you to let the surplus go for what you can get, within reason, thus avoiding profit being eaten up. Never sell a dog showing any signs of illness or skin trouble. Should you do so it will cause you more worry than the worth of the puppy and in the end it will no doubt be returned to you. Also, it is unkind to send a poor little animal away to a strange home unless it is a hundred per cent fit. On no account let your puppies go on approval. Once out of your hands you never know what infection they might pick up, and should a puppy be returned you may lose half your kennel in consequence; puppies quickly catch any disease that is going about. Invite your client to your Kennel; it is much more satisfactory to you both, and puppies are always at their best in their own surroundings.

Issue a diet sheet with every puppy you sell and hand it over with the pedigree. So many puppies go wrong immediately they have left the care of the breeder, owing to wrong feeding or, more often than not, being overfed. A healthy puppy is naturally greedy and will always be asking for more. If he is given as much as he asks for he will become upset inside and the buyer will at once think he has been sold a sick puppy, when actually it is nothing more than the outcome of an unsuitable diet – and too much of it.

Unless you are known in the dog world and have a ready sale for all your stock an advertisement in the general press or your local paper is the best way to dispose of your puppies. Do not misrepresent them, avoid over-statement, and always remember that the thing to aim at is a reputation for reliable dealing. Satisfied purchasers tell others. And it is the best form of advertisement; as time goes on you will become successful in your dog business and quickly dispose of your stock. You will make many friends, too, and how proud you will feel when your puppies are brought back to see you and their owners say, 'I wouldn't sell him back to you for double the money.' I always get great joy out of such a remark. Although it is the right thing to give everyone value for his money, I am equally against giving puppies away. How often I have heard said, 'I am only mating my bitch as my vet says it will be good for her to have a litter, but I shall not sell the puppies – I would rather give them away to good homes.' I always think this rather a stupid remark, as in my opinion this is when they are likely to find bad homes. If people are real dog lovers they will already have a dog, and if they cannot afford a pure bred one they will be happy with a cross-breed. So often the dogless person will accept a puppy becuse it is offered for nothing. They just love it as a baby; it will be so cute and amusing, it will probably have lovely long ears and such a doleful expression and everyone in the family will give it endless attention. But as it grows older and loses its attractiveness it will possibly become a poor, neglected, unwanted dog. I have seen this happen so many times. Eventually it may be given away to anyone who cares to have it, or even turned out into the street to fend for itself. Another thing I have come up against: all is well until the poor unfortunate puppy is ill; the owner at once finds it quite impossible to keep it and it is brought back to you with endless apologies and excuses. So my advice is: never give a puppy away unless you know the people well and they already have a dog.

Training the House Pet

Dogs, like human beings, have different temperaments, each individual having a distinct personality. Some are instinctively more responsive than others. No two dogs are alike in looks or character. Some are more quickly trained than others. The trainer will need to be patient and under-standing; he will also need to be kind but at the same time firm. Should a dog be needed either as a house pet or as a show dog, training should commence at an early age. A well-trained dog is a pleasure, an unruly one a nuisance.

Assuming your puppy is to be a pet in the house, his first lesson will be cleanliness. Make him understand that he must not misbehave himself; his favourite place will be your carpets. If he is allowed the run of the house, keep him away from your best rooms until he has learnt what is expected of him. Put him outside at the slightest hint that he is about to misbehave himself, also immediately after meals and first thing in the morning and last thing at night. A dog's memory is wonderfully retentive, and when he has thoroughly learnt a lesson he will not easily forget it. Cleanliness in flats is a difficult situation because it is not possible to turn your pet into a garden. I have often heard of puppies being successfully trained on a galvanized tray. The tray should be filled with sawdust and the puppy put on it several times a day, particularly after meals. He will quickly learn what is needed of him. When he becomes old enough to be taken for walks the tray can be done away with.

There are other house manners to be learnt. If you allow your dog to be present at meals, do not give him tit-bits. If you once start he will give you no peace until he has eaten almost everything on the table. I have yet to meet a cocker who is not always hungry; even if they have just eaten a big meal they will still tell you they are starving, so if yours persists in worrying for food shut him out of the room. Being a sensible dog he will soon get to know why he has been turned out. Another bad habit, if he is not checked, will be to jump on chairs and scratch up cushions, and perhaps shower the place with feathers. Then he will come to the door to meet you, looking very innocent, with feathers stuck all over his nose. I have had this happen on more than one occasion. Another important thing is not to allow your dog to jump up; there is nothing more annoying than to be jumped up at and pawed over each time you enter the house. He may seriously damage your best suit, or ruin your silk stockings. To come home and meet your dog should be a pleasurable experience, not one necessitating changing into old clothes before you dare make an appearance. Good manners in the road should also be taught; do not allow him to foul the pavements – you can always guide him into the gutter. Teach your puppy to walk quietly on the lead; he will probably want to run ahead and pull at the lead. Correct this at once. Nothing looks worse than to see a dog taking you for a walk instead of you taking him. Try to get him to walk just behind to your left; your task will be more simple if you carry some tasty tit-bit in your left hand and reward him occasionally. If your puppy sits down and refuses to walk at all do not pull him. Just get behind him and give him a pat; he will soon start off again. You can also train him to follow off the lead when required, but even the best-behaved dogs are safer attached to a lead when in a busy thoroughfare. Inevitably one day he will see a dog on the other side of the road, or more likely a cat, and will probably forget his training in his excitement and dart into the road and under a car or bus. I have seen it happen many times. Dogs are so often blamed for bad behaviour when it is usually the fault of the owner; if a dog is not well trained he will always be a nuisance. A cocker is a very faithful animal and is always anxious to please; therefore the greatest kindness his owner can do is to spend a little time in training him. He will be well rewarded; his friendship and devout affection are well worth cultivating.

If you consider him and treat him with the kindness he deserves you can have no better companion; he will almost know your thoughts, he will always be the same faithful little friend, whatever sort of mood you may be in, and will unfailingly greet you with a wag of the tail.

I have often been asked, 'Is it fair to make a pet of a cocker, as he is a sporting dog?' My answer is, 'Yes.' Most breeds originated from sporting stock, and if a cocker is given plenty of exercise and companionship he will be happy. On the other hand, there is commonsense in all things; for instance, it would be unfair to take a working cocker who had been regularly shot over and expect him to be happy in a London flat.

If you keep poultry you should let your puppy know from an early age that they are not to be molested. They are a great temptation to a young cocker; he will probably start by chasing them and pulling their tail feathers out, which will be great fun, but if this is not checked in the beginning you will probably go out one day and find all your hens killed. The same principles apply to chasing deer or sheep. If treated with a very firm hand at the start he will probably make a peace pact with all these and grow up to respect them. You will then be able to meet them with a free mind when out for your walk together. To my way of thinking there is no greater embarrassment than for an owner to take his dog where there are deer or sheep and suddenly find him giving chase with a herd or a flock ahead of him. Apart from the embarrassment, it is a serious offence. A real dog lover will find training less difficult. Dogs are gifted with a wonderful instinct which enables them to know their friends. This explains why people who are genuine dog lovers have more success in training and showing. Dogs put their trust in them and try to do everyting they can to please. I feel one can often judge people's character by their attitude towards animals, and those timid individuals who dislike and are afraid of dogs must not be surprised if they get bitten; dogs can quickly recognize enemies and are not above giving them a quiet nip. Dog-loving people who have an intimate knowledge of canine character seldom get bitten; they are usually given a welcome.

Dogs kept chained up often become very ferocious. You cannot blame them. If I were a dog kept on a chain I should bite everything on sight! Just think of it: every day on the end of a chain, day in and day out. I am sorry to say one will often see this in the country, the poor dog frequently without water, a dirty little crust thrown down for a meal, no one to say a friendly word, and kept for the sole purpose of giving warning of an approaching stranger. In time the system becomes weakened and the mind becomes numb, the outcome of an existence of lasting solitude. Nothing could be more cruel and any dog lover should fight against this cruelty by reporting such cases to the RSPCA.

Some people go to the other extreme and allow their dog to curl up and sleep on their bed. I think this is wrong. It is unhygienic and should the owner become ill the dog must find another sleeping place. He will be utterly miserable and unsettled; a cocker is a great one for routine where his bit of comfort is concerned. If you must have him in your room at night let him have his own basket, which will be much better for both owner and dog.

The Novice Exhibitor

If you have a nice dog, someone sooner or later is sure to suggest that you show it, and when you start showing take every opportunity of learning all you can on how best this can be done. In most areas there are ringcraft training classes and these present an ideal way of starting you off. You learn what you are supposed to do in the ring, the dog learns ring discipline and the more experienced exhibitors training their youngsters will give you a reasonable idea of how good your dog is.

Begin with local shows. These are all advertised in the two weekly dog papers and entries usually close about a month beforehand. Watch what the other exhibitors do. See that your dog is looking his best, and when your class is eventually called into the ring do not gaze absentmindedly about you. Keep your thoughts and attention on your dog the whole time until the judge has placed his winners. See that the dog is standing or is placed in his most attractive position. The judge might give him a side glance and catch him at an awkward angle which might lose you the card he had in mind for you. Should you not win anything do not go to the judge and tell him what you won at another show; perhaps the competition was not so keen on the day you won, and this judge might like a different type. It is a poor sort of judge who has no mind of his own and has to follow the placings of others or assess a dog on past performances. Should the appointed judge happen to be a friend of yours do not pretend, when you get to the show, never to have seen him before – he will think more of you if you just pass the time of day – and do not expect to receive awards with inferior specimens because you are a friend. Remember there are many judges sitting at the ringside, and a judge can quickly lose his reputation by 'putting up' poor specimens. Do not call the judge's notice to a fault by the way you set up your dog. In years past most dogs were shown standing naturally on a loose lead, but nowadays this is the exception rather than the rule. Never be disheartened if you do not win. Study the winners closely and compare their good and bad points with your own dog. Maybe you have not trimmed him correctly, or perhaps he has not been taught what is needed of him in the show ring.

A beginner would be wise to avoid big shows until experience has been gained. At the smaller local shows competition is not so keen; confidence can be gained and a lot learnt in the way of handling. I have often heard a novice say that he showed his dog but could not win a thing with him. Such people make up their minds that it is useless going on, so decide to sell. A dog is sold to a famous kennel and immediately he is shown he goes to the top, but it never occurs to the original owner that the experienced breeder has made a close study of training, handling and trimming. The dog with his new owner is trained to go into the ring with a gay appearance, is taught to stand and show off his best points, and is trimmed to perfection. A well-turned-out dog is able to cover many shortcomings in other points, for there is yet to be bred the cocker every judge will acclaim as perfect. If you have a good dog and he is put into the ring as he should be, his day will come, whoever the owner may be.

A novice need not feel he is a nobody in the show ring; he is the backbone of the dog world; without him shows would not go on. All exhibitors are only too pleased to welcome recruits if they have the love of their breed at heart. Needless to say, most breeders have.

Dog shows are of five different types: Championship, Open, Limited, Sanction and Exemption. A show of Championship status is the most important of all and is authorized by the Kennel Club to award Challenge Certificates. With most breeds, when a dog has won three Challenge Certificates under three different judges, such a winner is classed as a Champion, but it is not so with gundogs – they must pass a field test before being allowed to use this title. As the cocker spaniel is one of the gundog group, it is necessary to obtain a qualifying certificate at a recognized Field Trial or Show

Spaniels Field Day in accordance with Kennel Club Rules before one can obtain the title of Champion. Without this qualifying certificate, a dog with three Challenge Certificates under three different judges is known as a Show Champion (or Sh. Ch.) for short.

Open and Limited Shows are held under Kennel Club licence. At an Open Show anyone can compete, and champions may also compete. At a Limited Show, competition is confined to members of the society running the show, and Champions (or Show Champions) cannot compete.

Sanction Shows are confined to society members, and have a maximum of twenty-five classes with post-graduate as the highest class. Over the years the number of Sanction Shows held has fallen, but these and Limited Shows are ideal for the novice to make a start. The general standard of dogs shown is not as great as at Open and Championship Shows, and the tension for the nervous new exhibitor is not so great.

Exemption Shows are small, usually held in aid of a charity with four classes for pedigree dogs (not necessarily registered at the Kennel Club) and a number of 'Novelty' classes (e.g. 'The dog with the most appealing eyes' or 'The dog the judge would most like to take home'). They are usually enjoyable events, and many beginners start out showing at this type of show.

Bear in mind that dog showing is a form of competitive sport and should be taken as such. Do not listen to all the bits of tittle-tattle you will be certain to hear. When I was quite a novice there came to my hearing an unkind remark someone had made about my dog. I was greatly hurt and spoke to our greatest cocker authority about it. His answer was: 'Don't worry. You can take it as the greatest compliment; if your dog was a bad one they wouldn't bother to talk about him.' I have always remembered this and it has helped me many times; so now when I hear that one of my dogs is being talked about unkindly I feel considerable satisfaction and know that the dog has 'caught on'. Fortunately for most of us, all these little bits of scandal when investigated boil down to nothing; they usually come from a disgruntled exhibitor who has had a bad day, or from a newcomer to the breed who repeats hearsay what he has accepted as fact.

Another thing you often hear is that the poor unfortunate novice will never stand a chance of winning, however good his dog may be. This of course is nonsense; if his dog is good enough he will certainly win. Novice exhibitors have had sensational wins, and many comparatively recent recruits to the show scene are winning Challenge Certificates. So do not get disheartened if you have a good dog. Keep showing him, remembering all the well-known exhibitors of today were once beginners, and sure enough your day will come. When you have been fortunate enough to breed a dog worthy of winning a Challenge Certificate, and one that is sought after for stud, you have achieved something which all breeders are aiming at. It has probably been the outcome of many years' hard work and concentration, but you have reached your goal and it has been well worth all the heartbreaks and setbacks you no doubt endured.

Training for the Show Ring

You can commence training your puppy for the show ring very early in his life; even at the tender age of eight or ten weeks you can train him to stand – mastering this is a good start and should make the more serious training less difficult. Between the age of five or six months is quite soon enough to introduce him to the lead. Should he not take kindly to it, no attempt should be made to pull him. The lead should be kept fairly loose at first, or attach it to his collar and let him drag it about where he pleases. Finally, retain the lead in your hand and allow him to move at his own will – he will soon become accustomed to it. I have found that another successful way of training a puppy is to take him out with the adult dogs. He will be so intent on following them that he will completely forget he is being led.

Assuming your puppy is trained to the lead, now is the time to begin lessons for the show ring. Make sure you have your dog's attention, and reward good behaviour with a tit-bit. Simulate or reproduce in your own run, or in any surroundings to which the dog is accustomed, as near as possible the actual show ring, even to the extent of having a stranger to handle him, which can often be arranged when a friend calls.

When you have everything in order, attached him to a slip lead and put him through his paces, walk him round the home-made ring, pose and re-pose him, run him up and down the centre of the ring, and set him up again; and then get your friend, who is a stranger to the dog, to handle him as though he or she were the judge. If your puppy is sensible and free from nerves lessons of this sort every day for a week should be sufficient for him to know what is wanted. Firm nerves and self-possession are essential qualities in the show ring for both exhibit and exhibitor. Many good dogs leave the ring cardless owing to bad showing, due to nervousness. Should the handler be nervous in the ring, I am confident the nervousness can be transmitted through the lead to the dog, so you cannot expect your dog to be a fearless shower if you are all het up with nerves. After all, there is nothing to be nervous about – the onlookers are looking at your dog, not at you. I have met many novice exhibitors who become self-conscious immediately they enter the ring and this at once reflects on the dog.

The dog in training should be taken into crowds, particularly if owners live in quiet country districts, where their dogs are not used to meeting a lot of people. Your pupil should be taken through traffic and in the midst of noise. The trainer must have great patience and, above all, persistent kindness. He should use a quiet voice; dogs dislike being shouted at. Some dogs seem to be born with a natural aptitude for showing, others learn only by experience or have to be taught. Do not imagine that a perfectly trained dog will remain so if badly handled.

Having got your dog trained as you want him, you may enter him at a show. He will need to be in good condition; he must be firm with plenty of muscle but not fat; lean meat and plenty of exercise are in my opinion the best things for getting a dog into condition. When you have decided on your show send a postcard to the secretary asking for a schedule, if you have not already received one. He will be only too pleased to send you one by return. All shows are advertised in the dog papers for some time before the entries close. When the schedule arrives the next thing is to enter your dog to the best advantage. The definition of the different classes will be seen at the beginning of the schedule. These classes are so arranged that dogs which have done a certain amount of winning cannot enter in the lower classes, therefore your puppy will not have to compete with the well-known winners unless you unwisely enter him in the higher classes, which would be a great mistake on your first attempt. Also a puppy has very little chance of winning when he is competing against mature dogs. Your policy should be to enter him in classes where you think he may stand a chance of being in the first three; perhaps you could get advice from a regular exhibitor with your first entry.

When the show day arrives make a point of reaching there quite half an hour before the scheduled time for judging. If the show is benched, find your bench which will be numbered. If it is unbenched, settle your dog in where it will be comfortable and happy until it is time for him to go into the ring. When you have settled your dog in, discover the location of the cocker ring; this will avoid searching at the last minute, which might mean missing your class. Then a good grooming can be done, so that the dog will be ready when your class comes along. When you are at long last in the ring you will have been given a ring number, which you attach to yourself where it can be easily seen. Exhibitors will then be asked to move their dogs round the ring. Always keep the dog on your left side, that is, in full view of the judge, taking care not to tread on the heels of the person or the dog in front of you. The judge and the ring stewards must be obeyed; if you are asked to stand in a certain position or order, stay there until you are wanted again. When you are asked to move your dog, take him up and back briskly, in the direction in which the judge wants him moved. It will be chiefly the dog's action from the front, the rear and the side that he will be looking at. Sound movement will play a big part in the placing of your dog in the prize list; so many are good standing and will look the winner, but when they are asked to move – oh, dear, what a disappointment! If the movement is bad it will stop the dog, however good in other points, getting very high in the awards, particularly if competition is keen. The standard of the cocker is so high today that a bad mover will not be tolerated. Therefore too much attention cannot be paid to the movement of your prospective prize winner. Movement should give a clue to the general make and shape; there should be perfect freedom at shoulder, elbow, stifle and hock. The gait should be easy and straightforward, each leg swinging back and forth the same distance forward as it does backwards. Turned-in toes (known as pin toes) and side swing of either leg or foot, are to be deplored, as is any upward swing of the forefeet or any action similar to that of a hackney pony. Style is inborn and cannot be taught, but every dog can be trained to show the best style of which he is capable.

When the awards are given out, accept whatever they may be with a good heart; if your dog is not placed do not be disappointed. Dog showing will lose all its joy if you allow a bad day to worry you. After all, there will be another day and another judge who will perhaps like your dog better, as some judges like an entirely different type.

The decision of the judge is absolutely final. It is useless to make a fuss; this only makes you look unsporting, so however disappointed you may feel it is better to say nothing, as complaining will not help matters. You have taken your dog to the show of your own free will, for the judge's criticism, so you must accept it. If you do not agree with the placings, or if you are anxious to know why your dog was turned down, go up to the judge quietly after he has finished his judging and ask the reason. A judge will be only too pleased to tell you, provided you approach him in the right way; he will no doubt comment on the qualities and failings of your dog. Remember his criticism; it will greatly help you in the future.

Another very important thing to remember is the handling of your exhibit in the show ring. So much depends on this; a good handler can show off his dog to the best advantage and bring out his good points, whilst a bad handler can manage to disguise the good points of the very same dog. Other things being equal, the dog shown by an experienced handler will often beat the one in the hands of the inexperienced one, simply because the novice has not learnt the art of handling, and his dog has not been seen to the best advantage. At smaller shows, where you meet a lot of novice exhibitors, judges find many exhibits which flatly refuse to be handled. Often they will not even stand on their four legs, and when

Sh. Ch. Astrawin Amusing

Sixshot Gobble the Turkey

Thomas Fall

Sh. Ch. Val of Locknell

Thomas Fall

Sh. Ch. Lochranza Strollaway

Diane Pearce

Sh. Ch. Olanza Pipistrelle

Sh. Ch. Sorbrook Holly Berry

Ch. Ouaine Chieftain, Best Cocker and reserve Best in Show, Crufts 1970. Cup presented by Princess Margaretta of Sweden
Diane Pearce

Mr G. Caddy

Ch. Bournehouse Starshine

Anne Roslin-Williams

Sh. Ch. Ramiro of Ronfil

Ian Scott

Sh. Ch. Chrisolin Cambiare of Styvechale

asked to move they simply rush across the ring with their tails tucked beneath them, and their ears on top of their heads, looking in all directions. It is quite impossible to sum up a dog of this sort, and a judge is not to blame if an otherwise good specimen fails to get placed. So if you intend to take up showing make a point of knowing what is expected of your dog in the ring; it is of the greatest importance to accustom him to show himself off and to be at his natural best in the show ring. Again the value of local ringcraft training classes must be stressed. Both dog and novice exhibitor can benefit greatly from them.

After the Show

For several days after bringing a young dog back from a show he should be carefully watched, and should he appear languid, with an indifferent appetite, or the development of a temperature, professional advice should be sought. It is in fact a wise precaution to isolate after a show for at least a week, particularly when you have young dogs in your kennel. This will often save the introduction of infection amongst your other stock. On the other hand, the exhibitor would do well to have had his dogs immunized against hard pad and parvorvirus and, particularly if living in an urban environment, against leptospirosis. It must be admitted dog shows have their drawbacks, but the dog would never have reached its present high standard without them. The show is the only way the breeder has of showing off his stock, and without the endorsement of our judges the British cocker would never have gained a world-wide reputation and attained its present popularity.

Nervousness in Show Dogs

Many dogs suffer with nerves, and a veterinary surgeon cannot do much to help in such cases as medicinal treatment does little good. I have heard it said many times that highly bred show dogs are so often nervous, but I wonder if this is due to dogs not having being taken out until they become adults. Owners of valuable show dogs are so afraid of taking them out and picking up some infection. As a consequence, during puppyhood they see only little of the outside world, whereas an ordinary puppy purchased as a pet is immediately familiarized with strange sights and noises, taken amongst traffic, meeting different people and all sorts of dogs; therefore they seldom suffer with nerves. If you wish to conquer nerves you should take it in hand during puppyhood. One is sorry to see so many nervous dogs at the shows nowadays, and I do regret to say it is becoming more prevalent: tails tucked beneath them, for example, and no sign of the merry cocker wriggle which has always been so characteristic of the breed.

I think judges should penalize this very severely as, if it is allowed to go on, our little cocker will lose all its charm. Tail-wagging is a particular fetish of mine; I regard it as a most valuable asset to a show cocker. I am almost certain this tucked-in tail is the result of puppies having being kept in safe seclusion for too long. Let your puppies meet people and take them into traffic at an early age, even if you carry them under your arm. Were such a policy general I am sure we should see fewer nervous dogs in the show ring. It is worth a little risk. If I have a couple of promising puppies which I intend to run on I often put them in the car when I go shopping. They usually dislike it at first but I find that after the first two or three times they really enjoy it, particularly if you give them some tasty morsel once or twice during the journey. If your puppy is eventually to become a show dog it is certainly worth the little extra time spent in such training. Nothing can be more distressing to an owner than to arrive at a dog show with his exhibit absolutely petrified with nerves. Both finish up by having a miserable day, and the owner feels that he never wants to see another dog show, having got nowhere in the award list. I have, fortunately, never owned a nervous dog, and I am quite sure this is only because I get mine out early in life. Dogs are often just what you make them. The cocker, like all dogs, is a highly sensitive animal and, as I have said before, like human beings each has an individual temperament. You cannot treat them all alike.

All dogs dislike being handled roughly and by so doing a good-tempered dog can be quickly turned into a bad-tempered, nervous one. If you treat your dog kindly he will have complete trust in you, and once you have gained his confidence you create a duty never to let him down. Cockers are wonderfully loyal and I am sorry to say often lavish their affections on unworthy masters. Owners should return their dogs' devotion and the faith and trust put in them. It is the duty of all breeders to see that the right kind of people acquire their dogs. The British are a dog-loving people, but even we have too many dogs in the hands of the wrong kind of owners. The dog for many hundreds, perhaps thousands, of years has been in close association with mankind. The right kind of human companionship has become essential to his mental well-being and not even the company of his own kind can take its place. The more, therefore, one's cockers are about with one the better it is for them and the more intelligent they will become. When in kennels they should have the companionship of other dogs and, if possible, an outside run where they can see everything that is going on. It is a great mistake to tuck show dogs away where they never see anyone yet expect them to go to a dog-show, meeting hundreds of strange people, without a sign of nerves. If you hope to exhibit a dog and do well with him it will pay you to take him out as much as you can amongst people. The dog, being a highly sensitive animal with an acute instinct for self-protection, will often snap at strangers if he is nervous and highly strung and has not been in the habit of meeting many people. If he does this in the show ring, however good he may be the judge will not place him. Nervous dogs will require careful treatment, and a great deal of time and patience is sometimes necessary to educate them to sense kindness. I am sure that this policy would reduce the number of nervous pets.

An Intelligent Dog

I have so often heard people say, 'Oh, give me a mongrel every time for intelligence and companionship.' With this I cannot altogether agree. Although I do not wish to belittle the intelligence of the mongrel, nor have I any criticism to make regarding its devotion to its master, I have at different times owned some amazingly clever cocker spaniels. I once had a red cocker bitch named Plum, and she really was one of the most intelligent dogs I ever knew, for she used all her senses – in fact she was almost human. It was during a very hot summer's day, when the temperature was over 80°F (26.6°C), and she was nursing a litter of puppies. Each time I visited her I found the puppies soaking wet, which really puzzled me until I actually caught her in the act of dipping one into her water bowl. I was so amazed that I just stood and watched her whilst she returned the puppy to the nest and treated each of the others in the same manner, and finished by making herself as wet as possible. They did look an uncomfortable little lot by the time she had finished, but the procedure made me realize the common sense this little mother had got. She knew her puppies were too hot, so decided to make them cool. Needless to say, her water bowl was promptly removed.

Life, however, is the sum of things which one remembers, and when I look back and review the clever things this little cocker did I have little desire to argue whether she worked by instinct or reason.

All dogs like eggs, and eggs have a pleasant smell in a dog's nostrils. More than this, they seem instinctively to know they are of a brittle nature and need handling carefully. Each time my little bitch heard the cackling of a hen she would rush to the hen-house and wait at the gate to be let in. When I opened the gate she would go forth, collect the egg and bring it out in a most careful manner and lay it in my hand. She would then give one sharp little bark and go in and collect another, and so on until all the eggs in the nest had been brought to me. But alas! in the end she disgraced herself. It was not always convenient to be there to open the gate; the hens would cackle and she must get in at all costs so she commenced digging under the wire. Then we could not understand why there were no eggs. We knew the hens were in full lay; perhaps the rats were taking them. I went to investigate and found a sprinkling of egg shells in the hen-house, and then I noticed that Plum's ears were covered with yellow, which looked uncommonly like the yolk of an egg. This was indeed very suspicious. She knew she had done wrong and her brown eyes looked up with an appeal that no sentiment can exaggerate. I immediately forgave her, although I told her she would never in all her life be allowed to collect the eggs again.

Dogs certainly possess what we call a conscience – that is they are well aware when they have done wrong, and everyone who has kept cockers will have little doubt about the profound depth of their affection. Plum's instinct would always tell her when I was nearing home, and she would be waiting to welcome me with the utmost importance, wearing a broad smile, twisting her lips and showing her teeth. This was another of her marked characteristics. To the rest of the world she was rather indifferent, though always perfectly courteous and polite to everybody. She had a striking personality; she used to sit up for everything she wanted, although she had never been taught to do so as I am not in favour of dogs doing tricks. When Plum was six years of age she left us. This was a very sad day and marred my pleasure for some time. We had accepted an invitation to dine with friends that night but asked to be excused owing to the death of a 'dear little friend'.

Essential for the Novice to Remember

Fresh, clean water should always be available. On no account ever chain your cocker up; it is a cruel practice. One cannot imagine any dog-loving person doing such a thing, but I am sorry to say that, much to my horror, I once found a puppy I had sold being treated in this way. I promptly bought the poor darling back and found him a home where he was appreciated. If it is not convenient to let him have his full liberty build a run of some kind for him.

Always keep your kennels and feeding bowls scrupulously clean. A dog will not be healthy in a dirty kennel.

Brush and comb your dog daily and see that he is free from livestock. Don't forget that dirt will encourage fleas and skin disease.

A large raw bone is good for dogs of all ages, but never give game, poultry, rabbit or chop bones as they are liable to splinter and cause serious internal trouble.

Too much sloppy food upsets a cocker's insides and deprives his digestive organs of their exercise. Never over-feed or under-feed your dog; two good meals a day at regular times are sufficient.

Should you own only one house pet and be unfortunate enough to lose it through hard-pad, parvovirus or other infectious or contagious disease, do not buy another for several months; the infection may remain in your house and be passed on to the new arrival. Hardpad and parvovirus are very infectious and can be carried even on your clothing.

If you have several dogs do not show favouritism to one and neglect the others.

Never overcrowd; do not have more dogs than your kennel and grounds will take comfortably.

Ventilate your kennel well; cockers need plenty of fresh air; as do human beings; germs thrive in bad ventilation.

See that your dog has daily exercise, which he will greatly look forward to; it will also go a long way towards keeping him in fit condition.

Loneliness is irksome to a healthy cocker; his mind needs feeding as well as his body. A happy dog is a fit dog.

Do not expect your dog to obey you before he is thoroughly trained and knows what is expected of him.

Lastly, keep an eye on your dog's general condition. A dry nose, staring coat, running eyes or lassitude, are sure signs of something wrong.

5

Successful Kennels and Exhibitors of Post-war Years

Whilst, sadly, a number of the people who helped to re-establish the breed are gone, the memory of their dogs still remains, and their influence is still recognized by the growing band of enthusiasts, and the keenness and determination of many young exhibitors will ensure that progress, started by people like Mrs. Lucas-Lucas, the original author of this book, will be maintained.

For the benefit of those new to cockers who, I am sure, would like to know about post-war successes, brief notes of the well-known kennels and their most successful exhibits may be of interest.

Asquanne

Ann and Alan Webster have had both solid and particolour show champions. Their first was the blue roan bitch, Sh. Ch. Asquanne's Kims Superbe, a really free-striding showman, and later top winners included Sh. Ch. Asquanne's Genevieve, a black who amongst her many successes won a Challenge Certificate at Crufts in 1984, and was Reserve Best in Show all breeds at Paignton Championship Show. The latest Sh. Ch. is also black, Asquanne's Ghia.

Astrawin

Mrs Phyllis Wise and her late husband Stan have produced a large number of solid coloured top winners in the last thirty years. They have included the beautiful type red dog Sh. Ch. Astrawin April Fire, the glamorous Sh. Ch. Astrawin Authentic, another red dog, and the Crufts Best of Breed Bitch in 1961, Astrawin Aphrodite.

Bitcon

Moray Armstrong from Cumbria is one of the younger school who has had a succession of top particolour bitches since 1975. In 1978 his Sh. Ch. Bitcon Silver Model was runner up to the top cocker of the year, and in 1980 a bitch he bred, Sh. Ch. Bitcon Florin of Mistfall, achieved the top spot. His Sh. Ch. Bitcon Shy Talk was top puppy in 1985, and the latest Sh. Ch. is Bitcon Shawnee.

Bournehouse

Gordon Williams achieved a remarkable record when his beautiful home-bred blue roan bitch, Ch. Bournehouse Starshine passed the highest number of C.C.s won by a cocker. Her eventual total was 60. She also qualified in the field to become a full champion, as well as producing two show champion daughters. Mr Williams has now reverted to his other show breed, English setters, in which he had the marvellous success of Best in Show at Crufts.

Broomleaf

The late Mrs Kay Doxford had a long record of outstanding success and solid breeding has been greatly influenced by the stock she produced. High amongst the greats must be her red dog, Ch. Broomleaf Bonny Lad of Shillwater, and exhibitors in the early 1970s will remember the lovely red bitch, Sh. Ch. Broomleaf Blithe Spirit, Best in Show at the Cocker Spaniel Club in 1971, and C.C. winner at Crufts in 1970. The black dog, Sh. Ch. Blackbird of Broomleaf was Best of Breed at Crufts in 1965. Particolours were also kept, and Sh. Ch. Blueprint of Broomleaf was a good representative of these. More recently the black dog, Sh. Ch. Broomleaf Bright Memory has made his mark, having sired several show champions. When Mrs Doxford died the prefix passed to her companion of many years, Miss Poppy Becker (*see* Olanza prefix).

Bryansbrook

Brenda and the late Bryan Fosbrook bred a number of beautiful solids, and the climax was at Crufts in 1980 when Sh.

Ch. Bryansbrook High Society was Best of Breed. 'Oscar' went subsequently to Mr Eugene Phoa in Edmonton, Canada, and achieved the No. 2 English Cocker spot in Canada and No. 4 in USA. His photograph is on the front cover of this book.

Canigou

Mrs Patricia Bentley, another solid breeder gained success with both reds and blacks, the high spot being in 1986 when the black dog, Sh. Ch. Canigou Mr Happy was Cocker of the Year.

Canyonn

Mrs Susan Young has made an impact in later years with her home-bred blacks. Sh. Ch. Canyonn Christa and Sh. Ch. Canyonn Cassandra, Best of Breed at the last show in 1987, the Ladies's Kennel Association.

Cassa

The late Mrs Dora Kershaw and Mrs Eva Coulton bred very successfully during the 1950s, mainly with solids, but the tricolour dog, Ernocroft Expert achieved his show championship. Sh. Ch. Cassa Christina was a lovely type red bitch.

Cilleine

Mrs Denise Barney has had success with a show champion title for her black bitch, Cilleine Athene, but in recent years the most successful dog has been the blue roan, Sh. Ch. Cilleine Echelon. Home-bred, 'Edward' was Cocker of the Year for three years in succession (1981–1983), won 35 C.C.s and was Best of Breed at Crufts in 1984.

Classicway

Both Ernie and Mrs Daphne Darby have been showing cockers since their youth and, particularly in recent years, have been very successful with a number of particolour show champions including a dog, Sh. Ch. Classicway Concorde who went to Australia, Sh. Ch. Classicway Carrie Ann and Sh. Ch. Classicway Cressida. They have also been very successful with some terrier breeds.

Cochise

Success at the top started for Howard and Mrs Joy Blake with a beautiful orange roan bitch, Sh. Ch. Cochise Circe and from her and her line were produced a number of show champions including the blue dog, Sh. Ch. Cochise Czardas and the striking black and white bitch, Sh. Ch. Cochise Czoloushka.

Colinwood

It would be difficult to overstress the importance to and influence on the breed of the Colinwood kennels. Until his death these were run by Mr Alf Collins, and have since been successfully carried on by his daughter Phyllis, now Mrs Woolf and her husband, Peter. The tricolour dog, Ch. Colinwood Cowboy was the first post-war champion; the black dog Colinwood Black Eagle was Reserve Best in Show at Crufts in 1962, but it is Ch. Colinwood Silver Lariot who is best remembered. His 57 C.C.s remained a breed record for many years. Sh. Ch. Colinwood Bellboy is the latest champion from the kennel.

Coltrim

Ed and Mrs Joan Simpson made the blue roan, Coltrim Mississippi Gambler into a show champion. From 1978–1988 Ed was secretary of the Cocker Spaniel Club, recognized universally as the parent club of the breed.

Cornbow

The brothers Jack and Ron Clarke started the Cornbow kennels soon after the war, but their first big win must have given them immense pleasure. Mr H. S. Lloyd the 'Wizard of Ware' did not judge at championship shows over here until 1954 when he judged the bitches at the Midland Cocker Club Show. Cornbow Myosotis, a red bitch, won the brothers their first C.C., and she went on to be Best in Show. Ron has now left the partnership (see Roanwood). Amongst the well-known dogs with the Cornbow prefix have been the black show champions Sh. Ch. Cornbow Night Owl and Sh. Ch. Cornbow Venture.

Courtdale

Mrs Sylvia Jones does not show nowadays, but exhibitors of her successful show days will not forget at least two of her show champions, the delightful tricolour bitch, Sh. Ch. Courtdale China Model, and the blue roan dog Sh. Ch. Courtdale Flag Lieutenant. Flag was a dog of lovely type with a beautiful head, and his type was reproduced in his many successful offspring.

Courtmaster

Although a comparatively young couple, Doug and Mrs Sue Telford have produced two blue roan show champions, Courtmaster Je Suis and Courtmaster Abracadabra. Abracadaba was Best of Breed at Crufts in 1987.

Craigleith

The Craigleith cockers belonging to Mrs Mollie Robinson are well known all over the world. Since Ch. Craigleith Cinderella (a blue roan) won her first C.C. in 1961, they have maintained a lovely type through to Sh. Ch. Craigleith The Waltz Dream, the orange and white latest champion. Ch. Craigleith Cinderella and Sh. Ch. Craigleith Maggie May (black and white) were particular favourites. Cinderella won the C.C. at Crufts in 1962 and The Waltz Dream in 1981.

Crosbeian

The late Mrs Dorothy Trench was a greatly respected lady in the breed, and her show champions were the bitch, Sh. Ch. Crosbeian Thornfalcon Flamenco and the blue dog, Sh. Ch. Crosbeian Cascade.

Dellah

Leslie Page was a very successful exhibitor in the twenty years or so after the war, starting his C.C. winning career in 1949 with the orange roan, Sh. Ch. Dellah Pin Up Girl. Sh. Ch. Dellah Merrymaker of Wykey, a lovely type blue roan dog, won seventeen C.C.s, a particularly good record as he was being shown at the same time as the great Ch. Colinwood Silver Lariot. Mr Page is now recognized as one of the top gundog judges in the country, and is a member of the Kennel Club Judges Sub-Committee.

Gatehampton

Mrs Queenie Cloke is another who does not now exhibit but had one of the most highly respected solid kennels in the years after the war. Prominent amongst her winners were the red dog Sh. Ch. Gatehampton Dumbo and the black, Sh. Ch. Gatehampton Black Sambo of Lochnell.

Gladrien

One of the newer of the successful kennels belongs to Mrs Geraldine Kaufman. Her black dog Lorjos Something Impressive of Gladrien won the Gundog Group at the Scottish Kennel Club Show in 1985, but she made up her first show champion, Gladrien Gem Sparkle, another black, in 1987.

Glencora

The late Jimmy Auld had one of the most successful kennels in Scotland with the Glencora Cockers, both solid and parti-colour show champions being produced. The black dog, Sh. Ch. Glencora Black Ace was a particularly good cocker of lovely type, and Sh. Ch. Glencora Gallant Star was a very striking black and white.

Haradwaithe

Stuart Clayforth, and his partner R. Peters hit their high spot in 1986 when their blue bitch, Sh. Ch. Haradwaithe Sorceress won the Best of Breed award at Crufts.

Of Hearts

Hubert Arthur, in earlier years prominent in many gundog breeds, and well-known for his involvement with cockers in the immediate post-war years, made up the two blue roan litter brothers, Sh. Ch. Silver Mogul of Hearts and Sh. Ch. Shooting Star of Hearts. He and his wife Mrs Doris Arthur both now judge gundog groups at Championship shows.

Helenwood

Mrs Jackie Marris-Bray, another breeder who has lived with

top show cockers since her youth had Best of Breed at Crufts with Sh. Ch. Janeacre Night Skipper of Helenwood and since then she has produced a succession of top winners. A number of them have been black, including the latest Sh. Ch. Helenwood Ivanoshon, but amongst the reds have been the dog, Sh. Ch. Helenwood Haymaker and the lovely red bitch, Sh. Ch. Helenwood Amarella.

Of Ide

Joe Braddon is recognized as one of the world's top all-round judges. Many of the later people showing cockers do not appreciate the outstanding contribution he made to the breed in the 15 years or so after the war. He made up a considerable number of dogs and qualified most of them in the field. It is difficult to place any order of preference, but amongst the outstanding ones were the lovely type blue dog, Ch. Valstar Glow of Ide and the striking black and white, Ch. Domino of Ide.

Kavora

Miss Pam Trotman has been one of the most successful of cocker exhibitors in recent years, mainly with solids, though she has won a C.C. with a particolour. In 1969 and 1970 her red bitch, Sh. Ch. Kavora Merryborne Sweet Martini was outstandingly successful. She was runner up to the Cocker of the Year in 1969 and won the top spot in 1970. In recent years another red bitch, Sh. Ch. Kavora Charade has been amongst the top winning cockers in the breed, following on from several blacks being made up.

Leabank

The Leabank dogs of the late Mrs Margaret Stevens were generally excellent in type and probably the most successful was the blue roan bitch, Sh. Ch. Raneyl Late Summer of Leabank. The blue roan dog, Sh. Ch. Leabank Levity figures in many pedigrees.

Lindridge

A kennel that has come into great prominence in recent years is the Lindridge kennel of Mrs Angela Hackett. The first of her show champions was Sh. Ch. Lindridge Lucky Charm and her latest is the young blue roan dog, Sh. Ch. Lindridge Venture. Sh. Ch. Lindridge Gypsy Girl, cocker of the year in 1984 won three C.C.s whilst still a puppy, but at her first show out of the puppy classes, she clinched her title by winning the C.C. (A dog must win a C.C. after it becomes a year old to qualify for the Sh. Ch. title.)

Lizarn

Arnold and Mrs Elizabeth Hall, not now active exhibitors in the breed, showed both solids and particolours including the red bitch, Sh. Ch. Lizarn Late Summer Morn. Mr Hall now judges eighteen breeds in the Gundog Group, and has just given up his position as breed correspondent to the weekly *Dog World* after 20 years. He has run the Cocker of the Year and Cocker Puppy of the Year competitions since their inception (*see* page 138).

Lochdene

Mrs Patricia Shaw, formerly Mrs Tosh, who lives in Scotland has produced cockers of very high quality and type for many years. She has been particularly successful with her reds. In 1965 she won the C.C. at Crufts under Mrs Lucas-Lucas with Sh. Ch. Lochdene Pepper Pot. Sh. Ch. Lochdene Sorbrook Sundowner was a very successful red dog.

Lochnell

The late Mrs Marjorie Cameron was a popular figure at dog shows, and although she made up only one show champion herself, the lovely headed red dog, Sh. Ch. Val of Lochnell, she was a particularly successful breeder. Others which she bred achieved their title in other ownership, and ones which spring to mind are the black dog owned by the then Miss Phyllis Collins (now Woolf), Sh. Ch. Colinwood Jackdaw of Lochnell; Mr Jimmy Auld's black bitch, Sh. Ch. Black Jade of Lochnell; Mrs Cloke's Sh. Ch. Gatehampton Black Sambo of Lochnell and the red bitch owned by Mrs Lucas-Lucas, Sh. Ch. Sixshot Honeybird of Lochnell.

Lochranza
The Lochranza kennels was founded by Miss Joan Macmillan and she is now partnered by Mrs Jean Gillespie, with the assistance of Mr John Gillespie. Early after the war Miss Macmillan qualified the black dog, Ch. Lochranza Latchkey, and a few years later the red dog, Sh. Ch. Lochranza Dancing Master proved to be a great stud force. There have been many show champions produced over the years, and one of the most notable was a black dog, Sh. Ch. Lochranza Strollaway, Reserve Best in Show at Crufts in 1969.

Lucklena
The late Mr Arthur Mansfield had a remarkable record with the small kennel he was able to maintain. He had a succession of top cockers, starting with Ch. Lucklena Musical Maid, who qualified in the field and produced champion offspring. His last champion was made up not long before his death, with Ch. Lucklena Minstrel. Mr Mansfield lived in a built-up area in Derby but he trained and qualified six champions in the field, an outstanding achievement.

Matterhorn
Howard and Mrs Eirlys Jones had their big moment when Sh. Ch. Matterhorn Montana started in 1985 with Best of Breed at Crufts and ended it as Cocker of the Year. Amongst their other champions has been his black and white daughter Sh. Ch. Matterhorn Morning Mist.

Maxway
Ken McFarlane gained his best win with his blue dog, Sh. Ch. Maxway Music Maker when this young home-bred was Best in Show All Breeds at the Three Counties Championship Show in 1987. It was particularly pleasing for him as Music Maker is sired by his previous show champion, Tudorgold Nimrod Variations from Maxway.

Merryborne
Mrs Irene Martin now lives in Nevada, USA, but she had considerable success with her solids before moving over there. In 1971 she had Best of Breed at Crufts with her black bitch,

Sh. Ch. Merryborne Simone and at the same show won the Reserve Dog C.C. with the red dog, Sh. Ch. Merryborne Big Shot. She also bred Sh. Ch. Kavora Merryborne Sweet Martini (*see* Kavora).

Merrybray
The late George Dunn and his daughter Pat (now Mrs McEntee, living in Eire) owned many good particolours and pride of place must go to Sh. Ch. The Mataroa of Merrybray, a blue roan dog, much admired during his show career in between 1968 and 1971.

Merryworth
Mrs June Chadwick, who died in 1975, was a very successful breeder of particolours and very much in memory are the striking black and white bitch Sh. Ch. Merryworth Matches and the free-striding and sound blue roan dog, Sh. Ch. Merryworth Musical Box, Dog C.C. winner at Crufts in 1961.

Misbourne
Miss Dorothy Hahn is one of only two people still with us who have judged the breed at Championship Shows before the war. She won her first Reserve C.C. with Valcresta of Misbourne in 1949. A succession of show champions started in 1953 when Pickpocket of Misbourne won the C.C. at the London Cocker Spaniel Society under Mr Joe Braddon, and included the lovely black bitches Sh. Ch. Atway My Love of Misbourne, and Sh. Ch. Sweet Anice of Misbourne. The latest was Sh. Ch. Misbourne Postmark in 1980. The Misbourne prefix is now shared with partner Mr Peter Rudd.

Mistfall
Geoff and Mrs June Parkin have won well with the Mistfall particolours in recent years, both Mistfall Mood Indigo and Mistfall Mandalay gaining their show champion titles.

Moyhill
Jim Cudworth and the late Ted Fletcher won well with their blue roan dog, Sh. Ch. Buryhill Cedar, and later with the

home-bred blue roan dog, Sh. Ch. Moyhill Maxwelton at a time when Ch. Colinwood Silver Lariot was amassing his huge total of C.C.s. Their attractively marked tricolour bitch, Sh. Ch. Moyhill Miss Jazz also made her mark. Mr Cudworth is a well-known gundog judge who took the English Springer, Sh. Ch. Hawkhill Connaught into the record books in his breed.

Normanview

Slav and Mrs Daisy Baldwin own this Scottish kennel which has produced show champions in their own dogs, Normanview Thundercloud and his son Normanview Scots Grey, as well as Normanview Stormtrooper owned by Mr and Mrs J. Reid, also from Scotland.

Noslien

A very old-established Scottish kennel, originally in the name of the late Mrs Neilson and now run by her daughter Miss Pat Neilson. In 1966 both C.C.s at Crufts were won by their dogs, Sh. Ch. Noslien Nathaniel, a black dog was Best of Breed and the beautiful red bitch, Sh. Ch. Noslien Naughty Nineties won the bitch C.C. Since the war the 'of Ware' kennels is the only other one to achieve a similar double at Crufts.

Nostrebor

An old-established kennel owned by Mrs Doreen Robertson who made up three cockers, Ch. Nostrebor Riverbank Rogue, a very nice type blue roan dog, the attractive orange roan bitch, Sh. Ch. Nostrebor Nightlight and another orange roan, Sh. Ch. Nostrebor Nonchalant. Rogue won the Crufts Dog C.C. in 1955. Mrs Robertson does not now attend shows, but is well known for her weekly breed notes in *Dog World*.

Olanza

Miss Poppy Becker was associated with the Broomleaf kennels for many years, but at the same time managed to win at the top with her own Olanza breeding. She made up her first Sh. Ch. Olanza Pipistrelle in 1970, and has had continuous success leading to 1987 when the litter brother and sister Olanza Poacher's Moon and Olanza Promise Me both became show champions. Poacher's Moon crowned Miss Becker's year when he became top cocker of 1987.

Oxshott

The late Mrs K. Joyce Gold's dogs had a powerful influence on the breed in the early post-war years, with the blue roan dog, Ch. Oxshott Marxedes being one of the major stud forces. Mrs Gold also won with her blacks, including Sh. Ch. Crumpington Pendarcylla of Oxshott. She was one of the few successful in breeding between solids and particolours.

Ouainé

Ouainé is the prefix of Mrs Joyce Caddy, who is Secretary of the Cocker Spaniel Breed Council, and representative for the breed on the Kennel Club Breed Liaison Council. The best known of the Ouainé dogs has been Ch. Ouainé Chieftain, a lovely headed, very sound moving and free-striding dog with good ring presence, who was Reserve Best in Show at Crufts in 1970, and won Best in Show All Breeds awards at Paignton and the Scottish Kennel Club Championship Shows. 'Ringo' was top cocker of the year in 1969 and 1971, runner up in 1970, and Irish top cocker in 1972. Mrs Caddy also trained and qualified him for his full championship. Amongst her other show champions was Sh. Ch. Ouainé Chipaway, who was the last tricolour dog in the breed to gain his title.

Peasemore

Miss Margaret Annetts kept only a small kennel but she had two show champions, Sh. Ch. Peasemore Playgoer a blue roan dog, and Sh. Ch. Peasemore Pirouette a black and white bitch. Miss Annett does not now show, but occasionally attends shows in the south east.

Peelers

Mrs Marion France, daughter of the late Mr Dick Morgan, one of the best gundog trainers in the country, had great success with the Peelers solid cockers in the 1960s, winning Best in Show All Breeds at General Championship Shows with both Ch. Peelers Cornbow Myth and Sh. Ch. Peelers Public Order. She later handled Ch. Bournehouse Starshine during her extremely successful show career, and also handled Mr Gordon Williams' English Setter, Sh. Ch. Bournehouse Dancing Master, to a Best-in-Show at Crufts.

Pentavy

Mrs Kay Holmes had her first cocker just before the war and produced sound cockers over a long period. She bred and showed Sh. Ch. Pentavy River Patrol a black white and tan dog, but a lot of overseas travelling limits her present showing. She is chairman of the Cocker Spaniel Club.

Platonstown

The Platonstown solids, mostly black, have had great success in Great Britain and Eire for Mrs May Snary over a long period. In 1984 Sh. Ch. Platonstown Scooby Doo was Best in Show All Breeds at the Belfast Championship Show. Her first champion, Sh. Ch. Platonstown Lovely Cottage won her first C.C. in 1965.

Quettadene

Quettadene was originally the prefix of Mrs Woodbridge, known affectionately to all exhibitors as 'Woody'. She produced many beautiful solids, with the black bitches Sh. Ch. Quettadene Lucky Dip and Sh. Ch. Quettadene Dream Awhile being great favourites. She also bred, and co-owned with Mr Leslie Page, Sh. Ch. Quettadene Mark. When she died the prefix passed to Mrs Penny Lester, who had been associated with the kennels since childhood. Mrs Lester has continued the success story, and her beautiful black dog Sh. Ch. Quettadene Emblem is one of the current top stud dogs. Apart from being a Group winner himself, he sired the top cocker of the year in 1986 and the two top winners and top puppy in 1987.

Roanwood

Roanwood is the prefix of Mrs Shirley Clarke, though her interest is shared with her husband Ron, previously in partnership with his brother Jack with the Cornbows. Mrs Clarke was interested in obedience work with cockers before her marriage, but she and her husband have had great success with showing. Sh. Ch. Roanwood Ripple won twenty-five C.C.s, the record number for a black bitch. She was runner up to the Cocker of the Year in 1982, but tragically died young whilst in whelp. The first Roanwood dog champion, Sh. Ch. Roanwood Flint was made up at the last show in 1987.

Ronfil

Ron and Mrs Tydfil Bebb from South Wales share the interest in the dogs, which are in Mrs Bebb's name. They came to the fore in the early 1950s with the lovely dog, the black and white Sh. Ch. Ronfil Regent, and although housing only a comparatively small number of dogs have been consistently successful. The most successful from the point of view of C.C. winning was the blue roan dog, Sh. Ch. Ramiro of Ronfil who won nineteen C.C.s, a Reserve Best in Show and a Gundog Group, but many people also remember the lovely blue roan bitch, Sh. Ch. Ronfil Rememberance.

Scolys

The Scolys dogs of Mrs Dilys Schofield do not appear much in the show ring nowadays, but the name of Ch. Scolys Starduster is still well known from the many pedigrees on which his name appears. Mrs Schofield qualified both Starduster and Ch. Scolys Showpiece in the field. At the Show Spaniels Field Day, Starduster also won the Novice Stake.

Sixshot

The late Mrs Lucas-Lucas, original author of this book, had a particularly successful kennel. Although a few particolours were kept, it was with solids that the name Sixshot excelled. Before making up a champion, two black dogs, Sixshot Black Swan and Sixshot Willy Wagtail were great stud forces in their day. A succession of show champions came, starting with the lovely headed red dog, Sh. Ch. Sixshot Woody Woodpecker. A particular favourite of the reviser of this book was the beautiful black bitch, Sh. Ch. Sixshot Sugar Bird. Sadly Mrs Lucas-Lucas died in 1987.

Sorbrook

Mrs Jean Smith, in partnership with her husband John, has made the prefix 'Sorbrook' well known in many countries of the world. Since Sh. Ch. Amanda Jane of Sorbrook, there has been consistent winning, with Sh. Ch. Sorbrook Christmas Knight and Sh. Ch. Sorbrook Sorceress as the most recent. A number of the Sorbrook dogs figure prominently in pedigrees today, e.g. Sh. Ch. Sorbrook Christmas Knight is the sire of Sh. Ch. Quettadene Emblem.

Styvechale

A few years ago one of the sights of the year was the Stud Dog class at the Cocker Spaniel Club Show when Sh. Ch. Chrisolin Cambiare of Styvechale paraded with the huge number of progeny that he had sired entered at the show. Mrs Phyllis Masters, who has been one of the stalwarts of the breed for a very long time has also produced other show champions, including the blue roan bitch, first C.C. winner for Styvechale, Sh. Ch. Styvechale Startime, and the black and white dog, Serenader of Styvechale.

Tarling

Jim and Mrs Olive Norfolk made Sh. Ch. Coltrim Crackerjack of Tarling into a show champion. Mr Norfolk is an ex–Secretary of the Cocker Spaniel Club, at present Chairman of the Cocker Spaniel Breed Council, and is breed correspondent for the weekly paper, *Our Dogs*. Mrs Olive Norfolk was the founder of Cocker Spaniel Rescue which she started in 1968 and continued for many years, only giving it up when it had become an accepted part of cocker spaniel life, and when it was on a very sound financial footing.

Treetops

Mrs Judy de Casembroot has now retired from both showing and judging, but her name and her Treetops prefix will live on in the breed. Amongst her many achievements are having owned the only red cocker to have won a Best in Show All Breeds at a Championship Show, Sh. Ch. Treetops Turtle Dove. She is also the only person to have owned a Crufts Best in Show (a greyhound, Treetops Golden Falcon) and have judged Best in Show at Crufts as well. With Miss Hahn she is the only cocker judge to have judged the breed pre-war and to have won a pre-war C.C. with Turtle Dove in 1937. The kennel was founded on the beautiful black bitch, Treetops Treasure

Trove, who won at C.C. level, and was a good brood bitch, producing Treetops Talkie, a great stud force at the time. Treetops Terrific was the sire of Mrs Lucas-Lucas's Sixshot Black Swan.

Ware/Falconers

Reference has been made earlier in the book to the pre-eminence of the 'of Ware' cockers, and of the successes of such cockers as Whoopee, Exquisite Model, Sir Galahad and Tracey Witch. Mrs Jennifer Carey, daughter of Mr H. S. Lloyd, and grand-daughter of Mr Richard Lloyd who started the outstanding kennels in the early 1900s, has continued the Ware tradition since the death of her father and, whilst keeping a much smaller kennel than in the past, maintains the breeding and type which made them such a force in the past.

Weirdene

Richmond Weir from Falkirk in Scotland was a Championship Show exhibitor of top cockers at a very early age, his family having connections with the breed, and has had many champions in his kennels. He is proud of the fact of having made up show champions in six different colours. Two with great reputations were the black and white, Sh. Ch. Wells Fargo of Weirdene, and the blue roan Sh. Ch. Weirdene Questing Strathspey. Weirdene is another of the kennels with a great reputation abroad, and this breeding figures prominently in pedigrees worldwide.

Westdyke

Another Scottish kennel, with a good reputation for quality and type. Mr Willie Robertson does not show in England as much as he did in earlier years. Sh. Ch. Westdyke Weel Kent Man, a blue roan dog, was amongst his best.

Wilholme

Mrs Sally Shields and son David both exhibit the Wilholme particolours. They were originally based on the Reklawholm cockers of Mrs Prudence Walker who emigrated to the far west of Canada, and the same compact cobby type has been maintained. Sh. Ch. Wilholme Wrangler, made up in 1987, is their latest champion.

6

Cockers abroad

Since the war the popularity of the cocker spaniel – or English cocker spaniel as it is sometimes known – has grown tremendously in many other countries, and with English imports often the root stock, the quality in many of them is high.

In most countries the breed standards are those recognized by the international body, the FCI or Federation Cynologique Internationale, and in the case of the cocker it is that of the country of origin – Great Britain. In the United States of America the standard recognized is that of the English Cocker Spaniel Club of America, which unfortunately differs from ours in some respects – the main being height, which over there is 38–41 cm (15–16in) for bitches and 41–43 cm (16–17 in) for dogs. Presentation is geared towards glamourous dogs, and a lot of emphasis is placed on showmanship. The main club, the ECSCA, is a very active body and their annual 'Speciality' or Championship Show, attracts top dogs from all over the country. We think a journey from London to Edinburgh is a long way. What about San Francisco to New York?

In the USA English cockers are gaining in strength and popularity although they have a long way to go to catch up numerically with their cousin, the American cocker spaniel.

The *Jubilee Book* of the ECSCA, a marvellous record, published in 1986, points out that one of the greatest influences in the development of the cocker here was Ch. Obo, whilst Ch. Obo II imported into the USA in 1882 'in utero' is generally regarded as the father of the American Cocker. As differences in type developed, the American Kennel Club recognized the English Cocker Spaniel Club and classes for it were given at shows in 1936.

The opposite situation arose in Great Britain, and it was not until the mid-1960s that Mrs A. M. Jones, MBE, bought the first American show import, a red–buff bitch from Mr Dick Squiers called 'Squiers Ambassador' (later to be Mittina Squiers Ambassador). Challenge Certificates were first given at Crufts in 1970 when Miss Joan Macmillan of Lochranza fame was the judge.

It is really invidious to list names of people and dogs over there, but I feel I ought to mention the late Mrs Geraldine Dodge, architect of their Breed Standard for the English cocker spaniel, and revered so greatly by everyone; and Mrs Kate Romanski, present secretary of the ECSCA, a most efficient administrator and organizer of a very popular club. Many dogs deserve a mention, but amongst the greats have been Ch. Dunelm Galaxy, Ch. Treetops Tristan of Giralda (pre-war), Ch. Applewin Angus born in 1975 and Ch. Kenobo Capricorn, a great stud force who won Best in Show at the ECSCA Speciality at the age of ten years.

Two Crufts Best of Breed winners, Sh. Ch. Bryansbrook High Society and Sh. Ch. Matterhorn Montana have been exported to North America in recent years. High Society reached the No. 2 spot in the English Cockers in Canada and No. 4 in America, but whilst Montana gained his American title he did not prove to be quite as successful. In all, six Crufts Best of Breed dogs have found homes abroad: Sh. Ch. Lochranza Strollaway and Colinwood Black Eagle (South America), Sh. Ch. Lochranza Man of Fashion (Sweden, although he returned to spend his later years at Lochranza), Sh. Ch. Peelers Public Order (Italy) as well as the two already mentioned.

Over the years a number of Champions and other good winners have been exported to South American countries. For a long time exhibitors from those countries were able to visit England, but with currency changes and inflation exports to those countries have reduced.

The importance of English stock is always emphasized by the number of people from abroad who gather round the cocker ring at Crufts early in the morning, and maintain their positions during the long day's judging. There are usually contingents from France, Sweden, Norway, Finland, Holland and Denmark amongst others, who combine the show with visits to kennels in various parts of the country. Many British judges are appointed to judge at foreign shows, and most are impressed by the progress made in many countries, and by the high standard of their top winners.

The same applies to dogs in Australia and New Zealand. In recent years Mrs Jean Gillies of New Zealand has judged the breed at the Three Counties Championship Show, and Miss Viney Jenkins from Australia has judged a London Cocker Spaniel Society Open Show. An article in a book by Miss Jenkins a few years ago suggested that dogs in Great Britain were in general better in coat, bone and heads, and were rather more compact in body, though the best dogs in Australia would hold their own with top dogs here.

The rapport between breeders around the world is best demonstrated by the European Spaniel Congress, held every two years with representatives of all the spaniels discussing every aspect of their respective breeds. The Secretary of the ESC is Mrs Kay Baldwin, of Vailotest cocker note, a former Secretary of the London Cocker Spaniel Society, and a very hard-working and popular lady with cocker lovers everywhere.

One particularly interesting publication illustrating the standard is published by the Spaniel Club Français, entitled *L'English Cocker Spaniel* showing in diagrammatic form what the construction of the cocker should be (see page 44). There are a few points on which opinions over here would differ but French cocker owners have a real guide to what they should be looking for.

The world is certainly a small place for cocker spaniel lovers.

7

Top dogs: Cocker of the year; Puppy of the year

Top Dogs

In 1969 Mr Arnold Hall, breed correspondent for *Dog World* felt that interest in the breed could be created by devising a competition for the 'Cocker Spaniel of the Year'. He based this on a points system for Challenge Certificate and Reserve Challenge Certificate wins at Championship Shows throughout the calendar year. Only wins within the breed are counted, i.e., group or stakes wins are ignored. This has now been accepted as a prestigious award, and the winner receives a bannerette (originally a silken dog jacket) to commemorate the win. Since 1975 these have been donated by the London Cocker Spaniel Society.

The puppy of the year competition was introduced in 1983, and it is interesting that at the time of writing some of the past winners have become show champions. The points are confined to the Any Colour Minor puppy (6–9 months) and Puppy (6–12 months) classes at Championship Shows. The bannerettes for this competition are donated by the Cocker Spaniel Club.

Mr Hall, who has now given up writing the breed notes, continues to collate all the records of wins and generally run the competition.

COCKER OF THE YEAR

	Winner	*Runner up*
1969	Ch. Ouainé Chieftain	Sh. Ch. Kavora Merryborne Sweet Martini
1970	Sh. Ch. Kavora Merryborne Sweet Martini	Ch. Ouainé Chieftain
1971	Ch. Ouainé Chieftain	Sh. Ch. Broomleaf Blithe Spirit
1972	Sh. Ch. Lochranza Newsprint	Ch. Bournehouse Starshine
1973	Ch. Bournehouse Starshine	Ch. Lucklena Light Music
1974	Sh. Ch. Newsreader of Lochranza	Sh. Ch. Merryworth Mr Chips
1975	Sh. Ch. Newsreader of Lochranza	Ch. Bournehouse Starshine
1976	Ch. Bournehouse Starshine	Sh. Ch. Ramiro of Ronfil
1977	Sh. Ch. Raneyl Late Summer of Leabank	Sh. Ch. Kenavon Envoy
1978	Sh. Ch. Lochranza Man of Fashion	Sh. Ch. Bitcon Silver Model
1979	Sh. Ch. Lochranza Man of Fashion	Sh. Ch. Kavora Blackbird
1980	Sh. Ch. Bitcon Florin of Mistfall	Sh. Ch. Cilleine Athene
1981	Sh. Ch. Cilleine Echelon	Sh. Ch. Sorbrook Brambleberry
1982	Sh. Ch. Cilleine Echelon	Sh. Ch. Roanwood Ripple
1983	Sh. Ch. Cilleine Echelon	Sh. Ch. Lochranza Like Your Style
1984	Sh. Ch. Lindridge Gypsy Girl	Sh. Ch. Quettadene Emblem
1985	Sh. Ch. Matterhorn Montana	Sh. Ch. Quettadene Emblem
1986	Sh. Ch. Canigou Mr Happy	Sh. Ch. Quettadene Emblem
1987	Sh. Ch. Olanza Poacher's Moon	Sh. Ch. Asquanne's Ghia

PUPPY OF THE YEAR

1983	Haradwaithe Sorceress
1984	Mistfall Meddler
1985	Bitcon Shy Talk
1986	Asquanne's Ghia
1987	Quettadene Memento

8

The Cocker Spaniel as a Gundog

by P. R. A. Moxon

The training of cocker spaniels for the gun differs in no wise from that of other spaniels, except insofar as the cocker is inclined to be an individualist and requires greater firmness and tact in handling. When properly trained a cocker of working strain is one of the most useful dogs that a rough shooter can have, being keen, fearless in cover and water, and possessing a good nose for both fur and feather. In regard to retrieving, this varies from dog to dog, but some of the best retrieving gundogs I have seen have been cockers. With experience these little dogs can deal with any game, including cock pheasants and even hares.

The king-pin of gundog training is OBEDIENCE. A dog which is not obedient is not trained, no matter how brilliant a gamefinder it may be. A wild, unruly gundog of any breed is a curse to the shooter rather than a blessing, putting up game out of range of the gun and generally spoiling sport for everyone present. Wild dogs may develop wonderful noses and find plenty of game, it is true, but they spoil more sport than they provide, and this is particularly true of wild spaniels. The cocker is inclined to be wilful and therefore needs special attention paid to its preliminary 'hand' or obedience training. The trainer must be firm but kind, and very patient. The old saw about 'a woman, a spaniel and a walnut tree, the more you beat them the better they be' may be true about women and walnut trees – I don't pretend to know – but as far as cocker spaniels are concerned the less punishment that is given the better. This is not to say that punishment has to be altogether dispensed with, but I wish to dispel the illusion, still retained in some quarters, that 'the stick' is the only method whereby cockers can be trained. Punishment handed out indiscriminately and without showing the dog where it is at fault can produce only two types of gundog – the cowed cringing wretch that is the pity of all who behold it, or the hardened sinner who will please himself and accept a beating as a matter of course. No thinking man desires to own either type of spaniel.

What is required of a cocker spaniel in the field? Normally, the cocker is used to quest within gunshot for unshot game, flush it and retrieve the slain only upon command. It must remain steady when rabbits bolt or game gets on the wing, and is generally taught to drop both to flush and shot. There are some owners who not only use their cockers thus but also like them to act as retrievers pure and simple when game is being driven. To use a cocker in this manner, whilst by no means impossible, is asking a lot of a breed whose natural instinct is to be on the move the whole time. I have found that whilst certain individuals will take kindly to the idea of waiting in a butt or at a pheasant stand for driven game, the majority of cockers are far too restless and are inclined to become over-excited, whine and even yap when the birds come over and the guns start firing. Such dogs are a nuisance to both handler and to the other guns present, and generally end up by being tethered to their masters' sides if not removed from the shooting field altogether. My advice to cocker owners is, therefore, not to expect too much from the breed in this respect, but to use the dogs mainly, if not solely, for their natural work as questing dogs when game is walked up, plus, of course, retrieving when required.

Early Training

Training to come to call, to retrieve a small dummy, and to quest light cover can begin at a very early age – almost from the nest stage, in fact. The puppy should be taught its name and to come in to a particular whistle (I use two quick toots on a high-pitched staghorn whistle for this), and this is best accomplished by repeating the name, followed by the whistle signal, and the giving of an edible reward. This creates an association between name and whistle and something pleasant, and to puppies, like children, nothing is more pleasant than something to eat! Let the puppy run about on the lawn and suddenly call his name and give your whistle signal, and immediately he comes in make much of him. In cases of stubbornness run up to and past the puppy, repeating name and whistle, and in a very short time you will have a puppy obedient to call.

Retrieving a small dummy (which can be a ball, an old glove rolled up or a small, stuffed rabbit skin) can be commenced as soon as the above lesson has been learned. Most worth-while cockers have a natural retrieving instinct and if you throw your dummy a short way on bare ground even the youngest puppy will usually run after it and pick it up. Immediately this happens call and whistle him in and praise him, but do not snatch the retrieve away at once. Take it very gently and use only slight pressure on the lips if there is a tendency for the pupil to hang on. If a puppy seems to prefer running off with the dummy to his kennel or basket, place yourself in a position where you can intercept him on the inward journey, and adopt the same procedure. Encourage the puppy to come right up to you and stand with the dummy in his mouth in front of you. If you try to remove it too quickly he may get into the habit of circling round you, which must at all costs be avoided. A good, clean delivery is essential in a well-trained gundog.

At first the puppy can be allowed to run-in and pick up the dummy immediately it is thrown, but ultimately he must wait on the drop until you give the command to fetch. This cannot be taught until the puppy has learned to sit to command, which is the next important step in training, and for this reason dummy practice must not be overdone, but carried out sufficiently often to retain keenness and a willing return and delivery. As the puppy grows older, however, you can and should vary the practice by throwing the dummy into cover of gradually increasing degrees of thickness, rough grass, cabbages, light bracken, etc. to encourage the hunting instinct, love of cover and use of nose.

By the time the average puppy is five or six months old it should be sufficiently bold to withstand serious obedience training, the first stage of which is sitting to command. Individuals vary, of course, and as I point out in a book I recently published no hard and fast rules about age can be laid down. Bold puppies can be started earlier than shy ones, and really nervy dogs are best left until they are eight or nine months of age. In any event you should do everything you can to instil confidence and courage by taking the puppy about and letting it meet people and things – becoming generally world-wise, in other words. This will never occur if the puppy is kept rigidly in kennel between lessons, although of course you must not go to the other extreme and allow all and sundry to handle and fool about with the puppy. Common sense should dictate how much licence can be allowed in this respect.

Sitting to Command

Teaching a puppy to sit to command is most important and must be done very thoroughly. I try to teach my pupils to drop to the word 'Hup!', to a *single, long* blast on the whistle and to the raised hand. Spaniels should also drop to shot, and I am assuming that you have already accustomed yours to the sound of gunfire so that it is neither gun-shy nor gun-nervy. Firing a gun at feeding-time at gradually decreasing distances from the kennel or house is probably the best way of getting a puppy used to gunfire. Once sitting to command has been learned by the pupil, the report of the gun must also be made to signify an immediate drop.

A leather slip-lead is useful for early training – one which has a loop at one end for your hand and a ring through which the lead can be passed to form a running noose at the other. The noose is slipped over the puppy's head and he is gradually taught to walk without lagging behind or pulling ahead by manipulation of the lead. Jerk the lead sharply and give the erring pupil an 'electric shock'. Usually there is a certain amount of reluctance to behave on the lead at first but puppies can be gradually accustomed to wearing collar and lead from an early age. This will be helpful when serious training starts.

To teach the drop, have your puppy walking on the slip lead at your left side, preferably on the lawn or in a field away from all distractions. Walk the puppy along, stop suddenly, raise your right hand and give the previously decided command to drop. The puppy does not understand what you require, so show him by pressing him firmly down on his haunches with the left hand whilst holding the lead tight with the right. Gradually straighten your back and stand still. If the puppy moves, manipulate the lead to force him back into a sitting position, repeating the command sharply. Keep him thus for a few moments, then pat him and walk on, repeating the procedure over and over again for ten minutes or so. Training lessons should always be short in the early days – ten to fifteen minutes being plenty long enough, otherwise the pupil is apt to become bored and dispirited. It is far better to give two or even three short spells of training per day than one over-long lesson. A bored puppy will never learn properly and will prove a real problem to deal with.

If your puppy takes to his dropping lessons and quickly gets the hang of them you need not give an edible reward each time he drops, but a difficult or reluctant puppy can be encouraged in this way if it really seems necessary. Bribery is best dispensed with altogether if possible and if used should never be carried on for too long. A puppy appreciates a pat and a word of praise, however, and I make a point of showing my approval in this way every time the pupil does well. The next step in training is to get the puppy to remain on the drop until given the command to move. This can be commenced as soon as he has thoroughly learned to drop quickly to command and to the whistle, if used – if not, it can be introduced at once by being blown immediately after the vocal command. In a very short while a puppy will respond to the whistle without any spoken command at all, and the voice is 'kept in reserve', as it were. The lead is dispensed with as progress advances.

By backing away slowly from the seated puppy you will soon discover whether he is of the restless type or not. Most pups very naturally try to follow their handler the moment he moves away, and now your patience is going to be truly tested. If, when you back away, the puppy moves, repeat the command to drop and reseat him in his original position by taking him by the slack skin under the throat. This must be done *every time he moves*, without exception. Some people 'peg down' their pupils with a short chain and peg, thus forcibly

C. M. Cooke

Sh. Ch. Bitcon Silver Model

Hartley

Sh. Ch. Cilleine Echelon

Ian Scott

Sh. Ch. Roanwood Ripple

Anne Roslin-Williams

Sh. Ch. Kavora Charade

Mr. K. MacFarlane with Sh. Ch. Maxway Musicmaker, Best in Show all breeds, Three Counties Ch. show, 1987.

Hartley

Sport & General

A good delivery. Pinehawk Hobo retrieving to James Wylie

Sport & General

The object achieved.
A small Cocker retrieving a hen pheasant

Sport & General

Typical scene at a Spaniel Field Trial

restraining the puppy from moving when they back away. This is quite in order in the case of a very stubborn, wilful puppy, but I prefer to do without mechanical aids as far as possible, except the lead in early lessons. However, more of this anon. As soon as the puppy seems to have the right idea, try walking away instead of backing. This will lead to more trouble between you and your pupil, in all probability, but with patience and perseverance on your part you should be able to walk away and leave him on the drop quite happily after a few lessons. If you reseat the puppy every time he makes a move from the very beginning you will quickly establish your mastery over him. Omit to do so once or twice and he will be encouraged to repeat the offence. Never allow a pupil to get the better of you if it can possibly be avoided, or he will tend to lose respect for you and the bond between handler and dog, so necessary for complete success, will be weakened. Cocker spaniels are restless animals by nature and most trainers experience rather more difficulty in obtaining discipline from this breed than from some of the other gundogs.

Dropping at a Distance

Once your puppy will drop to command promptly and remain on the drop whilst you walk away, and even hide out of sight, you can teach him to drop at a distance. In some cases it will be found that the pupil sits to command and/or whistle even when at a distance from his handler, simply because you have so thoroughly taught association of ideas between command and the action of dropping. Where special lessons are required, the following method of teaching to drop at a distance will be found very efficient and quick. Simply seat your pupil, walk away about fifteen or twenty yards and whistle him up. Immediately he get within a few feet of you give the command (vocal or whistle) to drop. Success being achieved, walk on again, repeat the process but each time give the order to sit a little sooner, so that ultimately the puppy will go down instantly at any point between his original position and yourself. Thereafter let him run about in front of you and practise him at dropping wherever he may be in relation to yourself. In some cases it may be found necessary to use a check cord to instil obedience at a distance. This is a cord about ten to fifteen yards long with a ring at one end to make a noose for the pup's head. A few knots are tied in the cord (sash cord does very well) and the dog is made to wear it. When the command to drop is given you stand sharply on the cord, thus bringing the pup up with a jerk. This same cord can be used to restrain a puppy from running home (as some will) when the first obedience lessons are given.

Steadiness to thrown dummy

From this point on your puppy should never be allowed to run-in again to the thrown dummy. At first let him wear a short lead or cord and drop him beside you, holding the lead under your foot. Throw the dummy out and restrain the puppy for half a minute or more before allowing him out to retrieve, commanding him to sit should he stand up and struggle to go after the dummy, as he almost certainly will. Continue the exercise until you can safely dispense with the lead, but always be on the alert and position yourself so that you can intercept the puppy should he attempt to run-in to the thrown dummy. Keep him on the drop for an appreciable time before sending him out to retrieve, and always despatch him with the same command: 'Fetch it!', 'Hi, lost!', 'Seek!', or what you will. Readers may consider that I have used up a lot of space in dealing with preliminary obedience. I can assure them from personal experience that this is no waste, for half the battle in dog training is won if the initial work is thoroughly carried out. Field work on game will come naturally to a good cocker, but it will be useless unless you have got the dog under control and working for *you* instead of for himself.

Dropping to shot. Retrieving practice

Your puppy must now be taught to drop to shot. Using a blank-cartridge pistol or a shotgun, you simply give a sharp command to drop and immediately throw up the gun and fire. In a very short while the shot acts as another signal to drop, although later on when the 'real thing' is being hunted you will probably find your pupil stands rather than drops to shot. Provided no movement is made this is all right, but insisting upon a complete drop is better. Naturally, no puppy should receive these gunfire lessons until he is completely confident and unafraid of the report. Further steadiness practice can be given by throwing the dummy into cover of gradually increasing degrees of thickness and firing the gun whilst the dummy is in the air, thus simulating real shooting conditions. The pupil is despatched to retrieve after a wait on the drop, and as progress is made so the retrieves can be made more difficult by being made longer and longer and the cover more formidable. *Always whistle up* the pupil at the moment his head goes down to pick up. Artificial drag lines can be laid with the dummy at this juncture, thus giving the pupil a 'line' to follow as he will later have in the field when sent for wounded birds. The line should be laid upwind at first, out of sight of the pupil and without yourself fouling the scent. This can be accomplished by using a long pole, or fishing rod and line, with the dummy attached and held as far from you as possible, or by getting an assistant to hold the other end of a long rope, to the centre of which the dummy has been tied. Later on, when experience has been gained, dead birds and rabbits can be used in just the same way.

Advanced retrieving practice can be given with the dummy as soon as the puppy is really obedient. This includes dropping the pupil and walking out yourself to throw the dummy, and the ever-useful 'going back' lesson. Drop the dummy in full sight of the puppy, walk him on and send him back over ever–increasing distances for it. As this is learned, do not let him see the dummy fall – send him out on a 'blind retrieve' for it. Whistle immediately he picks up. In the shooting field he will often be called upon to look for game which he did not see fall. This lesson will also encourage use of nose and a speedy return. If you wish to put a real 'finish' upon your pupil, utilize this lesson for dropping him on the way out to his retrieve, using a check cord if necessary. This lesson, tactfully conducted, will get him under even better control and may well come in useful if ever you run in trials and you see the dog making for the wrong bird. A dog which can be stopped and redirected on a retrieve is well on the way to becoming trained. Use clear-cut hand signals to help your pupil wherever possible, especially for indicating the direction of a retrieve. Encourage a love of cover and let the dog quest it freely, trying at first to find game-free cover until steadiness work has been given.

Working in water. Jumping fences and gates

Any retrieving gundog worthy of the name must face water and retrieve therefrom. Most cockers of working strain take to water very quickly and love working in it. Introduction to it should be made on a warm day and force should not be used. Choose a pond or stream with gently shelving banks and throw a ball or dummy a little way in. If this does not work throw in something eatable, or make use of a trained and keen water dog as an example. Wade in and paddle about yourself if you feel inclined – anything to encourage the puppy and promote confidence in water. Once he will swim a little way encourage him farther and farther out until you can see that he really has the idea. Then teach him to go across water and climb the opposite bank to seek the dummy. Tact and perseverance on your part are almost sure to be successful – completely water-shy cockers are a rarity – but you must be gentle and patient.

Jumping fences and gates is taught quite easily once a puppy is well grown and confident. Just take him for walks and climb easy fences yourself and walk on. If there are no suitable, easy places nearby it is worth while constructing a jump and bribing the puppy over it either with the dummy or with food, or allow an experienced dog to set an example. Do not let the first places be too difficult, of course, and avoid barbed wire and fences which are not fairly solid to start with. Confidence must be created – once you have your puppy jumping for the love of it you will have no more trouble. All that remains to be done is to practice retrieving over jumps of different kinds.

Introduction to game

Up to this point all training has been conducted artificially, using a dummy for retrieving practice. The dummy has been gradually increased in size and weight so that by the time your pupil is ready to retrieve real game it is of a fair size and weight. The change-over will not therefore strain the neck muscles of a small cocker and cause a poor delivery. The first rabbits and birds used for retrieving must be *fresh shot but cold*, and quite free from blood and damage. In the first instance drop the bird in full view of the dog, as you have been doing with the dummy, walk him on and send him back for it. Whistle him up the moment his head goes down to retrieve, and if he hesitates run away as you did in the early lessons. If the puppy refuses to pick up, or starts to play with the bird, take it and throw it like a dummy, running away and calling him up the moment his head goes down to it. Few cockers refuse to retrieve game after a while. Those which do require special treatment which cannot be discussed here owing to lack of space. Common sense should dictate the steps to be taken when difficulties are encountered. Once a puppy is accustomed to picking up cold birds, and does not attempt to play with or bite them, he can be tried with warm game or rabbits in the same way. Always remember to hurry the puppy up by whistling and calling the moment he picks up, so that there is not time for him to think about playing with the game. Scent trail lessons, as previously given with the dummy, can now be carried out with advantage, using dead birds or rabbits. Never use the same specimen for more than one, or at the outside two, retrieves. To use the same bird or rabbit again and again leads to bad delivery, if not refusal to retrieve, and hard mouth.

Questing for game and steadiness

Our cocker spaniel, having been taught obedience and control and to retrieve from cover and water, must now have more advanced tuition in questing for game and remaining steady to it. Spaniels are natural questers and quickly learn to quarter their ground in a systematic manner with very little aid from their handler. Use a separate command for questing – I always snap my fingers and say, 'Hi, seek!' for this, starting the pupil off to one side of me. It is necessary that a spaniel quest within gunshot range, so when the limit of about 20 or 25 yards is reached I attract his attention by name or whistle and wave my hand over to encourage him to quest on the other side. All this time I am walking steadily forward and keeping the dog on the move. The puppy which does not quickly 'cotton on' to the idea is made to drop by whistle when he reaches the limit of his range to one side, and then waved over. If all else fails, small pieces of biscuit can be thrown out to right and left to encourage the puppy to 'weave' about, but previous lessons have usually instructed him to watch your hand movements closely and work to them. If the puppy ranges too far whistle him back with your usual 'come back' whistle, and back away yourself. The ideal place for these early questing lessons to be taught in is a smallish meadow of rough grass, light clover or spring wheat –somewhere where the puppy can easily be seen but with enough cover to interest him and make him work. Naturally, though it is an advantage that there should be some scent of game or rabbits in such a place it is to be hoped that actual game will not be present as the pupil has yet to learn to be steady. An accidental flush might ruin chances of future steadiness, so after one or two lessons as suggested above the next step is to introduce him to game, or rather rabbits, and teach strict steadiness.

Most professional trainers use a rabbit pen for this purpose – a specially constructed enclosure of a quarter of an acre or more, containing live rabbits and natural cover, If you can construct such a pen – even a small one containing only one or two rabbits – or have access to one belonging to someone else, a great deal of work and worry will be avoided. Failing this, turning a tame rabbit out on the lawn or in the cabbage patch for a few moments will prove a great help. You will have to adapt your training to whatever system you can evolve with the time and space at your disposal.

When using a rabbit pen, introduce the puppy into it on a lead or check cord. Walk him round until you find a rabbit, and immediately the latter bolts give the command to drop and jerk the puppy down. Carry this on for ten or fifteen minutes, making the pupil drop each time a rabbit bolts, using the voice, whistle and lead to ensure prompt obedience. After a few lessons the puppy will show signs of knowing what is required, and is then worked with the cord trailing, so that if he does break away after bunny you can stop him and make him sit. Punishment should not be given unless absolutely essential, and should be given in such a manner that the dog knows what it is for. Always punish in the act of committing the crime if possible, or at any rate take the puppy back to the exact spot where he did wrong and whip him there. Never, never beat a dog when he returns to you – always take him back to the scene of his crime. Punishing by holding and shaking is usually more effective than a whipping, and afterwards give him a minute of two on the drop to meditate upon his crime.

As soon as the puppy becomes reliable when close to you, let him quest naturally if the pen is large enough, dropping him by voice or whistle should he show signs of chasing. Keep the check cord in reserve for cases of flagrant disobedience. In many instances the pupil does not drop after a time, but simply stands and watches the rabbit away. Insist on a drop, at any rate to begin with. Take the gun or pistol into the pen at this stage and fire it as the rabbit bolts, thus creating a 'natural' situation which will always be occurring in the future. Some cockers will show a tendency to 'point' their rabbits – this is to be encouraged; stand stock still when it occurs. Keep the puppy pointing for as long as possible, then walk in and push the rabbit up yourself, making the pupil drop as you do so. If you always allow the dog to push the rabbit out himself he will soon cease to point and flush at once. When a spaniel is questing in the pen and puts up a rabbit make him hunt in a different direction after the rabbit bolts. Never allow him to follow the rabbit. If the pen is large enough, walk down the middle of it, making the puppy range from side to side in front of you and within range. Retrievers and many spaniels are made to retrieve the dummy in the pen from nearby grazing rabbits (some of which are usually tame or semi-tame for this purpose), and this is a further aid to steadiness.

However, in a small pen or on the lawn with only one

rabbit, such refinements are not possible, and so you will have to proceed as above on any available field or cover where rabbits can be found in sufficient quantities. It naturally takes longer to steady a puppy on natural ground, but it can be and often is done. Provided the pupil has never been allowed to self-hunt and chase game and rabbits, steadiness is not really difficult to inculcate in any gundog, for by this system of training the puppy is taught right before it learns to do wrong, and obedience is acquired gradually and naturally. Once the puppy shows that he has the right idea on rabbits he can be taken into fields and woods where all types of game will be encountered, made to quest and have shots fired over him. Do not shoot to kill until you are completely sure of his reactions and feel confident of his steadiness.

First shooting experience

The first shooting expedition is best undertaken alone or with one friend to shoot whilst you do the handling. Make the puppy quarter the ground and drop to shot and rise of game. Never send him to retrieve if he has shown the slightest unsteadiness and, whilst the early retrieves in the shooting field must be reasonably easy, avoid sending him for birds which lie in the open and can be found by sight alone – this will only encourage unsteadiness. Never send him for birds which show any signs of life until he is proficient at retrieving stone-dead ones, and always watch closely and whistle him up the moment his head goes down to pick up. Keep the dog on the drop for fully half a minute, or even longer, after every shot and fall, and despatch to retrieve by command and signal as previously.

As experience is gained on dead birds and rabbits the pupil can be trusted to try for wounded birds or 'runners'. Avoid putting the dog on to them whilst they are still in sight, and do not be disappointed by early failures or signs of hard mouth. The retrieving of runners is a knack gained only by experience and many young dogs will maul their first few birds and rabbits. Do all you can to get your dog back to you quickly by *whistling him up the moment he puts his head down to retrieve*, running away from him if necessary. This is why you should always at first try to follow your puppy when out after a retrieve (live or dead) which is in cover but do not, of course, go right up to him. Try to see what is taking place and whistle him up, returning to your original position at the run if necessary. Do not allow your dog to retrieve every bird or rabbit shot – select those which require use of nose and hunting in cover, picking up the easy ones yourself whilst the dog remains on the drop.

Your dog is now well on the way to being trained, and all that is required is further experience. Readers may think that I have made it all seem beautifully easy and have glossed over the snags that are likely to be encountered. If you have the right dog and teach him the right way training *is* easy, but of course many little things arise to trip up the unwary. I cannot go into details nearly as fully as I should wish in a short chapter on training – it is easier to write a book than a chapter on this vast subject!

General suggestions and advice

As a conclusion I will offer some words of advice which should help the novice handler. Choose your puppy from working parents, preferably those with field trial blood in their veins. Commence training to answer name and retrieve a small dummy as early as possible, deferring strict discipline until you know he can 'take it'. Try to 'think like a dog' and, when things go wrong, try to see the situation from the dog's point of view, and apply the remedy at once. Punishment should be given only when really necessary and should be made to fit the crime. It must always be administered at the actual spot where the dog did wrong, or whilst the crime is being committed. Remember that the lessons, though the earlier ones can be intermingled to add variety, must be given in their proper order and that no new lesson should be started until the latest one has been thoroughly mastered by the pupil. Do not make the mistake of hurrying him on to 'more interesting work'.

Plug away at the hand-training and obedience until you really have an obedient, steady dog. Give short but frequent spells of training, encourage use of nose and confidence in thick cover and water from the start. Make the change-over from dummy work to the real thing as gradual as possible, and when shooting starts think about your dog rather than your shooting – otherwise you will have wasted a lot of time. When guns go off and game falls, think first of the dog and be ready to prevent him running in or chasing – say 'Hup!' or 'Sit!' or blow your whistle as a matter of course – always expect the worst, in other words! Then you will not go wrong. Choose your words of command and signals and whistles and stick to them, always using the same one for the same action. Use your hands sensibly to give signals which are clear-cut and definite. Train your puppy away from distractions and other dogs and people. If he seems to be getting bored or restless stop the lesson and put him away for a few hours – a bored puppy does not learn. Be patient but firm at all times, and try to wind up each lesson on a note of success – do not let the pupil 'best' you. He must go back to his kennel feeling you are boss, not that he has won a victory of wills over you.

If you aspire to run your cocker in field trials your training should be just the same but, if it is possible, more thorough and prolonged. There are plenty of stakes run for cocker spaniels only. For trials your dog must be mute, of course – a dog which gives tongue whilst questing is 'out' as far as present-day trials are concerned. You will find that field trials are a very enjoyable and sociable type of sport and both you and your dog would benefit from watching and competing. The field trial people are a friendly lot and anxious to help newcomers to the game. Quite apart from this, it will be doing cocker spaniels as a breed a great service to train them and enter them at trials, for they are, after all, *gun*dogs and deserve to be used as such. Spaniels are the shooter's 'maid-of-all-work' and cannot be beaten for rough shooting, especially in dense woods and other places where birds and rabbits have to be flushed from thick cover. If you train a dog properly it is a joy to shoot over, and I offer the hope that my few words on the subject will go some way towards restoring the merry little cocker to its rightful place as 'the sporting spaniel'.

To those who wish to go thoroughly into this absorbing hobby I offer the suggestion that they should read my book, *Gundogs: Training and Field Trials* (Popular Dogs Publishing Co. Ltd) in which the subject is dealt with comprehensively and in considerable detail.

9

Some commoner health problems

by F. Andrew Edgson, MRCVS

A cocker spaniel, like any other dog, can fall foul of various infections or conditions which may arise from accident or advancing years. The duty of the owner is to try to protect his or her charge from these, and today this can be done more effectively than ever before. The dog born today is indeed fortunate compared with his ancestors of even ten or twenty years ago, and anybody who has the responsibility of owning a dog and does not take all the measures available to him to protect his charge is living in the past, and putting his charge in jeopardy.

A healthy dog is a happy dog and a pleasure to have with you. If he has, for instance, a dirty mouth or bad ears he will not only be unhappy but objectionable to have with you. A regular grooming, and making sure that he is free of parasites are obvious 'musts', but how often do many owners check to make sure that claws are not too long, not cracked or split, and that the teeth are free from tartar, and the ears free of wax? These are points which a spaniel will particularly appreciate with his soft mouth, jowl and pendulous ears, more than some other less well-endowed breeds. The very points which make him such a fine specimen do put him in need of just that little extra attention from time to time.

In all diseases, protection is better than cure. Even with modern anti-sera, antibiotics and chemotherapeutics, any disease is almost always bound to leave behind its damage, however promptly and effectively the infection is diagnosed, treated and arrested. This is why, when efficient, modern, vaccines are available to prevent infections, every advantage should be taken of them.

The diseases which can kill or harm your dog are as follows:

Distemper, 'Hard–pad' and Parvoviruses

With the progress which veterinary science has made within the past few years, the most important and dangerous infectious disease, 'hard-pad', and its closely associated disease, distemper, are both nowadays preventable. It is very much, of course, up to the owner of the dog, or to the dog breeder to take the steps which he can to protect his animals, and the breeder or dog owner who today does not vaccinate against at least one disease is as negligent as the mother who does not have her child immunised against diphtheria. Today there is no excuse whatsoever for outbreaks of 'hard–pad' or distemper resulting from shows or other doggy occasions. If all dog owners took the simple steps which are readily available to them, you would only read about these diseases in books. Anybody who has had the misfortune to have to nurse a dog through 'hard–pad' or distemper would say that an effective and active immunisation is an absolute godsend, and yet even today some people do not take this precaution which is easily available to them.

'Hard–pad' and distemper are caused by an ultra-microscopic virus, and the vaccines which are in current use are freeze-dried and are prepared by mixing the culture with a dilutent immediately before it is administered to the dogs. The virus which is injected is one which is grown on live cells and as a result produces a good immune response within the animal but without producing the disease in any way. Within recent years another vaccine has become available against yet another, but more recent, disease which can cause a high mortality rate, especially in puppies. This is a vaccine, or group of vaccines against the canine parvovirus, an acute infection which can affect the heart muscle of very young dogs and, in older dogs, the alimentary tract, liver and associated organs. Sudden death is the only symptom observed in young puppies with the heart muscle being affected. In older dogs the very debilitating 'V & D' symptoms (vomiting and diarrhoea) are the ones most likely to be observed and even with intensive care involving continuous transfusions, death is still a possible outcome. As in all vaccination programmes, circumstances dictate the use and timing of the vaccine of choice. Parvovirus vaccines can be administered alone, or incorporated with other vaccines against other 'doggy' diseases.

So far as re-vaccination is concerned, it would seem to be highly desirable to boost the immunity which is conveyed by all vaccines at regular intervals, as lack of contact with actual infection may allow the resistance within the animal's body to wane and therefore if re-vaccination is not carried out the degree of immunity after several years may not be sufficiently strong to resist a virulent natural strain of the virus.

Combined vaccines immunising not only against 'hard-pad', distemper and parvo, but also against the fox encephalitis virus (HCC) or Rubarth's disease, a virus disease which attacks liver tissue, are available. Rubarth's disease is an infection of particular importance to the young or very young puppy and in some instances can produce the 'fading' of puppies syndrome.

Non-viral diseases against which vaccination is to be recommended are the two leptospiral diseases of dogs – leptospira icterohaemorrhagiae, and leptospira canicola, the former being rat-borne and an organism which attacks the liver tissues, and the latter being carried by dogs and producing severe or chronic kidney damage of an acute or chronic type. Today it is possible to immunise against several of these diseases in two or three combinations, thereby reducing the number of injections that each puppy will require in order to become immunized. Your veterinary surgeon can best advise you on important details such as local risks, best age to vaccinate, whether to use a single or multiple vaccine and the most economic way of doing this. None of these modern vaccines are cheap, but there is nothing more distressing, or expensive, than a dead dog.

Disorders of the alimentary tract

The symptoms which are seen in cases of these disorders are commonly shown by vomiting with or without diarrhoea, or constipation. As already mentioned, parvo is a factor to be considered under this group of symptoms.

A dietary indiscretion may be the cause of vomiting and after the offending food has been ejected the dog is frequently perfectly all right again. In all cases of vomiting, however, where this symptom persists the cause should be ascertained, as it may be of a serious nature. In the puppy, in particular, foreign objects such as buttons, stones, needles, bones, may be swallowed and these can produce trouble either in the stomach itself or in the lower parts of the gut such as the small intestine or colon. If you suspect that your dog has swallowed some foreign object, the most important thing is to not give any laxative or purgative such as liquid paraffin or castor oil, and to consult your vetinary surgeon, who may wish to examine him by special procedures such as X-rays, to ascertain if your suspicions are correct and whether or not an operation is indicated. In all cases of vomiting, the dog should not be allowed water, although a little barley water or milk and water (half-milk, half-water) may be given.

In any case of vomiting, the dog should not be allowed to have any further food until he has been examined by a veterinary surgeon. In elderly dogs a chronic degenerative nephritis is a common cause of vomiting and this is due to the animal's kidneys being unable to excrete in the urine all the waste products which should be eliminated in this fashion. Again pyometra, an infection of the uterus, which is not uncommon in the virgin bitch after the age of five or six years, is accompanied by an increase in thirst and vomiting. It will be seen therefore that vomiting is not always a straightforward condition such as an upset 'tummy'.

In puppies worms will cause the symptoms of vomiting and diarrhoea and a worm may sometimes been seen in the vomit or in excreta. Before dosing this type of case for worms the gastritis should be settled down by a careful milk and fish diet for a few days and a little raw white of egg beaten in a quarter of a pint of milk is a useful bland feed in such instances.

Enteritis

This is symptomized by loose motions or diarrhoea and occasionally if a gastro-enteritis is present, vomiting may also be seen. The cause is almost invariably a dietary indiscretion which has either produced a direct inflammation of the small and large intestines or which contained harmful bacteria that have produced the inflammation. Today there are many effective remedies that can be prescribed for such cases and your veterinary surgeon will be able to advise and treat the case accordingly. However, supportive treatment in the way of careful feeding is important and arrowroot cooked and mixed with boiled fish or hard-boiled egg makes a good, if rather uninteresting, convalescent diet and this should be continued until the diarrhoea has ceased. A periodic diarrhoea in older dogs is sometimes not a simple matter. It may be due to parasites such as tapeworms or other intestinal invaders but occasionally one comes across the animal, just as in humans, who cannot digest adequately certain factors in his diet. Fat, for instance, is not completely digested by some dogs but tests which can be carried out by your veterinary surgeon will elucidate such more complicated cases.

In all cases of abdominal pain it is as well to consult your veterinary surgeon as foreign bodies can, having negotiated the stomach, become lodged in the small intestine. Again diarrhoea may be a constant or intermittent symptom with such foreign bodies or the cause of abdominal pain may be due to bacterial infection which again can be treated effectively.

Conditions of the ear

The cocker spaniel, by virtue of the pendulous ears, is more prone to conditions of the ear than other breeds. When an ear is affected, the dog holds its head to one side, shakes its head or scratches at the offending ear. The cause may be quite simple such as a little natural secretion may have accumulated and caused a local irritation but there may be an inflammation of the outer-ear canal, this condition frequently being referred to by breeders as 'canker'. However, a foreign body may have got into the external meatus of the ear and this will have to be removed by your veterinary surgeon under anaesthetic.

A gentle cleaning with a little cotton wool moistened with water will generally remove any accumulation of wax quite satisfactorily. If when the ear is handled or squeezed there is a squelching sound, or if there is a slightly offensive smell at all, it is most probable that an infection is present in the outer-ear canal. In such cases remove any matted hair around the opening of the ear canal and any discharge may then be removed with cotton wool and warm water. Foreign bodies are particularly common in the summer or autumn with dogs that are exercised in fields. The signs of a grass-seed having gained access to the outer-ear canal are acute discomfort, the holding of the affected side down, and a constant shaking of the head. The dog very rarely tries to scratch the ear in such cases as the discomfort is usually too great for this to be tolerated. It is important, if circumstances suggest such a cause, that your veterinary surgeon examine the ear, quite promptly, with a special instrument, as the sooner the offending grass seed or awn is removed the better. Under no circumstances should the ear be probed as this merely forces the seed or foreign body further down the ear canal. It may be necessary for the veterinary surgeon to administer a general anaesthetic to retrieve the offending grass-seed and therefore the animal should not be given any food at all until the examination has been made.

Pyometra or metritis

This is an important and serious condition (pus in the womb) in which the uterus is infected. It is usually confined to maiden bitches of six years or more, but it is occasionally seen in young bitches as the result of infection which is usually acquired at the time of whelping or contracted even from the stud dog. In the case of the older bitch which has not been bred from, the uterine tissues begin to deteriorate in the course of time and this makes them more likely to become infected with harmful bacteria. In young bitches accidentally infected after mating, or whelping, there is no degeneration of the uterine tissues but infection occurs from the outside, usually with the commoner groups of micro-organisms. All bitches should have at least one litter which will, to a large extent, prevent this very dangerous condition.

There are two main types of pyometra, the open and closed types. The latter is by far the more acute because the infection is pent up in the uterus, and there is no draining of the infected material. Accordingly the infection tends to be absorbed more rapidly into the bloodstream, producing a septicaemia. The symptoms of pyometra will vary, but a fever is almost always present, usually from 103 °F (39.5 °C) upwards; there is a loss of appetite, and a vaginal discharge in the open type is present and is usually of a brownish or pinkish colour, and as this condition becomes worse a great thirst with frequent vomiting and finally prostration is seen. In cases which are not treated, a toxaemia can quickly develop, particularly in the closed type and this can rapidly prove fatal if the condition is not relieved by treatment or surgery. A case of pyometra which is of the closed type may become an open type, and an open type may, on occasions, become closed, but in all instances where this condition is suspected your veterinary surgeon should be consulted, straight away. The operation for the relief of pyometra is referred to as an ovario-hysterectomy and this means that the bitch is unable to breed following the surgical removal of both the ovaries and the uterus. Where the bitch is a brood bitch or where she is very old and weak, more conservative treatment may be decided upon, and this is often successful provided it is begun at an early stage, but whatever the type of pyometra and whatever the age of the bitch, early treatment is of paramount importance.

Although pyometra can appear at more or less any time in a bitch's life, the danger period is about four to six weeks from the end of the last season, and any signs of increased thirst, slight abdominal enlargement, and other similar symptoms should be regarded as being highly suspicious of this condition.

Interdigital cysts

The cocker spaniel, owing to the large amount of hair or feathers around the feet, is perhaps more prone to this condition than many other breeds. It is usually caused initially by hair becoming caked with mud or dirt and being allowed to chafe the tender skin between the individual toes of the dog. A secondary infection occurs in the chafed area of skin and ultimately a small abscess will form between the toes. On occasions a grass-seed or barley awn can also work up in between the toes, penetrate the skin, and then produce a similar type of inflammation. Daily care of the feet is important if the dog is allowed to come into contact with mud, and this is best carried out by thoroughly washing away the mud, using a little warm water and mild soap. It is important not to use any strong antiseptics which might irritate the delicate skin. On occasions where interdigital cysts do occur, these are best treated by a veterinary surgeon, but you can well clean and clip away the hair around the offending area before the dog is examined. Interdigital cysts can on occasions be extremely difficult to treat as the shape of the foot in certain dogs makes them more prone to this condition, and where this is the case, your veterinary surgeon would be best able to advise you on preventive measures or on actual treatment.

Bad breath

This is usually due to an infection of the gums and/or teeth. Dogs, as they get older, are liable to accumulate tartar on their teeth and unless this is removed, the added amounts of tartar gradually press down on the gums causing them to become inflamed and recede. When this happens, the bacteria which are normally present in the mouth and in food collect in the tartar and a foul odour is the result. Regular cleaning of the dog's teeth is almost as important as cleaning your own teeth. A soft tooth brush used once a fortnight or so should be quite adequate in keeping a dog's mouth clean. Should an accumulation of tartar already have appeared on the teeth, this should be removed by your veterinary surgeon or, if you are skilled at this task, by yourself, using a teeth scaler.

Generally speaking, however, there is usually a fair degree of inflammation of the gums around the tartar-encrusted teeth and a thorough cleansing of the mouth for several days following the de-scaling with a little cotton wool soaked in a weak solution of a mild antiseptic, or glycerine and thymol, will usually settle this down. If, however, this should persist, then it is advisable to ask your veterinary surgeon to prescribe something more effective.

APPENDIX A

KENNEL CLUB LIAISON COUNCIL REPRESENTATIVE, BREED COUNCIL, AND BREED CLUBS AND SECRETARIES, 1987

Cocker Spaniel Representative to the Kennel Club Breed Liaison Council:
Mrs J. Caddy, Grandview, Monksilver, Taunton, Somerset TA4 4JE. Tel: (0984) 56247

Cocker Spaniel Council was formed in 1968 and continues to form a body to which all Breed Clubs other than the Cocker Spaniel Club belong. Meetings are held bi-annually at which delegates from all member clubs meet to discuss all aspects of the breed. The Secretary is: Mrs J. Caddy, addess as above

Cocker Spaniel Breed Clubs and Secretaries

The Cocker Spaniel Club
Chairman: Mrs L. G. Holmes, Monkton House, Pinhoe, Exeter, Devon Tel: (0392) 67384
Secretary: Mr D. Havell, Barwick House, 19 Imperial Road, Egerton, Huddersfield, West Yorks HD3 3AF. Tel: (0484) 520155

Black Cocker Spaniel Society: Mrs D. Porter, Gristwood, Beech Hill Road, Headley, Hants GU35 8DR. Tel: (0428) 713082

Cheshire Cocker Spaniel Club: Mrs A. Rathbone, 4 Harper Avenue, Newcastle, Staffs. Tel: (0782) 624090

Coventry Cocker Spaniel Club: Mrs M. Allard, 49 Angela Avenue, Potter's Green, Coventry CV2 2GH Tel: (0203) 616893

Devon & Cornwall Cocker Spaniel Club: Mr M. Owens, 299 Fort Austin Avenue, Crownhill, Plymouth PL6 5TQ. Tel: (0752) 775830

East Anglian Cocker Spaniel Club: Mrs O. Norfolk, Tarlings, West Hanningfield, Nr Chelmsford, Essex CM2 8UU. Tel: (0245) 400428

East of Scotland Cocker Spaniel Club: Mrs M. Hynd, 31 Iona Road, Dunfermline, Fife, Scotland KY11 4ED. Tel: (0383) 724879

Hampshire & Sussex Cocker Spaniel Club: Mrs R. Gill, Stone House, Bowyers, Liss, Hants GU33 6LJ. Tel: (0730) 892679

Home Counties Cocker Spaniel Club: Mrs F. Harness, Hillside, Colliers End, Ware, Herts SG11 1EN. Tel: (0920) 66329

Cocker Spaniel Club of Lancashire: Mrs D. M. Schofield, Cobbles, Norcott Brook, Nr Warrington, Cheshire WA4 4DX. Tel: (092 573) 353

London Cocker Spaniel Society: Mr R. W. Crisp, Layham, 192 Westmoreland Avenue, Limbury, Luton, Beds LU3 2PU. Tel: (0582) 508088

Midland Cocker Spaniel Club: Mr R. M. A. Pain, 57 New Inns Lane, Rubery, Birmingham B45 9TS. Tel: (021 453) 3215

North of England Cocker Spaniel Association: Mrs J. Hill, 2 Park Avenue, Timperley, Cheshire WA14 5AX. Tel: (061 962) 5278

North of Ireland Cocker Spaniel Club: Mr T. J. Gracey, 67 Knockvale Park, Belfast BT5 6HJ. Tel: (0232) 651394 or 471335

North Midlands & Eastern Counties Cocker Spaniel Club: Mrs W. M. Prince, Church Farm, The Green, Findern, Derby. Tel: (0283) 701896

North Wales Cocker Spaniel Club: Mr M. J. Holt, 'Chalfont', Nant Mawr Road, Buckley, Clwyd CH7 2PU. Tel: (0244) 544042

Particoloured Cocker Spaniel Club: Mr T. Browne, 26 Grosvenor Road, Shipley, West Yorks BD18 4RN. Tel: (0274 592) 555

Red & Golden Cocker Spaniel Club: Mrs V. H. Bidston, Nursery Lane, Hookwood, Horley, Surrey RH6 0HG. Tel: (0293) 784032

Rotherham & District Cocker Spaniel Club: Mrs A. Richardson, 65 High Street, Bolton-on-Dearne, Rotherham, South Yorks S63 8LH. Tel: (0709) 893425

Cocker Spaniel Club of Scotland: Mr & Mrs A. Crichton, 148 Glasgow Road, Garrowhill, Glasgow G69 3EU. Tel: (041 771) 2691

South Wales & Monmouthshire Cocker Spaniel Club: Mrs E. Jones, 2 Springfield Close, Cwmbach, Aberdare, Mid-Glamorgan CF44 0EL. Tel: (0685) 872387

Ulster Cocker Spaniel Club: Mr T. J. Cardy, Mount Keepe, Glen Road, Lower Castlereagh, Belfast BT5 7LT. Tel: (0232) 791267

West of England Cocker Spaniel Club: Mr T. Crocker, 36 Willis Road, Kingswood, Bristol BS15 4SS. Tel: (0272) 616407

Yorkshire Cocker Spaniel Club: Mr D. W. Shields, Meadowfields, 40 Thornton Road, Pickering, North Yorks YO18 7HZ. Tel: (0751) 72641

The Spaniel Club Francais: President: M. M. Dumand, Les Loges, 45700 Chevillon, Sous Huillard, France.

The English Cocker Spaniel Club of America: Hon. Secretary: Mrs Kate Romanski, P.O. Box 223, Sunderland, MA 01375 USA. Tel: (217) 423-0250

The Cocker Spaniel Club of Ireland: Hon. Secretary: Mrs Angi Carroll, 15A Grange Court, Marley Grange, Rathfarnham, Dublin 16, Eire. Tel: 01-941265

The Dublin Cocker Spaniel Society: Hon. Secretary: Mrs Norma Wooldridge, Ballinacor Estate, Rathdrum, Co. Wicklow, Eire. Tel: 0404-46507

The Black, Red or Golden Cocker Club of Ireland: Hon. Secretary: Mrs P. Murphy, Auburndale, Grange, Magenby, Carlow, Eire.

APPENDIX B

BRITISH CHAMPIONS from 1948 to December 1987

Key to colours:

B/R = Blue roan
B/R/T = Blue roan and tan
Ln/W = Lemon and white
O/W = Orange and white
Lr = Liver
Lr/W/T = Liver, white and tan
Lr/W = Liver and white
B/T = Black and tan
B/W = Black and white
B/W/T = Black, white and tan
Ln/R = Lemon roan
O/R = Orange roan
Lr/R = Liver roan
Lr/R/T = Liver roan and tan
Tri = Tricolour

	Name of champion	*Sex*	*Colour*	*Sire*	*Dam*	*Owner*	*Breeder*	*Date of Birth*
1947	Colinwood Cowboy	D	B/W/T	Blackmoor Brand	Colinwood Cigarette	A.W. Collins	Owner	6.10.44
	Golden Rod of Ide	D	Golden	Sixshot Black Swan	Lotus Flower of Sorrelsun	J.H.J. Braddon	Mrs L.M. Bently	24.7.41
	Blue Flash of Ide	D	B/R	Cartref Contender	Merryworth Mayflower	J.H.J. Braddon	Mrs S. Ryder	11.11.44
1948	Broomleaf Bonny Lad of Shillwater	D	Golden Red	Blare of Broomleaf	Caroline of Shillwater	Mrs K. Doxford	Mrs D.H. Webb	20.10.46
	Oxshott Marxedes	D	Light B/R	Falconers Mark of Ware	Berrazanne of Oxshott	Mrs K.J. Gold	Owner	5.5.46
	Rodwood Lass of Sandover	B	Tri	Falconers Mark of Ware	Mareway Marie	J.H.J. Braddon	J. Chapman	4.9.45
1949	Lochranza Latchkey	D	Black	Treetops Foxbar Cognac	Lochranza Lotinga	Miss J. Macmillan	Owner	2.2.47
	Harley Cherrybank Gentleman	D	B/R	Blackmoor Brand	Springbank Blue Cap	S.F. Topott and Mrs G. Broadley	R. Roger	2.8.47

1950	Valstar Glow of Ide	D	B/R	Ch. Blue Flash of Ide	Cobnar Mist	J.H.J. Braddon	T. Hodgkinson	27.5.48
	Colinwood Son of a Gun	D	B/W/T	Colinwood Roughrider	Downpour of Dondeau	A.W. Collins	H.D.P. Becker	26.3.48
1952	Domino of Ide	D	B/W	Ch. Blue Flash of Ide	Ch. Rodwood Lass of Sandover	J.H.J. Braddon	Owner	26.5.51
	Talwrn Riverbank Rainmaker	B	B/R	Harley Riverbank Recall	Riverbank Regina	Mrs J. Rothwell	Mrs G.L. Thomas	25.2.50
1953	Colinwood Haybury Howitzer	D	B/W	Ch. Colinwood Son of a Gun	Haybury Hushabye	A.W. Collins	Lady Helen Berry	2.3.50
	Solinda of Traquair	B	Golden	Ch. Broomleaf Bonny Lad of Shillwater	Sweet Sue of Traquair	R.H. Wylde	Mrs R. Kay-Walker	16.6.48
1954	Colinwood Firebrand	D	B/W	Ch. Colinwood Cowboy	Pierette of Jessely	A.W. Collins	Mrs M.V. Jessup	20.3.51
	Dennydene Dousonne of Ide	D	B/R	Carwyns Shandy	Ravensclough Twilight	J.H.J. Braddon	Mrs G.M. Briston	19.9.52
	Springbank Trudy	B	B/W	Springbank Marquis of Bromwyn	Springbank Tessina	Miss V. Ferguson	Owner	5.1.51
1955	Nostrebor Riverbank Rogue	D	B/R	Harley Riverbank Recall	Riverbank Regina	Mrs E.S. Robertson	Mrs G.L. Thomas	26.7.52
1956	Colinwood Silver Lariot	D	B/R	Joywyns Blue Flash	Truslers Misty Morn	A.W. Collins	Miss H.M. Allen	26.8.54
1957	Lucklena Musical Maid	B	B/R	Ch. Domino of Ide	Lucklena Melodious Maid	A.S. Mansfield	Owner	7.11.55
1961	Craigleith Cinderella	B	B/R	Goldenfields Minstrel Boy	Craigleith Heathermaid	Mrs L. Robinson	Owner	23.12.59
1961	Lick Bla Berenice	B	O/R	Chayn Janitor	Lick Bla Betsy	Mrs I.M.G. Agnew	Miss D. Fagan	20.6.55
1962	Wake Early of Weirdene	B	O/W	Colinwood Singing Cowboy	Sh. Ch. Weirdene Learigg Annitra	R. Weir	J. Auld	10.6.56
1966	Lucklena Musical Director	D	B/R	Ch. Colinwood Silver Lariot	Ch. Lucklena Musical Maid	A.S. Mansfield	Owner	14.11.61

	Name of show champion	*Sex*	*Colour*	*Sire*	*Dam*	*Owner*	*Breeder*	*Date of Birth*
1967	Peelers Cornbow Myth	B	Black	Sh. Ch. Quettadene Mark	Cornbow Carmabar Dusky Donna	Mrs M. France	J. and D.R. Clarke	20.10.65
1968	Lucklena Blue Music	D	B/R	Lucklena Roydwood Recorder	Lucklena Silver Chord	A.S. Mansfield	Owner	21.5.66
	Saffron of Settnor	B	O/W	Dorna Dambuster	Courtdale Blue Willow of Settnor	Mrs J. Owen	Owner	13.11.62
1969	Ouainé Chieftain	D	B/R	Crackshill Tricolour of Ide	Ouainé Panderosa	Mrs E.J. Caddy	Owner	1.2.68
	Scolys Starduster	D	Light B/R	Goldenfields Minstrel Boy	Scolys Sweet Solera	Mrs D. Schofield	Owner	11.2.65
1971	Cretoka Alfredo	D	B/R	Ch. Scolys Starduster	Cretoka Marigold	Mrs K. Creamer	Owner	11.10.68
1972	Light Music of Lucklena	D	B/R	Sh. Ch. Courtdale Flag Lieutenant	Lucklena Merry Music	A.S. Mansfield	Mrs R. Gibbs	29.7.71
	Scolys Showpiece	B	Light B/R	Sh. Ch. Courtdale Flag Lieutenant	Scolys Silver Laughter	Mrs D. Schofield	Owner	17.6.70
	Bournehouse Starshine	B	B/R	Ch. Scolys Starduster	Merrybray Marie Celeste	G.F. Williams	Owner	24.5.71
1977	Silver Music of Lucklena	B	B/R	Ch. Light Music of Lucklena	Scolys Snowdrift	A.S. Mansfield	Mrs D.J. Staton	10.11.73
1981	Lucklena Minstrel	D	B/R	Ronfil Remezzo	Ch. Silver Music of Lucklena	A.S. Mansfield	Owner	25.9.79

APPENDIX C

BRITISH SHOW CHAMPIONS from 1947 to December 1987

	Name of show champion	Sex	Colour	Sire	Dam	Owner	Breeder	Date of Birth
1947	Hyperion of Ware	D	B/R	Falconers Padlock of Ware	Bellarton Erica	H.S. Lloyd	Dr C.S. Glass	22.5.44
	Harmac Hycilla	B	B/R	Maxim of Sunnybank	Mistress of Cabinhill	Mrs F.E. McGladery	Mrs E.W. Stewart	10.5.43
	Foxbar Sandylands Silk	B	Black	Sixshot Black Swan	Sandylands Red Sue	Mrs C.R. Robb	Mrs G. Broadley	28.1.44
1948	Golden Rule of Ide	D	Golden	Golden Rod of Ide	Ringlands Pin-up Girl	J.H.J. Braddon	Mrs N.E. Staff	1.9.46
	Tracey Witch of Ware	B	B/R	Falconers Padlock of Ware	Whist	H.S. Lloyd	Miss D. Weldon	10.5.45
	Countess Chloe of Ware	B	O/W	Falconers Padlock of Ware	Serenity of Ware	H.S. Lloyd	Mrs M.R. Jones	1.3.46
1949	Treetops Timber Wolf	D	Black	Treetops Foxbar Cognac	Treetops Truly	Mrs J. de Casembroot	Owner	5.8.46
	Marcus of Akron of Ware	D	B/R	Falconers Mark of Ware	Kyra of Akron	H.S. Lloyd	J.C. Spiller	5.11.45
	Aberthaw Commander of Reaghbel	D	B/R	Aberthaw Merchantman	Queen of Belreagh	J. Thaw	T.J. Cardy	24.4.46
	Dellah Pin-up Girl	B	O/R	Augustus of Wykey	Dellah Joyful Girl	D.L. Page	J. Blackmore	2.7.45
	Golden Valerie of Durban	B	Golden	Sixshot Willy Wagtail	Belle Maison	J.A. Carr	T.W. Malpas	5.10.46
	Arlette of Oxshott	B	Black	Arlequin	Red Rougette of Oxshott	Mrs K.J. Gold	A.G. Brown	25.5.44
1950	Joywyns Blueboy of Ware	D	Light B/R	Fantee Silver Sentinel	Cartref Charmer	H.S. Lloyd	Miss J. Ruben	7.4.49
	Broomleaf Black and Tan	B	B/T	Ch. Broomleaf Bonny Lad of Shillwater	Butterfly of Broomleaf	Mrs K. Doxford	Owner	6.3.48

	Name of show champion	Sex	Colour	Sire	Dam	Owner	Breeder	Date of Birth
	Lochranza Lisbon Story	B	Red	Treetops Truce	Lochranza Laughing Imp	Miss J. Macmillan	Owner	14.6.47
1951	Blue Flint of Ide	D	B/R	Harley Sandylands Flare	Falconers Fuschia	J.H.J. Braddon	Mrs E.K. Dudgeon	11.7.48
	Sixshot Woody Woodpecker	D	Red	Sixshot Willy Wagtail	Sixshot Nightingale	Mrs V. Lucas-Lucas	Owner	18.9.48
	Golden Star of Ulwell	D	Golden	Sixshot Willy Wagtail	Romance of Ulwell	Mrs D. Garrington	Owner	10.4.46
	Broomleaf Primula of Kenavon	B	Golden	Sixshot Willy Wagtail	Bran of Broomleaf	Mrs K. Doxford	Mrs S. Barnes	12.12.46
	Treetops Tender	B	Red	Treetops Tenant	Mimosa of Dorswick	Mrs J. de Casembroot	Mrs H. Wicks	12.7.46
	Valstar Willow	B	B/W	Ch. Colinwood Cowboy	Cobnar Mist	F. Duke	T. Hodgkinson	7.9.47
	Pennoncelle of Oxshott	B	Black	Oxshott Penndarcye	Reeta of Oxshott	Mrs K.J. Gold	Mrs V. Fisher	20.7.47
	Sunkist Lotus Lily	B	Golden	Sh. Ch. Golden Rule of Ide	Crocus of Aingarth	Mr and Mrs D. Mackenzie	J. Lindsay	8.5.48
	Crumpington Penndarcylla of Oxshott	B	Black	Oxshott Penndarcye	Crumpington Honeypot	Mrs K.J. Gold	Mrs M. Barrett	21.12.48
1952	Craigomus Critic of Ide	D	Red	Sh. Ch. Golden Rule of Ide	Crocus of Aingarth	J.H.J. Braddon	Owner	8.5.48
	Jaycee Marxedeson	D	B/R	Ch. Oxshott Marxedes	Jaycee Motala Turquoise	J.H. Connolly	Owner	1.6.49
	Witchdoctor of Ware	D	B/R	Falconers Mark of Ware	Sh. Ch. Tracey Witch of Ware	H.S. Lloyd	Owner	25.10.50
	Scarcroft Georgiana of Rafborn	B	Black	Ahmed of Scarcroft	Super Black	Sq Ldr and Mrs J.D. Hill	S.B. Asquith	17.5.48

	Bonny Lass of Kenavon	B	Red	Ch. Broomleaf Bonny Lad of Shillwater	Bramble of Kenavon	Miss B.M. Mingay	Owner	4.3.48
	Broomleaf Ballet Shoes	B	Red	Broomleaf Kim of Churdles	Brown Bess of Broomleaf	Mrs K. Doxford	Miss G. Anslow	28.5.50
	Courtdale China Model	B	B/W/T	Sh. Ch. Ronfil Regent	Polly of Halford	Mrs S.G. Jones	Mrs I.C. Burford	29.6.50
1953	Ronfil Regent	D	B/W	Ch. Colinwood Cowboy	Dream Delight	Mrs T.M. Bebb	Owner	12.10.48
	Bramlyn Sunflower	B	Red	Treetops Truce	Bramlyn Brown Sugar	Mrs M. Mather	Mrs M.H. Bowden	21.8.49
	Ernocroft Expert	D	B/R/T	Ernocroft Highlandie Laddie	Ernocroft Evenmist	Mrs E. Coulton and Mrs D. Kershaw	Miss D. Whitehead	22.10.49
	Treetops Trader	D	Black	Treetops Foxbar Cognac	Treetops Trillion	Mrs J. de Casembroot	Owner	15.12.49
	Derrydale Duskie	B	B/R	Ernocroft Expert	Treetops Sheba of Woodlands	Mrs M. Bullivant	Owner	25.5.51
	Sixshot Sugar Bird	B	Black	Sixshot Willy Wagtail	Dorswick Love in a Mist	Mrs V. Lucas-Lucas	Mrs H.C. Wicks	19.6.51
	Blue Queen of Ide	B	B/R	Ch. Blue Flash of Ide	Blue Gown of Ide	J.H.J. Braddon	A.E. Morris	1.5.52
	Lochranza Eldwythe's Enchanter	B	Black	Ch. Lochranza Latchkey	Ch. Solinda of Traquair	Miss J. Macmillan	R.H. Wylde	16.10.51
1954	Colinwood Jessely Journeyman	D	B/W Ticked	Ch. Colinwood Cowboy	Pierette of Jessely	A.W. Collins	Mrs M.V. Jessup	21.7.52
	Springbank Silver Flame	D	B/R	Springbank Covenmore Silver Flare	Ch. Springbank Trudy	Miss V. Ferguson	W. Sunderland	22.7.52
	Weirdene Learigg Annitra	B	B/W	Aberthaw Commander of Reaghbel	Learigg Ladybird	J. Auld	Miss J. Donaldson	26.6.50
	Bluedapple Jaycee Orange Belle	B	O/R	Sh. Ch. Jaycee Marxedeson	Jaycee Orange Flower	Dr A.J. Clements	J.H. Connolly	20.5.50
1955	Sixshot Storm Bird	D	Red	Sh. Ch. Sixshot Woody Woodpecker	Sixshot Cuckoo	Mrs V. Lucas-Lucas	Owner	5.7.52

Year	*Name of show champion*	*Sex*	*Colour*	*Sire*	*Dam*	*Owner*	*Breeder*	*Date of Birth*
	Colinwood Black Sombrero	D	Black	Colinwood Gamekeeper	Colinwood Chance Step	A.W. Collins	Owner	27.2.53
	Glendorgal Spritely Lad	D	B/R/T	Marcus of Akron of Ware	Salwood Sprite	Mrs M. Salter	Mr and Mrs D.G. Brewer	5.10.49
1955	Treetops Walkie Talkie	D	Black	Sh. Ch. Treetops Trader	Treetops Tiller Girl	Mrs J. de Casembroot	Owner	27.6.53
	Pickpocket of Misbourne	D	Black	Ch. Broomleaf Bonny Lad of Shillwater	Swanette of Misbourne	Miss D.M. Hahn	Owner	1.5.52
	Merryworth Matches	B	B/W	Ch. Colinwood Firebrand	Merryworth Magical	Mrs E.F. Chadwick	Owner	13.1.54
	Nostrebor Nightlight	B	O/R	Nostrebor Hillrise Hilary	Nostrebor National	Mrs E.S. Robertson	Owner	1.9.51
	Goldenfields Merry Maiden	B	B/W	Mantop Merry Legs	Goldenfields Merry Miss	Miss D. Robinson	Owner	11.11.52
	Cassa Cristina	B	Red	Rivoli Watmor Coppersmith	Cassa Crisp	Mmes E. Coulton and D. Kershaw	Owners	29.10.51
	Betrothal of Broomleaf	B	Red	Ch. Broomleaf Bonny Lad of Shillwater	Sh. Ch. Broomleaf Primula of Kenavon	Mrs K. Doxford	Owner	2.6.50
	Wendayle Valjolie of Misbourne	B	Black	Sh. Ch. Pickpocket of Misbourne	Wendayle Valetta	Miss D.M. Hahn	Mrs D.M. Cole	12.7.53
	Lady Caradon of Ide	B	B/W	Colinwood Roughrider	Ardenoak Starshine	J.H.J. Braddon	L. Hughes	9.11.52
	Lavender of Charmace	B	B/R	Charmace Checkmate	Fair Maid of Cheltenham	P. Stevenson and P.S. Moaby	Owners	22.1.52
1956	Bartonblount Double Six	D	B/W	Ch. Blue Flash of Ide	Dollishill Merry Minx	J.H.J. Braddon	Mrs T.W. Mellor	22.2.53
	Gatehampton Dumbo	D	Red	Broomleaf Ernocroft Event	Gatehampton Sunrise	Mrs A.L. Cloke	Owner	20.6.53

	Gatehampton Jennifer	B	Black	Lochranza Eldwythe's Earl	Gatehampton Silver Cloud	Mrs A.L. Cloke	Owner	23.4.53
	Treetops Tudor Queen	B	Black	Treetops Trigger Happy	Treetops Tilda	Mrs J. de Casembroot	Mrs P. Price	3.7.53
	Darnmill Dolly Blue	B	B/R	Sh. Ch. Joywyns Blueboy of Ware	Darnmill Buryhill Pipistrelle	H.S. Lloyd	Mrs E. Cunningham	12.9.52
	Cassa Chance	B	Red	Sh. Ch. Sixshot Woody Woodpecker	Roscott Susie	Mrs D. Kershaw	Mrs L. Barringer	26.1.54
	Broomleaf Camellia of Dorswick	B	Red	Sh. Ch. Sixshot Woody Woodpecker	Honeysuckle of Dorswick	Mrs K. Doxford	Mrs H.C. Wicks	18.12.52
1957	Golden Wagson of Ulwell	D	Golden	Goldenstar of Ulwell	Olicana Caramel of Ulwell	Mrs D. Garrington	Owner	29.6.53
	Falconers Herald of Ware	D	B/R	Thornfalcon Fanfare of Ware	Falconers Brenda of Ware	H.S. Lloyd	Owner	15.3.56
	Colinwood Outrider	D	B/W	Ch. Colinwood Firebrand	Truslers Tracery	A.W. Collins	Miss H.M. Allen	11.2.54
	Dellah Merrymaker of Wykey	D	B/R	Sh. Ch. Joywyns Blueboy of Ware	Dellah Merry Maid of Wykey	D.L. and Mrs Page	Mrs N. Basnett-Broughall	27.4.55
	Cassa Contessa	B	Red	Ernocroft Esquire	Cassa Cristina	Mrs D. Kershaw	Owner	27.10.54
	Silver Cloud of Ormeau of Ware	B	B/W/T	Sh. Ch. Colinwood Cobbler	Crofthill Cascade	Miss J. Lloyd	J. Duncan	18.6.56
	Noslien Nola	B	Black	Noslien Nickel Coin	Lass of Carrick	Miss P. Neilson	Miss I.S. Johnston	24.12.55
1958	Winter Harvest of Weirdene	D	Dark B/R	Aust. Ch. Wings Ashore of Weirdene	Weirdene Trech Zenda	R. Weir	Owner	10.10.57
	Lochdene Lac d'Amour	B	Black	Talwrn Pia Gynt	Broomleaf Bright Budget	Mrs P.G. Tosh	Owner	5.6.55
	Broomleaf Black Eyed Susan	B	Red	Billy Budd of Broomleaf	Bubbly of Broomleaf	Mrs K. Doxford	Owner	19.10.55
1959	Valjoker of Misbourne	D	Black	Sixshot the Black Cockatoo	Sh. Ch. Wendayle Valjolie of Misbourne	Miss D.M. Hahn	Owner	11.1.57

	Name of show champion	Sex	Colour	Sire	Dam	Owner	Breeder	Date of Birth
	Buryhill Cedar	D	B/R	Ch. Valstar Glow of Ide	Sh. Ch. Darnmill Dolly Blue	J.P. Cudworth and E. Fletcher	Mrs E. Cunningham	3.9.54
	Tideway Cabin Boy of Eastlands	D	B/R	Ch. Colinwood Silver Lariot	Tideway Hightide of Eastlands	Mrs M. Harrison	Mrs D.P. Shakespeare	28.7.56
	Black Jade of Lochnell	B	Black	Treetops Walkie Talkie	Limelight of Lochnell	J. Auld	Mrs M. Cameron	19.6.56
1960	Colinwood Cobbler	D	B/W	Colinwood Jester of Glenbogie	Colinwood Silver Slipper	J. Auld	Miss P.M. Collins	16.2.54
	Sixshot Shorelark	B	Red	Sh. Ch. Sixshot Stormbird	Sixshot Moorhen	Mrs V. Lucas-Lucas	Owner	31.3.56
	Broomleaf Boots & Shoes	B	Red	Bootboy of Broomleaf	Sh. Ch. Broomleaf Ballet Shoes	Mrs K. Doxford	Owner	27.10.56
	Astrawin Aphrodite	B	Black	Sixshot the Black Cockatoo	Astrawin Arabesque	Mr and Mrs S. Wise	Owners	8.6.57
	Tangee of Tolstem	B	Red	Lochranza London Tan	Tango of Scarlac	Mrs O. Birch	Owner	2.2.56
1961	Sixshot Otto the Owl	D	Red	Sh. Ch. Sixshot Woody Woodpecker	Sh. Ch. Sixshot Sugar Bird	Mrs V. Lucas-Lucas	Owner	30.11.57
	Gay Domino of Ide	D	B/R	Ch. Domino of Ide	Gaytime of Ide	J.H.J. Braddon	Owner	11.1.58
	Atway My Love of Misbourne	B	Black	Sh. Ch. Valjoker of Misbourne	Black Nun of Atway	Miss D.M. Hahn	Miss A. Gurney	4.7.58
1962	Lochranza Dancing Master	D	Red	Lochranza Eldwythe Exceed	Lochranza Dancing Shoes	Miss J. MacMillan	Miss J. Coull	22.12.57
	Silver Mogul of Hearts	D	B/R	Ch. Colinwood Silver Lariot	Ch. Lucklena Musical Maid	T.H. Arthur	A.S. Mansfield	13.8.58
	Wells Fargo of Weirdene	D	B/W	Weirdene Barnscar Fisher	Weirdene Trech Zenda	R. Weir	Owner	17.11.59
	Colinwood Cheyenne	D	B/R	Ch. Colinwood Silver Lariot	Craigleith Geisha Girl	A.W. Collins	Mrs M. Robinson	10.7.58

	Merryworth Musical Box	D	B/R	Ch. Colinwood Silver Lariot	Merryworth Music	Mrs E.F. Chadwick	Owner	14.9.58
	Shooting Star of Hearts	D	B/R	Ch. Colinwood Silver Lariot	Ch. Lucklena Musical Maid	T.H. Arthur	A.S. Mansfield	13.8.58
	Lochranza Merryleaf Eigar	D	Black	Sh. Ch. Lochranza Dancing Master	Merryleaf Corinne	Miss J. Macmillan	Mrs K.R. Farquhar	22.3.61
	Colinwood Morning Star	B	B/R	Ch. Colinwood Silver Lariot	Colinwood Venus	A.W. Collins	Mrs G.M. Champion	31.12.58
	Lochranza Floral Dancer	B	Red	Sh. Ch. Lochranza Dancing Master	Lochranza Lusaka	Miss J. Macmillan	Owner	2.2.59
	Winter Yana of Weirdene	B	O/R	Sh. Ch. Winter Harvest of Weridene	Lochranza Hightrees Orange Petal	R. Weir	Mr and Mrs T. Thomson	28.4.59
	Miss Julie of Jaycee	B	B/W	Sh. Ch. Dellah Merrymaker of Wykey	Penny Piece of Jaycee	J.H. Connolly	Owner	11.7.59
	Bouffante of Broomleaf	B	Red	Bally Atom of Broomleaf	Barbecue of Broomleaf	Mrs K. Doxford	Owner	20.6.59
	Lucklin Black Velvet	B	Black	Treetops Top Bid	Linde of Lochnell	J. Auld	J. Fletcher	16.5.56
	Marstondale Nanette	B	B/R/T	Ch. Domino of Ide	Marstondale Fan's Lady	Miss M. Martin	Owner	10.11.57
1963	Lochranza Hightrees Red Admiral	D	Golden	Sh. Ch. Lochranza Dancing Master	Hightrees Sunflower	Miss J. Macmillan	Mrs E. Ridout	14.7.61
	Glencora Black Ace	D	Black	Sixshot the Black Cockatoo	Sh. Ch. Black Jade of Lochnell	J. Auld	Owner	30.4.61
	Moyhill Maxwelton	D	B/R	Sh. Ch. Colinwood Cobbler	Moyhill Wise Girl of Kilbride	J.P. Cudworth and E. Fletcher	Owners	12.6.59
	Glencora Generous Gift	B	Black	Black Cockade of Lochnell	Why Chance of Weirdene	J. Auld	R. Weir	7.5.61
1964	Carmabar Glengharrie	D	Black	Carmabar Garry	Carmabar Donna Dimple	J. and D.R. Clarke	Mrs E. Caffyn	24.10.60
	Gatehampton Black Sambo of Lochnell	D	Black	Red Bracken of Lochnell	Kirkdon Hazari Harosa	Mrs A.L. Cloke	T.E. Heavisides	16.5.62

Year	*Name of show champion*	*Sex*	*Colour*	*Sire*	*Dam*	*Owner*	*Breeder*	*Date of Birth*
	Glencora Gallant Star	D	B/W	Colinwood Texan	Glencora Treasure	J. Auld	Owner	8.5.60
	Segedunum Aide de Camp	D	B/R	Merryworth Muleteer	Saddlebow Gerda	G. Stalker	A.P. McCullum	24.12.60
	Sixshot Dan the Duck	D	Golden	Sh. Ch. Sixshot Stormbird	Sixshot Garden Warbler	Mrs V. Lucas-Lucas	Owner	15.1.63
	Weirdene Questing Strathspey	D	B/R	Weirdene Questing Solitaire	Questing Beryl	R. Weir	Dr M. Burns	4.8.61
	Colinwood Bunting	B	Black	Sh. Ch. Valjoker of Misbourne	Colinwood Moorhen	A.W. Collins	D.M. Griffin	26.8.60
	Crosbeian Thornfalcon Flamenco	B	B/W	Ch. Colinwood Silver Lariot	Thornfalcon Blue Frosting	Mrs D.M. Trench	Miss B. Seymour-Nicholls	27.9.59
	Crackshill Alpine Crocus of Kenavon	B	Golden	Sh. Ch. Lochranza Merryleaf Eigar	Crackshill Tawny Toes	Miss B. Mingay	Miss B. Ritchie	15.8.62
	Moyhill Miss Jazz	B	B/W/T	Sh. Ch. Colinwood Cobbler	Moyhill Wise Girl of Kilbride	J.P. Cudworth and E. Fletcher	Owners	12.6.59
	Peasemore Pirouette	B	B/W	Thornfalcon Foxtrot	Colinwood Blue Lace	Miss M. Annetts	Owner	21.1.59
	Quettadenes Lucky Dip	B	Black	Sh. Ch. Valjoker of Misbourne	Quettadenes Jolly Whisper	Mrs E. Woodbridge	Owner	27.7.61
	Ronfil Remembrance	B	B/R	Courtdale Colinwood Seahawk	Ronfil Courtdale Royal Doulton	Mrs T.M. Bebb	Owner	10.11.61
1965	Courtdale Flag Lieutenant	D	Light B/R	Courtdale Colinwood Seahawk	Courtdale Kinkellbridge Gina	Mrs S.G. Jones	Mrs G. Anstey	3.1.63
	Lochranza Quettadene Marksman	D	Black	Sh. Ch. Lochranza Dancing Master	Quettadene Prudence	Miss J. Macmillan	Mrs E. Woodbridge	8.10.62
	Quettadene Mark	D	Black	Sh. Ch. Lochranza Merryleaf Eigar	Quettadene Prudence	Mrs E. Woodbridge and D.L. Page	Mrs E. Woodbridge	28.6.64
	Topbrands Blue Prince	D	Light B/R	Friesian Lad	Topbrands Sylvaqueen	L. Alsop	Owner	14.11.61

	Astrawin Amusing	B	Black	Sh. Ch. Valjoker of Misbourne	Astrawin Artemis	Mr and Mrs S. Wise	Owners	19.4.63
	Cochise Circe	B	O/R	Sh. Ch. Wells Fargo of Weirdene	Cochise Chiyoko	Lt Cdr & Mrs H. Blake	Owners	1.6.63
	Donvale Demara	B	B/R	Colinwood Tenderfoot	Donvale Delia	H. Hubbard	Owner	25.8.62
	Eldwythe Mornessa Milora	B	Red	Sh. Ch. Lochranza Dancing Master	Eldwythe Elza	Mrs M. France	Mr and Mrs Greenaway	11.7.62
	Goldenfields Geisha Girl	B	B/W/T	Can. Ch. Craigleith Vagabond King	Goldenfields Starlet	Miss D. Robinson	Owner	27.9.61
	Lochdene Pepper Pot	B	Golden	Sh. Ch. Glencora Black Ace	Lochdene Bubble Gum	Mrs P.G. Tosh	Owner	23.5.62
	Westside Story of Weirdene	B	Black	Black Cockade of Lochnell	Aust. Ch. Why Chance of Weirdene	R. Weir	Owner	7.5.61
1966	Astrawin April Fire	D	Golden	Sh. Ch. Lochranza Merryleaf Eigar	Astrawin April Flame	Mr and Mrs S. Wise	Owners	4.7.63
	Blackbird of Broomleaf	D	Black	Sh. Ch. Lochranza Merryleaf Eigar	Sh. Ch. Broomleaf Black Eyed Susan	Mrs K. Doxford	Owner	21.11.62
	Colinwood Jackdaw of Lochnell	D	Black	Sh. Ch. Blackbird of Broomleaf	Lochranza Red Sash of Lochnell	Miss P. Collins	Mrs M. Cameron	2.5.64
	Lochranza Darnclever	D	Black	Sh. Ch. Lochranza Hightrees Red Admiral	Lochranza Dancing Lesson	Miss J. Macmillan	Miss J. Macmillan and Miss J. Coull	27.3.64
	Val of Lochnell	D	Golden	Valentine of Lochnell	Alexandra of Lochnell	Mrs M. Cameron	Owner	30.10.61
	Noslien Nathaniel	D	Black	Noslien Napoleon	Treetops Noslien Nandina	Miss P. Neilson	Owner	5.2.63
	Craigleith Maggie May	B	B/W	Sh. Ch. Wells Fargo of Weirdene	Craigleith Princess Ida	Mrs M. Robinson	Owner	19.7.64
	Noslien Naughty Nineties	B	Red	Sh. Ch. Lochranza Dancing Master	Noslien Nainsook	Mrs J.A. Neilson	Owner	25.11.60

	Name of show champion	*Sex*	*Colour*	*Sire*	*Dam*	*Owner*	*Breeder*	*Date of Birth*
	Quettadene Dream Awhile	B	Black	Sh. Ch. Lochranza Merryleaf Eigar	Quettadene Prudence	Mrs E. Woodbridge	Owner	5.11.63
	Noslien Nasturtium	B	Red	Sh. Ch. Treetops Walkie Talkie	Noslien Nainsook	Mrs J.A. Neilson	Owner	12.8.59
	Scotswood Honeysuckle	B	Golden	Sh. Ch. Glencora Black Ace	Goldenfields Generous Offer	Mrs R. Bryden	Owner	22.2.64
	Lochranza Merry Borne Honey Amber	B	Red	Sh. Ch. Lochranza Merryleaf Eigar	Lochranza Honeyglow	Miss J. Macmillan	Mrs I. Martin	27.11.63
1967	Blue Print of Broomleaf	D	B/R	Craigleith Oliver	Blue Gleam of Broomleaf	Mrs K. Doxford	Owner	10.8.65
	Glencora Black Knight	D	Black	Sh. Ch. Glencora Black Ace	Sh. Ch. Glencora Generous Gift	J. Auld	Owner	7.5.65
	Lochranza Clever Dick	D	Black	Sh. Ch. Lochranza Darnclever	Lochranza Lusaka	Miss J. Macmillan	Owner	5.5.66
	Ouainé Parrandero	D	B/R	Ch. Colinwood Silver Lariot	Ouainé Pandora	Mrs J. Caddy	Owner	8.11.61
	Crosbeian Cascade	D	B/W	Glencora Moyhill Mallory	Crosbeian Conchita	Mrs D.M. Trench	Owner	8.7.65
	Bella Bambina of Sonning	B	B/W	Pentavy Patrol	Brass Cordial of Sonning	Mrs A. Forward	Owner	10.5.65
	Broomleaf Thulemoor Tulip	B	Golden	Treetops Top Bid	Thulemoor Darling Bud	Mrs K. Doxford	Mrs B. Merton	10.7.63
	Gatehampton Lochranza Fascination	B	Red	Lochranza Honey Beau	Rivoli Lochranza Caramel	Mrs A.L. Cloke	Miss J. Macmillan	25.10.65
	Nostrebor Nonchalant	B	O/R	Freshet Florin of Quatford	Minnon of Quatford	Mrs E.S. Robertson	Mrs N. Parker-Smith	15.8.65
	Platonstown Lovely Cottage	B	Black	Sh. Ch. Lochranza Merryleaf Eigar	Patbarossa Unity	Mrs M. Snary	Owner	9.8.63

	Winning Ways of Weirdene	B	B/R	Rockstone Rambler	Questing Sapphire	R. Weir	Miss J. Bartlett	22.6.64
1968	Lochranza Strollaway	D	Black	Sh. Ch. Lochranza Hightrees Red Admiral	Lochranza Dancing Lesson	Miss J. Macmillan	Miss J. Macmillan and Miss J. Coull	4.6.66
	Peelers Public Order	D	Black	Sh. Ch. Quettadene Marksman	Sh. Ch. Eldwythe Mornessa Milora	Mrs M. France	Owner	12.8.66
	Broomleaf Blithe Spirit	B	Red	Bugle Call of Broomleaf	Sh. Ch. Bouffante of Broomleaf	Mrs K. Doxford	Owner	28.10.66
	Craigleith Sweet Charity	B	B/W	Sixshot the White Stork	Sh. Ch. Craigleith Maggie May	Mrs M. Robinson	Owner	17.1.67
	Waving Petals of Weirdene	B	O/R	Sh. Ch. Wells Fargo of Weirdene	Witch Broom of Weirdene	R. Weir	Owner	30.5.67
	Laughing Sunbeam	B	Red	Sh. Ch. Lochranza Dancing Master	Courtdale Zip of Garlieston	Miss S.A. Chalkley	Owner	24.2.65
	Megina Mischief	B	B/W	Sh. Ch. Courtdale Flag Lieutenant	Megina Career Girl	Mrs R. Greatorex	Mr and Mrs R. Greatorex	1.12.64
	Lochdene Peppermint	B	Black	Sh. Ch. Glencora Black Knight	Sh. Ch. Lochdene Pepper Pot	Mrs P. Tosh	Owner	16.9.66
	Hazari Honey Puff	B	Golden	Sh. Ch. Gatehampton Black Sambo of Lochnell	Quettadenes Laughing Viola of Sandover	Mrs A. Bailey	Owner	4.12.63
1969	The Mataroa of Merrybray	D	B/R	Sh. Ch. Courtdale Flag Lieutenant	Merrybray Honeysuckle	G. and Miss P. Dunn	Owners	5.2.67
	Noslien Night Porter	D	Black	Noslien Napoleon	Treetops Noslien Nandina	Miss P. Neilson	Owner	5.3.63
	Hightrees Gunsmoke	D	B/R	Hightrees Dusty Miller	Hightrees Pearl Blush	Mrs E. Ridout	J. Gillespie	18.4.66
	Kavora Merryborne Sweet Martini	B	Red	Sh. Ch. Lochranza Darnclever	Merryborne Martine	Miss P. Trotman	Mrs I. Martin	9.11.66

Year	Name of show champion	Sex	Colour	Sire	Dam	Owner	Breeder	Date of Birth
	Merryborne Simone	B	Black	Sh. Ch. Lochranza Quettadenes Marksman	Lochranza Honey Glow	Mrs I. Martin	Owner	8.6.67
	Wedgewood of Weirdene	B	Dark B/R	Welded Link of Weirdene	Wong Sue of Weirdene	R. Weir	Owner	25.5.67
	Lochranza Bittersweet	B	Black	Sh. Ch. Lochranza Quettadenes Marksman	Lochranza Monk-spring Marigold	Miss J. Macmillan	Owner	29.5.66
	Sunreef Plees Be Luverly	B	Golden	Sh. Ch. Astrawin April Fire	Sunreef Miss Bee-Yootiful	Misses M. Scarr and M. Harris	Owners	9.8.66
1970	Astrawin Authentic	D	Golden	Valdoonan of Misbourne	Astrawin Antanamaria	Mr and Mrs S. Wise	Owners	1.9.67
	Merryborne Big Shot	D	Red	Sh. Ch. Lochranza Quettadenes Marksman	Lochranza Honey Glow	Mrs I. Martin	Owner	8.6.67
	Lochranza Peelers Legal Love	B	Black	Sh. Ch. Lochranza Quettadenes Marksman	Sh. Ch. Eldwythe Mornessa Milora	Miss J. Macmillan	Mrs M. France	12.8.66
	Olanza Pipistrelle	B	Black	Butterprint of Broomleaf	Black Pansy of Andana	Miss P. Becker	Owner	31.8.68
	Goldenfields Penny Black	B	Black	Sh. Ch. Lochranza Strollaway	Goldenfields Scilla	Mrs F.M. Wilkinson	Miss D. Robinson	17.9.68
1971	Scotswood Warlord	D	Golden	Sh. Ch. Colinwood Jackdaw of Lochnell	Scotswood Flip	Mrs R. Bryden	Owner	14.10.67
	Platonstown Buzzardway Sambo	D	Black	Tam O Shanter of Sorbrook	Cholesbury Red Cinders	Mrs M. Snary	T. Sanderson	29.7.69
	Kavora Merrymaker	D	Red	Sh. Ch. Lochranza Quettadenes Marksman	Sh. Ch. Kavora Merryborne Sweet Martini	Miss P. Trotman	Owner	27.11.68

	Lochranza Seamile Talkabout	D	Black	Lochranza William Tell	Lochranza Evening Star	Miss J. Macmillan	Mr and Mrs Sealey	28.6.69
	Whatmore of Weirdene	D	B/R	Weirdene Lochranza Pearl Diver	Woodcote Honey of Weirdene	R. Weir	Owner	16.4.68
	Colinwood Turtle Dove	B	Golden	Colinwood Summerleaf of Lochnell	Sh. Ch. Colinwood Bunting	Mr and Mrs P.C. Woolf	Mrs P.C. Woolf	10.9.67
	Sixshot Honeybird of Lochnell	B	Golden	Sh. Ch. Val of Lochnell	Gold Dahlia of Lochnell	Mrs V. Lucas-Lucas	Mrs M. Cameron	16.9.69
	Leabank Limerick	B	B/R	Leabank Luckstone	Leabank Love in a Mist	Mrs M.E. Stevens	Owner	12.12.67
	Amanda Jane of Sorbrook	B	Black	Cornbow Manfred	Quettadenes Bernadette	Mr and Mrs J. Smith	Owners	28.11.68
	Noslien Never Naughty	B	Red	Sh. Ch. Lochranza Its a Pleasure	Sh. Ch. Noslien Naughty Nineties	Mrs J.A. Neilson	Owner	5.9.67
1972	Glencora Meadow Prince	D	Black	Sh. Ch. Glencora Black Ace	Lochranza Meadow Sweet	J. Auld	Owner	3.8.69
	Valsissimmo of Misbourne	D	Black	Sunglint of Sorbrook	Valswytch of Misbourne	Mrs P. Price	Miss D.M. Hahn	6.3.70
	Lizarn Late Summer Morn	B	Golden	Butterprint of Broomleaf	Lizarn New Pence	Mr and Mrs A. Hall	Owners	18.9.69
	Scolys Spinning Water of Digbrow	B	B/R	Ch. Ouainé Chieftain	Scolys Silver Laughter	Mr and Mrs J.E. Brown	Mrs D. Schofield	6.11.69
1973	Pentavy River Patrol	D	B/W/T	Ch. Ouainé Chieftain	Pentavy Prairie Rose	Mrs K.G. Holmes	Owner	27.9.69
	Lochranza Newsprint	D	Black	Butterprint of Broomleaf	Sh. Ch. Lochranza Bittersweet	Miss J. Macmillan	Owner	27.3.71
	Peasemore Playgoer	D	B/R	Peasemore Blue Peter	Peasemore Prelude	Miss M. Annetts	Owner	3.8.69
	Bronze Knight of Broomleaf	D	Red	Sh. Ch. Scotswood Warlord	Black Frost of Broomleaf	Mrs K. Doxford	Owner	11.6.71
	Janeacre Night Skipper of Helenwood	D	Black	Sunglint of Sorbrook	Janeacre Maid Marion of Lochnell	Mrs J.H. Marris-Bray	Mr and Mrs J. Holdsworth	28.7.72

Year	*Name of show champion*	*Sex*	*Colour*	*Sire*	*Dam*	*Owner*	*Breeder*	*Date of Birth*
	Startime of Glencora	D	B/R	Sh. Ch. Glencora Gallant Star	Rosecourt Raindrop	J. Auld	Miss J.G. Wilson	15.3.71
	Asquanne's Kim Superbe	B	B/R	Lucklena Roydwood Recorder	Merry of Brenshu	Mrs A. Webster	Owner	9.7.66
	Rosecourt Reverie	B	B/R	Sh. Ch. Moyhill Maxwelton	Rosecourt Sealrock Sapphire	Miss J.G. Wilson	Owner	25.6.69
	Glencora Foxglove	B	B/W/T	Glencora Game One	Confetti of Charmace	J. Auld	Owner	27.3.69
1974	Merryworth Mr Chips	D	B/R	Ouainé Gustav	Merryworth Maggie May	Mrs E.F. Chadwick	Owner	12.11.71
	Lochdene Sorbrook Sundowner	D	Golden	Sunglint of Sorbrook	Butterkist of Sorbrook	Mrs P. Shaw	Mr and Mrs J. Smith	16.4.70
	Cochise Czardas	D	B/R	Ch. Ouainé Chieftain	Sh. Ch. Cochise Circe	Lt Cdr and Mrs H. Blake	Owners	7.3.70
	Sorbrook Playboy	D	Black	Cornbow Manfred	Fyne Lady of Sorbrook	J. Oulton	Mr and Mrs J. Smith	7.8.70
	Olanza Pipers Dream	B	Black	Butterprint of Broomleaf	Bramclere Olanza Pipers Tune	Miss P. Becker	Mrs R. Warren	30.5.70
	Sorbrook Holly Berry	B	Red	Lochranza Quettadene Diplomat	Quettadene Bernadette	Mr and Mrs J. Smith	Owners	27.5.71
	Colinwood Fine Lace	B	Black	Colinwood Summer Leaf of Lochnell	Colinwood Wild Thyme	Mr and Mrs P.C. Woolf	Owners	16.6.70
	Wait for Me of Weirdene	B	O/R	Sh. Ch. Whatmore of Weirdene	Why Tell of Weirdene	R. Weir	Owner	17.8.70
	Cochise Czoloushka	B	B/W	Ouainé Gustav	Sh. Ch. Cochise Circe	Lt Cdr and Mrs H. Blake	Owners	25.11.71
	Astrawin Arkadina	B	Black	Sunglint of Sorbrook	Sh. Ch. Astrawin Amusing	Mr and Mrs S. Wise	Owners	25.5.70

	Delstar of Digbrow	B	B/W	Ch. Scolys Starduster	Sh. Ch. Scolys Spinning Water of Digbrow	Mr and Mrs J.E. Brown	Owners	22.11.71
	Kirkdon Peaches n' Cream	B	O/W	Cochise Casimir	Kirkdon Orange Sparkle	T.E.W. Heavisides	Owner	24.9.72
1975	Benedict of Broomleaf	D	Black	Sh. Ch. Bronze Knight of Broomleaf	Sh. Ch. Olanza Pipistrelle	Mrs K. Doxford	Miss P. Becker	16.8.73
	Helenwood Checkmate	D	Black	Sh. Ch. Janeacre Night Skipper of Helenwood	Helenwood Celebration	Mrs J. Marris-Bray	Owner	2.5.74
	Chrisolin Cambiare of Styvechale	D	B/W	Aust. Ch. Scolys Strike Lucky	Chrisolin Cantata	Mrs P.L. Masters	Mrs C. Gardner	2.1.74
	Ramiro of Ronfil	D	B/R	Yardew Constellation	Ronfil Rhaiwen of Colene	Mrs T.M. Bebb	Mrs I. White	7.3.74
	Burnished Gold of Bryansbrook	B	Golden	Sunglint of Sorbrook	Colinwood Spun Gold	B. Fosbrook	E. Taylor	2.6.73
	Bitcon Blue Model	B	B/R	Sh. Ch. Leabank Levity	Hightrees Love Serenade	M. Armstrong	Owner	24.11.72
	Misbourne Sweet Anice	B	Black	Valdikler of Misbourne	Sweet Rebecca of Misbourne	Miss D.M. Hahn	Owner	26.12.72
	Konigsea Night Glint of Platonstown	B	Black	Sunglint of Sorbrook	Konigsea Karen	Mrs M. Snary	P. Bradford	12.1.74
1976	Blenkarn Claudio of Cochise	D	B/R	Sh. Ch. Cochise Czardas	Blenkarn Blue Star	Lt Cdr and Mrs H. Blake	Mrs B.W. Hodgetts	14.2.74
	Kenavon Envoy	D	Black	Lochranza Quettadene Diplomat	Kenavon Autumn Crocus	Mr and Mrs E.W. Darby	Miss B. Mingay	1.7.73
	Leabank Levity	D	B/R	Ch. Scolys Starduster	Sh. Ch. Leabank Limerick	Mrs M.E. Stevens	Owner	28.11.70
	Kavora Hi-Jinx	D	Red	Sunglint of Sorbrook	Kavora Lochranza Dancing Pupil	Miss P. Trotman	Owner	13.7.71
	Lochranza Farmers Boy	D	Red	Sh. Ch. Bronze Knight of Broomleaf	Lochranza Dairymaid	Miss J. Macmillan and Mrs J. Gillespie	Miss J. Macmillan	22.9.73

Year	*Name of show champion*	*Sex*	*Colour*	*Sire*	*Dam*	*Owner*	*Breeder*	*Date of Birth*
	Rengil Ransy of Platonstown	D	Black	Sorbrook Sweet William	Rengil Renede	Mrs M. Snary	G. Wood	15.7.74
	Misbourne Paper Chase of Lochranza	D	Black	Sh. Ch. Newsreader of Lochranza	Sweet Rebecca of Misbourne	Miss J. Macmillan and Mrs J. Gillespie	Miss D.M. Hahn	29.8.74
	Bournehouse Shine-On	B	B/R	Sh. Ch. Merryworth Mr Chips	Ch. Bournehouse Starshine	G.F. Williams	Owner	3.4.74
	Bitcon Blue Berry of Mossdew	B	B/R	Sh. Ch. Leabank Levity	Hightrees Love Serenade	Mr and Mrs A. Moody	M. Armstrong	26.10.73
	Styvechale Startime	B	B/R	Aust. Ch. Scolys Strike Lucky	Styvechale Sleighbells	Mrs P. Masters	Owner	17.10.73
1977	Bobbinbraes Echo	D	Golden	Sh. Ch. Quettadene Mark	Ebony Spice of Bobbinbrae	Mrs H. Woodhouse	Owner	19.12.74
	Ouainé Chipaway	D	B/W/T	Waylight of Weirdene	Ouainé Panderosa	Mrs J. Caddy	Owner	11.11.72
	Normanview Thundercloud	D	B/R	Normanview Silver Waters	Normanview Silver Salver	Mr and Mrs J.R. Baldwin	Owners	2.7.72
	Lochranza Man of Fashion	D	Black	Lochranza Night to Remember	Lochranza Dolly Posh	Miss J. Macmillan and Mrs J. Gillespie	Owners	31.3.76
	Bitcon Silver Model	B	B/R	Ch. Scolys Starduster	Sh. Ch. Bitcon Blue Model	M. Armstrong	Owner	5.11.75
	Helenwood Chrysilla	B	Black	Sh. Ch. Janeacre Night Skipper of Helenwood	Helenwood Tanfaisie	Mrs J. Marris-Bray	Owner	23.9.74
	Bournehouse Silver Star	B	B/R	Sh. Ch. Merryworth Mr Chips	Ch. Bournehouse Starshine	J. Oulton	G.F. Williams	3.4.74
	Raneyl Late Summer of Leabank	B	B/R	Sh. Ch. Leabank Levity	Raneyl Pretty Miss	Mrs M.E. Stevens	F. Salisbury	31.8.73
	Bryansbrook Butterkiss	B	Golden	Quettadene Golden Miller of Glowhill	Bryansbrook Ebony Bloom	Mr and Mrs B. Fosbrook	Owners	9.11.74
	Kavora Black Pearl of Lochranza	B	Black	Sh. Ch. Lochranza Newsprint	Kavora Belinda	Miss J. Macmillan and Mrs J. Gillespie	Miss P. Trotman	20.8.72

1978	Broomleaf Bright Memory	D	Black	Sh. Ch. Benedict of Broomleaf	Butter Candy of Broomleaf	Mrs K. Doxford	Owner	7.4.76
	Coltrim Crackerjack of Tarling	D	B/R	Ch. Scolys Starduster	Nostrebor Nonsense	Mrs O. Norfolk	Mr and Mrs A.E. Simpson	3.2.74
	Serenader of Styvechale	D	B/W	Sh. Ch. Chrisolin Cambiare of Styvechale	Styvechale Silver Leaf of Hobmoor	Mrs P.L. Masters	D. Worrall	25.8.75
	Sorbrook Beechnut	D	Golden	Sh. Ch. Janeacre Night Skipper of Helenwood	Sorbrook Sweet Pepper	Mr and Mrs J. Smith	Owners	2.8.75
	Normanview Scots Grey	D	B/R	Normanview Thunderstrike of Merrybray	Normanview Nightingale	Mr and Mrs J.R. Baldwin	Owners	26.9.75
	Cilleine Soldier Boy	D	Black	Bugle Boy of Cilleine	Kavora April Morn of Cilleine	Mrs D.M. Barney	Owner	20.1.77
	Black Silk of Broomleaf	B	Black	Sh. Ch. Benedict of Broomleaf	Butter Candy of Broomleaf	Miss P. Becker	Mrs K. Doxford	7.4.76
	Burnt Toast of Broomleaf	B	Red	Brandy Butter of Broomleaf	Bright Glint of Broomleaf	Mrs K. Doxford	Owner	24.9.75
	Merrybray Montana	B	O/R	Mandate of Merrybray	Merrybray My Gem	G. and Miss P. Dunn	Owners	5.8.75
	Kavora Nightlight	B	Black	Sh. Ch. Janeacre Night Skipper of Helenwood	Kavora Joanna	Miss P. Trotman	Owner	16.3.76
	Konigsea Kankara of Platonstown	B	Black	Brandy Butter of Broomleaf	Konigsea Klansee	Mrs M. Snary	P. Bradford	25.10.75
1979	Rockaydons Jet Jasper	D	Black	Sh. Ch. Helenwood Checkmate	Rimaelia Gold Cheri	Mrs K.M. Simms	M. Simms	12.6.74
	Cornbow Night Owl	D	Black	Sh. Ch. Janeacre Night Skipper of Helenwood	Mint Toes of Cornbow	J. Clarke	Owner	15.7.74
	Kavora Blackbird	D	Black	Sh. Ch. Bonninbraes Echo	Kavora Jenny Wren	Miss P. Trotman	Owner	12.8.77

	Name of show champion	Sex	Colour	Sire	Dam	Owner	Breeder	Date of Birth
	Westdyke Weel Kent Man	D	B/R	Sh. Ch. Chrisolin Cambiare of Styvechale	Westdyke Wise Words	W. Robertson	Owner	15.5.78
	Noslien Nebula	D	Red	Sh. Ch. Lochranza Farmers Boy	Noslien News Snip	Miss P. Neilson	Owner	15.4.76
	Colinwood Witchcraft	B	Black	Colinwood Tango	Colinwood Wood Sorrel	Mr and Mrs P. Woolf	Owners	5.10.74
	Astrawin Amberran	B	Golden	Astrawin April Legacy	Astrawin Alcamilla	Mr and Mrs S. Wise	Owners	25.3.76
	Rengil Rensheen	B	Black	Platonstown Star Quality of Rengil	Rengil Renlibby	Mrs M. Snary	G. Wood	24.11.77
	Styvechale Shine-On of Cilleine	B	Black	Sh. Ch. Cilleine Soldier Boy	Styvechale Shining Shoes	Mrs D.M. Barney	Mrs P.L. Masters	18.1.78
	Bitcon Rhapsody	B	B/R	Sh. Ch. Ramiro of Ronfil	Sh. Ch. Bitcon Blue Model	M. Armstrong	Owner	20.3.78
	Bitcon Florin of Mistfall	B	B/R	Sh. Ch. Leabank Levity	Renanda Love Story	G. Parkin	M. Armstrong	29.10.77
1980	Misbourne Postmark	D	Black	Misbourne Valbengy	Sh. Ch. Misbourne Sweet Anice	Miss D.M. Hahn	Owner	7.7.78
	Broomleaf Butter Crisp	D	Golden	Kavora Copper King of Covana	Butter Candy of Broomleaf	Mrs K. Doxford	Owner	3.1.78
	Platonstown Super Duper	D	Black	Sh. Ch. Rengil Ransy of Platonstown	Sh. Ch. Konigsea Night Glint of Platonstown	Mrs M. Snary	Owner	17.9.76
	Lochranza Black Onyx	D	Black	Sh. Ch. Lochranza Man of Fashion	Kavora Black Pearl of Lochranza	Miss J. Macmillan and Mrs J. Gillespie	Owners	1.12.77
	Davorey Lucky Sentinel	D	B/R	Davorey Charlie George	Emma Jane of Hightrees	Mrs Pykett	Owner	17.5.77
	Browster Jonjo	D	Black	Persuader of Browster	Browster Victorian Rose	J.W. Tyson	Owner	4.4.78

	Bryansbrook High Society	D	Golden	Sh. Ch. Lochranza Man of Fashion	Bryansbrook Butterkiss	Mr and Mrs B. Fosbrook	Owners	31.3.78
	Matterhorn Manhattan	D	B/W	Sh. Ch. Chrisolin Cambiare of Styvechale	Matterhorn Masquerade	H.M. Jones	Owner	24.10.78
	Cognac of Curagowrie	D	Red	Curagowrie Beau Brett	Braunspath Susette	Mrs F. Curran and Mrs R. Hume	D.P. Kincaid	15.1.76
	Wilholme Waltztime	B	B/R	Helenwood Firecrest	Wilholme Witchcraft	D.W. Shields	Owner	2.9.76
	Canigou Mary Isabella	B	Golden	Canigou Isobert	Canigou Christine Mary	Mrs P. Quinn	Owner	23.5.78
	Kavora Night Star of Olanza	B	Black	Sh. Ch. Janeacre Night Skipper of Helenwood	Kavora April Star	Miss P. Becker	Miss P. Trotman	30.9.78
	Cilleine Athene	B	Black	Sh. Ch. Lochranza Newsprint	Kavora April Morn of Cilleine	Mrs D.M. Barney	Owner	8.10.78
	Bitcon Babycham	B	B/R	Hightrees Sweet Talk of Lochranza	Renanda Love Story	M. Armstrong	Owner	7.2.79
	Weirdene Wonderful One	B	B/R	Weirdene Worthy Friend	Weirdene Westerly Sunset	R. Weir	Owner	17.8.77
	Astrawin Asugar	B	Golden	Brandy Butter of Broomleaf	Astrawin Adulation	Mr and Mrs S. Wise	Owners	6.5.78
1981	Cilleine Echelon	D	B/R	Hightrees Sweet Talk of Lochranza	Styvechale Stardew of Cilleine	Mrs D.M. Barney	Owner	18.2.80
	Sorbrook Brambleberry	D	Black	Sh. Ch. Broomleaf Bright Memory	Sh. Ch. Sorbrook Holly Berry	Mr and Mrs J. Smith	Owners	25.11.78
	Cochise Chirichua	D	B/R	Harwenprince Sonata	Cochise Caparica	Lt Cdr and Mrs H. Blake	Owners	2.1.79
	Broomleaf Barley Brew	D	Golden	Brandy Butter of Broomleaf	Hilgard Heidi	Mrs K. Doxford	Mr and Mrs J. Fisher	21.6.78
	Pandorek Crispin	D	O/W	Coltrim Confederate of Craigleith	Pandorek Pattimac	Mrs P. Mace	Owner	24.8.79

Year	*Name of show champion*	*Sex*	*Colour*	*Sire*	*Dam*	*Owner*	*Breeder*	*Date of Birth*
	Craigleith the Waltz Dream	B	O/W	Craigleith the Waltz King	Craigleith Candy Kisses	Mrs M. Robinson	Owner	14.1.78
	Teifi Nightshade	B	Black	Chasbo Mr Mallaby of Trulynn	Brombank Black Silk of Teifi	D. Rees	Owner	31.7.79
	Helenwood Capelle	B	Red	Sh. Ch. Janeacre Night Skipper of Helenwood	Clonwilliam Sunblest of Helenwood	Mrs J.H. Marris-Bray	Owner	12.1.78
	Cochise Cshakira	B	B/R	Harwenprince Sonata	Cochise Caparica	Lt Cdr and Mrs H. Blake	Owners	2.1.79
	Quettadene Black Jade	B	Black	Sh. Ch. Broomleaf Bright Memory	Cornbow Tantaliza	Mrs P.M. Lester	Owner	3.7.79
	Roanwood Ripple	B	Black	Persuader of Browster	Roanwood Isadora	Mrs S. Clarke	Owner	4.2.80
	Richbet Snowfall of Matterhorn	B	B/R	Matterhorn Masterpiece	Galen Loving Words	H.M. Jones	R.A. Lewis	1.4.79
	Gemma of Asquanne	B	Black	Bugle Boy of Cilleine	Kavora April Morn of Cilleine	Mr and Mrs A. Webster	Mrs D.M. Barney	23.6.79
1982	Colinwood Bellboy	D	B/R	Frant Blue Stone	Colinwood Rhapsody	Mr and Mrs P.C. Woolf	Owners	27.9.78
	Helenwood Haymaker	D	Golden	Sonic Sandmark	Sh. Ch. Helenwood Chrysilla	Mrs J.H. Marris-Bray	Owner	20.7.78
	Glowhill Peter Pan	D	B/R	Sh. Ch. Chrisolin Cambiare of Styvechale	Glowhill Blue Wings	Mrs J.E. Hill	Owner	29.9.79
	Dearnewood Star Venture	D	B/R	Sh. Ch. Leabank Levity	Scolys Silver Cygnet	R. and Mrs A. Richardson	Owners	7.6.78
	Mistfall Mood Indigo	B	B/R	Sh. Ch. Dearnewood Star Venture	Snowgate Blue Lady	G. Parkin	Owner	24.1.80
	Astrawin Avocet of Cabourne	B	Black	Sh. Ch. Kavora Black-bird	Astrawin Adulation	Mr and Mrs I. Hillier	Mr and Mrs S. Wise	11.10.79

	Chrisolin Moonlight Magic of Classicway	B	B/R	Falconers Envoy of Ware	Chrisolin Cantata	Mr and Mrs E.W. Darby	Mrs C.M. Gardner	5.4.78
	Lindridge Lucky Charm	B	B/R	Sh. Ch. Cilleine Echelon	Sh. Ch. Lindridge Silver Charm	Mrs A. Hackett	Owner	9.7.81
1983	Ouainé Juryman	D	B/R	Ouainé Diogenes	Ouainé Santa Rosa	Mrs J. Caddy	Owner	26.6.79
	Matterhorn Mick the Miller	D	B/W	Coltrim Confederate of Craigleith	Matterhorn Masquerade	H.M. Jones	Owner	28.1.81
	Coltrim Mississippi Gambler	D	B/R	Matterhorn Masterpiece	Coltrim Dakota Sioux	Mr and Mrs A.E. Simpson	Owners	17.12.80
	Platonstown Cracksman	D	Black	Sh. Ch. Lochranza Newsprint	Sh. Ch. Konigsea Night Glint of Platonstown	Mrs M. Snary	Owner	1.11.78
	Lochranza Like Your Style	D	Red	Lochranza Country Style	Lochranza Candy Floss	Miss J. Macmillan and Mrs J. Gillespie	Owners	16.9.81
	Asquanne's Omen	D	B/R	Commander of Courtdale	Asquanne's Leanne	Mr and Mrs A. Webster	Owners	2.9.81
	Lindridge Silver Charm	B	B/R	Sh. Ch. Chrisolin Cambiare of Styvechale	Lindridge Spot On	Mrs A. Hackett	Owner	31.5.78
	Olanza Pure Magic	B	Black	Sh. Ch. Broomleaf Bright Memory	Kavora Night Star of Olanza	Miss P. Becker	Owner	27.6.81
	Bitcon Hot Gossip	B	B/R	Bitcon Silver Rebel	Renanda Love Story	M. Armstrong	Owner	6.12.80
	Canyonn Christa	B	Black	Lochranza Double Top	Canyonn Celebrity	Mrs S. Young	Owner	7.11.80
	Asquanne's Genevieve	B	Black	Persuader of Browster	Sh. Ch. Gemma of Asquanne	Mr and Mrs A. Webster	Owners	7.12.81
1984	Cynacre Gemini	D	Black	Sh. Ch. Bidston Top of the Pops	Cynacre Holly Red	Mr and Mrs A. Softley	Owners	12.6.81
	Matterhorn Montana	D	B/W	Sh. Ch. Matterhorn Mick the Miller	Sh. Ch. Richbet Snowfall of Matterhorn	H.M. Jones	Owner	7.7.82

	Name of show champion	*Sex*	*Colour*	*Sire*	*Dam*	*Owner*	*Breeder*	*Date of Birth*
	Rosaday Super Trooper	D	Black	Sh. Ch. Platonstown Super Duper	Misbourne Sweet Lizbie	Mrs S. Sadler	Owner	29.7.81
	Quettadene Emblem	D	Black	Sh. Ch. Sorbrook Christmas Knight	Quettadene Fascination	Mrs P.M. Lester	Owner	30.4.83
	Cornbow Venture	D	Black	Bobbinbraes Solitaire of Cornbow	Cornbow Nightshade	J. Clarke	Owner	13.9.81
	Bidston Top of the Pops	D	Black	Sh. Ch. Broomleaf Bright Memory	Bidston Easter Bonnet	Mrs M.D. Robson	Mrs P.S. Hillary	9.9.79
	Classicway Crocus Time	B	B/R	Sh. Ch. Cilleine Echelon	Adargi Joyful Girl of Classicway	Mr and Mrs E.W. Darby	Owners	14.9.81
	Shanaz Short and Sweet	B	B/R	Hightrees Sweet Talk of Lochranza	Sapphire of Shanaz	Mrs W. Reid	Owner	24.9.81
	Kavora Charade	B	Red	Sh. Ch. Broomleaf Barley Brew	Kavora Ebony Spice	Miss P. Trotman	Owner	16.7.82
	Mistfall Mandalay	B	B/R	Bitcon Silver Rebel	Sh. Ch. Mistfall Mood Indigo	G. Parkin	Owner	9.6.82
	Lindridge Gypsy Girl	B	B/R	Styvechale Storm Cloud	Sh. Ch. Lindridge Silver Charm	Mrs A. Hackett	Owner	13.8.83
	Haradwaithe Sorceress	B	B/R	Haradwaithe Quick-silver	Mistfall Moviestar of Haradwaithe	S.E. Clayforth and R. Peters	Owners	11.11.82
1985	Manuchi Top of the Class of Krismoor	D	Golden	Canigou Isobert	Kitimat Orange Princess	Miss C.J. Littlemore	Mr and Mrs D.A. Guy	27.7.82
	Sorbrook Christmas Knight	D	Black	Willowside Buffalo Bill	Sorbrook Penny Royal	Mr and Mrs J. Smith	Owners	24.12.81
	Platonstown Scooby Doo	D	Black	Sh. Ch. Platonstown Super Duper	Platonstown Nice and Easy	Mrs M. Snary	Owner	25.7.83
	Tudorgold Nimrod Variations from Maxway	D	B/R	Sh. Ch. Coltrim Mississippi Gambler	Tudorgold Raindrop Prelude	K. McFarlane	Miss O.M. Tennant	22.6.83

	Helenwood Avalaf	D	Black	Sh. Ch. Broomleaf Bright Memory	Sh. Ch. Helenwood Capelle	Mrs J. Marris-Bray	Owner	5.11.83
	Classicway Carrie Ann	B	B/R	Sh. Ch. Cilleine Echelon	Adargi Joyful Girl of Classicway	Mr and Mrs E.W. Darby	Owners	14.9.81
	Courtmaster Je Suis	B	B/R	Sh. Ch. Cilleine Echelon	Wild Oats of Ware	D. and S. Telford	Owners	1.10.81
	Rosaday Leading Lady	B	Black	Sh. Ch. Platonstown Super Duper	Misbourne Sweet Lizbie	Mrs S. Sadler	Owner	29.7.81
	Eilans Black Charlotte of Charbonnel	B	Black	Sonic Sailor of Charbonnel	Eilans Midnight Merryem	Miss S. Lloyd	Mrs E. Medcalf	3.1.84
	Okell Ole	B	B/R	Sh. Ch. Colinwood Bellboy	Shielwood Crown Jewel of Okell	Miss J. Walker	Owner	23.7.81
1986	Classicway Concord	D	B/R	Normanview Midnight Runner of Classicway	Classicway Candice of Sudawn	Mr and Mrs E.W. Darby	Mrs S.D. Eaton	24.1.85
	Canigou Mr Happy	D	Black	Sh. Ch. Quettadene Emblem	Canigou Isabella Coral	Mrs P.L. Bentley	Owner	15.6.84
	Normanview Stormtrouper	D	B/R	Normanview Blue Rondo	Normanview Night Lady	Mr and Mrs J.L. Reid	J. and Mrs D. Baldwin	18.11.81
	Kendra Harmony Child	B	B/R	Styvechale Stormcloud	Kendra Graceful Child	Mr and Mrs K. Morrisson	Owners	24.9.82
	Brightgrass Ballpoint	B	Black	Brightgrass Bounty	Brightgrass Bryony	Mrs J. Irwin	Owner	12.5.82
	Classicway Charmaine	B	B/R	Normanview Midnight Runner of Classicway	Sh. Ch. Classicway Carrie Ann	Mr and Mrs J. Perry	Mr and Mrs E.W. Darby	16.10.83
	Squiresbrook Electra	B	B/R	Bowerleas Braemore of Laicsyde	Styvechale Sainete	Mrs S.M. Jones	Mrs D.J. Staton	13.12.82
	Matterhorn Morning Mist	B	B/W	Sh. Ch. Matterhorn Montana	Matterhorn Madrigal	H.M. Jones	Owner	9.6.83
	Sorbrook Sorceress	B	Black	Sorbrook Charcoal	Sorbrook Jezebel	Mr and Mrs J. Smith	Owners	16.3.84

Year	*Name of show champion*	*Sex*	*Colour*	*Sire*	*Dam*	*Owner*	*Breeder*	*Date of Birth*
	Mossdew Imagination	B	B/R	Sh. Ch. Cilleine Echelon	Wyrepark Passing Fancy	R.W. Jackson	Mr and Mrs Moody	4.9.82
	Helenwood Amerella	B	Golden	Sh. Ch. Bidston Top of the Pops	Sh. Ch. Helenwood Capelle	Mrs J.H. Marris-Bray	Owner	26.3.82
	Canyonn Cassandra	B	Black	Sh. Ch. Quettadene Emblem	Sh. Ch. Canyonn Christa	Mrs S. Young	Owner	7.11.84
	Bitcon Shy Talk	B	B/R	Mistfall Meddler	Bitcon Artists Model	M. Armstrong	Owner	20.7.84
1987	Wilholme Wrangler	D	B/R	Styvechale Stormcloud	Wilholme Who Loves Ya Baby	Mrs S. Shields	D.W. Shields	4.9.82
	Asquanne's Cougan at Sundeala	D	B/R	Sh. Ch. Asquannes Omen	Cascade at Derlan	Mrs B.E. Davies and R. Bebb	Mr and Mrs A. Webster	7.3.85
	Courtmaster Abracadabra	D	B/R	Normanview Midnight Runner of Classicway	Courtmaster Santa Lucia	D.J. and Mrs S. Telford	Owners	23.5.85
	Curagowrie Culture Club	D	Black	Sh. Ch. Bidston Top of the Pops	Curagowrie Coquet	Mrs F. Curran and Mrs R. Hume	Mrs F. Curran	6.10.85
	Maxway Music Maker	D	B/R	Sh. Ch. Tudorgold Nimrod Variations from Maxway	Orange Meringue from Maxway	K. McFarlane	Owner	9.7.84
	Misbourne Sweet Prince of Perrytree	D	Golden	Perrytree Gentleman Jake	Misbourne Sweet Trista	Mrs J. Rowland	Miss D.M. Hahn	30.3.85
	Cleavehill Pot of Gold	D	Red	Beligar Pot Black	Canyonn Christina	Mrs E. Buttrick and Mrs J.M. Taylor	Mrs J.M. Taylor	17.3.84
	Lindridge Venture	D	B/R	Mistfall Meddler	Sh. Ch. Lindridge Gypsy Girl	Mrs A. Hackett	Owner	29.10.85
	Olanza Poachers Moon	D	Black	Sh. Ch. Quettadene Emblem	Olanza Princess Gem	Miss P. Becker	Owner	22.8.85
	Roanwood Flint	D	Black	Sh. Ch. Quettadene Emblem	Roanwood Isadora	Mrs S. Clarke	Owner	12.9.85

Classicway Cressida	B	B/R	Sh. Ch. Cilleine Echelon	Adargi Joyful Girl of Classicway	Mr and Mrs E.W. Darby	Owners	12.7.84
Gladrien Gem Sparkle	B	Black	Lorjos Something Impressive of Gladrien	Fonesse Fame	Mrs G. Kaufman	Owner	16.8.83
Asquanne's Ghia	B	Black	Sh. Ch. Quettadene Emblem	Sh. Ch. Asquanne's Genevieve	Mr and Mrs A. Webster	Owners	6.10.85
Lynwater Tawny Owl	B	Golden	Sh. Ch. Noslien Bebula	Lynwater Kestrel	Miss F. Wormell	Owner	1.3.82
Olanza Promise Me	B	Black	Sh. Ch. Quettadene Emblem	Olanza Princess Gem	Miss P. Becker	Owner	22.8.85
Towbray Tosca	B	B/R	Bowerleas Braemore of Laicsyde	Towbray Sweet Surprise	Mrs H. Ladanowski	Owner	3.8.84

APPENDIX D

BRITISH FIELD TRIAL CHAMPIONS from 1947–December 1987

	Name of show champion	*Sex*	*Colour*	*Sire*	*Dam*	*Owner*	*Breeder*	*Date of Birth*
1947	Glennewton Julius	D	Black	Glennewton Buoy	Glennewton Jane	J. Forbes	Owner	1.8.44
1948	Lash of Mansergh	D	B/W	Brisk of Mansergh	Frolic of Mansergh	Major G. Roslin Williams	J.A. Barrow	13.5.46
1949	Newton of Chrishall	D	B/W	Spey of Corran	Judy of Chrishall	J. Kent	Owner	14.10.45
1950	Glennewton Timothy	D	Ln/W	Shorefield Quickstep	Glennewton Bunty	J. Forbes	Owner	4.4.47
	Young Punch of Elan	D	B/R	Silver Flash of Elan	Alberstan Wendy of Elan	Lt Cdr E.A.J. Collard	Owner	2.10.47
	Meadowcourt Breckonhill Beau	B	Lr/W	Rivington Goldfinch	Breckonhill Besom of Mansergh	R.B. Weston Webb	G. Curle	8.3.47
1951	Brackenbank Breckonhill Blackie	D	Black	F.T. Ch. Glennewton Julius	Breckonhill Besom of Mansergh	R.N. Burton	G. Curle	5.3.49
	Desire Me	B	B/W	F.T. Ch. Newton of Chrishall	Jigs Sally	J. Scott	Owner	10.3.48
1952	Merlin Micky	D	Black	F.T. Ch. Glennewton Julius	Merlin Miz	Lt Col R.H. Ogden	H. Ogden	23.6.50
	Shawfield Glenfire	D	B/R	Blanco of Mansergh	F.T. Ch. Desire Me	J. Scott	Owner	14.4.50
	Geisha Girl of Elan	B	B/W	F.T. Ch. Glennewton Julius	Sally of Elan	Lt Cdr E.A.J. Collard	Owner	1.8.46
	Shaflyde Jean	B	B/W	Blanco of Mansergh	F.T. Ch. Desire Me	Mrs E.M. Scott	J. Scott	14.4.50
1953	Dan Buoy of Elan	D	B/W Ticked	Glennewton Buoy	F.T. Ch. Geisha Girl of Elan	Lt Cdr E.A.J. Collard	Owner	19.3.52
	Debdenhall Timothy	D	Ln/W	F.T. Ch. Glennewton Timothy	Tanhouse Blackie	W. Grant Fiske	J.W. Hicks	22.9.51

	Glennewton Podge	D	B/W	Glennewton Benjamin	Glennewton Jenny	J. Forbes	Owner	24.4.51
	Rockstead Footsnap	D	B/R/T	Magic Needle	Rockstead Footshoe	R. Macdonald	H. Wilcock	1.10.50
	Juliet of Elan	B	Black	F.T.Ch. Glennewton Julius	Sally of Elan	Lt Cdr E.A.J. Collard	Owner	29.5.48
1954	Skipper of Elan	D	B/W	F.T. Ch. Young Punch of Elan	Geisha Girl of Elan	Lt Cdr E.A.J. Collard	Owner	5.3.49
	Buoy of Elan	D	B/W Ticked	Glennewton Buoy	F.T. Ch. Geisha Girl of Elan	Lt Cdr E.A.J. Collard	Owner	19.3.52
	Galbry Dandy Boy	D	B/W/T	F.T. Ch. Young Punch of Elan	Galbry Kite	J.M. Hannah	Owner	2.7.52
	Shaflyde Wilfred	D	B/W	Blanco of Mansergh	Judy of Mansergh	Mr and Mrs J. Scott	J. Scott	14.4.50
1955	Merlin Mark	D	Black	Lanegate Darkie	Merlin Mischa	Lt Col R.H. Ogden	Mrs M. Noble	27.2.52
	Merlin Minimus	B	Black	F.T. Ch. Glennewton Julius	Merlin Miz	Major H. Peacock	H. Ogden	23.6.50
1956	Black Buoy of Elan	D	Black	F.T. Ch. Buoy of Elan	Juliet of Elan	Lt Cdr E.A.J. Collard	Owner	19.7.54
	Jordieland Bunty	B	B/R	Greylag Seorus	Kilterson Queen Bee	J.H. Windle	J. Hutcheson	8.9.52
	Stockbury Elizabeth	B	Lr	Brownie of Poughley	Stockbury Madge	W.S. Fuller	Owner	9.5.53
1957	Bronze Buoy of Elan	D	Ln/W	F.T.Ch. Buoy of Elan	F.T. Ch. Juliet of Elan	Lt Cdr E.A.J. Collard	Owner	18.7.54
	Carswell Solomon	D	Lr/W	F.T. Ch. Galbry Dandy Boy	Galbry Blondeye	Mrs P.M. Badenach-Nicholson	J.M. Hannah	6.7.54
	Brookville Sandy	D	Golden	F.T. Ch. Skipper of Elan	F.T. Ch. Juliet of Elan	H. Martineau	Lt Cdr E.A.J. Collard	20.2.55
	Galbry Daniel	D	B/W/T	Galbry Oscar	Glad Tydings	J.M. Hannah	J.H. Windle	6.7.56
	Simon of Elan	D	Black/B/R	F.T. Ch. Buoy of Elan	Trudy of Elan	Lt Cdr E.A.J. Collard	Owner	14.4.57
	Deewood Wendy	B	Black	F.T. Ch. Glennewton Julius	Merlin Miz	T. Ellis	Mrs T.A. Watt	10.3.53
	Meadowcourt Gay	B	Ln/W	F.T. Ch. Buoy of Elan	Meadowcourt Breckonhill Beau	Mrs S. Weston-Webb	R.B. Weston-Webb	28.3.56

	Name of show champion	Sex	Colour	Sire	Dam	Owner	Breeder	Date of Birth
1959	Greatford Crick	D	Black	F.T. Ch. Glennewton Julius	Merlin Miz	Lady Portarlington	Mrs T.A. Watt	13.6.56
	Debdenhall Terra	B	Lr/W	F.T. Ch. Debdenhall Timothy	Stockbury Jill	W.G. Fiske	Owner	24.3.58
1961	Greatford Buoy	D	B/W	F.T. Ch. Buoy of Elan	Greatford Rikka	Major H. Peacock	F.J. Cheney	24.7.58
	Headland Blue Zulu	D	B/R	F.T. Ch. Merlin Micky	Blue Tandy	Miss P.E. Brown	Owner	12.5.58
1962	Henhamlodge Dynah	B	B/W	F.T. Ch. Buoy of Elan	Mahneh Lodge Kim	J.W. Smith	Owner	25.3.59
	Henhamlodge Byng	D	B/W	F.T. Ch. Buoy of Elan	Mahneh Lodge Kim	R.S. Wilkins	J.W. Smith	25.7.58
	Gem of Elan	B	B/W	F.T. Ch. Buoy of Elan	Maybelle	Lt Cdr E.A.J. Collard	H.T. Davis	16.8.57
	Scamp of Elan	D	B/W	F.T. Ch. Brookville Sandy	Gem of Elan	Lt Cdr E.A.J. Collard	Owner	19.6.60
	Colognac Cherry of Elan	B	B/W Ticked	F.T. Ch. Buoy of Elan	Colognac Teazle	Lt Cdr E.A.J. Collard	Mrs M.P. Alexander	29.3.58
1963	Swift of Elan	D	B/R	F.T. Ch. Simon of Elan	Beta of Elan	Lt Cdr E.A.J. Collard	Owner	9.8.61
	Bliss of Elan	B	B/W	F.T. Ch. Buoy of Elan	Exton Freckles	Lt Cdr E.A.J. Collard	Mrs T.A. Watt	21.3.61
	Headland Hazel of Monnow	B	B/W	F.T. Ch. Buoy of Elan	Headland Blue Hen Spider	H.J. Timms	Miss P. Brown	23.5.61
	Lanegate Linda	B	B/W	F.T. Ch. Buoy of Elan	Maybelle	Mrs R. Hall	H.T. Davis	16.8.57
1964	Exton Monty	D	Liver	Exton David	Exton Mousie	Mrs T.A. Watt	Owner	19.5.61
	Greatford Darkie	D	Black	Jan Boy	Exton Mousie	Major H. Peacock	Mrs T.A. Watt	8.4.60
	Jet of Elan	B	Black	F.T. Ch. Brookville Sandy	F.T. Ch. Gem of Elan	Lt Cdr E.A.J. Collard	Owner	19.6.60
1965	Headland Irish Moss	D	Lr/W	F.T. Ch. Buoy of Elan	Headland Blue Connemara	Miss V. Pinney	Miss P.E. Brown	10.2.62
1966	Exton Duncan	D	Liver	F.T. Ch. Exton Monty	Della of Trundles	Mrs T.A. Watt	Owner	24.5.64

1967	Pinehawk Rebb	D	B/W	F.T. Ch. Swift of Elan	Bright of Elan	J. Wylie	Mr and Mrs T.P. Hall	11.3.65
1968	Goldspan Bray	D	Black	Goldspan Je T'Adore	F.T. Ch. Henhamlodge Dynah	Mrs P. Leigh	J. Smith	29.3.65
	Goldspan Je T'Adore	D	Black	F.T. Ch. Debdenhall Terra	F.T. Ch. Deewood Wendy	Mrs P. Leigh	T.P. Hall	9.3.62
	Jimmy of Elan	D	Lr/R	F.T. Ch. Swift of Elan	F.T. Ch. Jet of Elan	Lt Cdr E.A.J. Collard	Owner	1.6.63
	Exton Busy	B	Liver	Wood Spice	Dinah of Poughleywood	Mrs T.A. Watt	Owner	10.8.64
	Exton Jenny	B	Lr/W	F.T. .Ch. Exton Monty	Della of Trundles	Mrs T.A. Watt	Owner	21.2.66
	Gale of Elan	B	B/R & Black	F.T. Ch. Swift of Elan	F.T. Ch. Gem of Elan	J. Forbes	Lt Cdr E.A.J. Collard	23.4.65
	Whisper of Corsewall	B	B/W	Galbry Jordieland Podge	Galbry Mona	Mrs P.M. Badenach-Nicholson	Mrs Carrick-Buchanan	14.8.63
1969	Danny of North Standen	D	Liver	F.T. Ch. Jimmy of Elan	Dainty of Ladbroke	Lord Rootes	Owner	1.4.68
	Glennewton Keeker	D	B/W	F.T. Ch. Wilfred of Cromlix	F.T. Ch. Bliss of Elan	Hon Mrs N. Hopkinson	Lt Cdr E.A.J. Collard	18.7.66
	Templebar Blackie	D	Black	F.T. Ch. Wilfred of Cromlix	F.T. Ch. Jet of Elan	Mr and Mrs T.P. Hall	Lt Cdr E.A.J. Collard	22.4.67
	Wilfred of Cromlix	D	B/W	F.T. Ch. Merlin Micky	Nix of Cromlix	Lady Auckland	Owner	28.11.61
	Monnow Mayfly	B	O/W	F.T. Ch. Pinehawk Rebb	F.T. Ch. Headland Hazel of Monnow	H.J. Timms	Owner	1.9.67
1970	Exton Sarah	B	B/W	F.T. Ch. Exton Monty	Exton Fizz	Mrs T.A. Watt	Owner	4.5.67
	Speckle of Ardoon	B	Lr/R	Tireragh Silver Starlight	Colleen of Elan	W.C. Sloan	Owner	1.7.69
1971	Jorrocks of Elan	D	B/W	F.T. Ch. Swift of Elan	F.T. Ch. Gem of Elan	Lt Cdr E.A.J. Collard	Owner	18.7.66
	Exton Dainty	B	B/W	F.T. Ch. Exton Monty	Exton Fizz	Mrs T.A. Watt	Owner	15.8.68
1972	Ardnamurchan Mac	D	Black	F.T. Ch. Templebar Blackie	Templebar Gail	W. Mathew	Mr and Mrs T.P. Hall	17.4.69

	Name of show champion	*Sex*	*Colour*	*Sire*	*Dam*	*Owner*	*Breeder*	*Date of Birth*
	Templebar Tammy	B	Black	F.T. Ch. Templebar Blackie	Templebar Gail	Mr and Mrs T.P. Hall	Owners	17.4.69
1973	Goldspan Tojo	D	Lr/W	Lanegate Spot	Della of Trundles	Mrs P. Leigh	Mrs T.A. Watt	22.1.70
	Morborne Tees	D	B/R	Harpersbrook Sobers	Morborne Spey	F. Cheney	Owner	29.7.71
	Burnhatch Fly	B	Ln/W	F.T. Ch. Templebar Blackie	Templebar Tanya	Hon Mrs F. Hopkinson	Mr and Mrs T.P. Hall	23.7.69
	Diasan Meg	B	B/W	F.T. Ch. Ardnamurchan Mac	Monnow Elizabeth	H. Carpenter	P. Hayward	27.9.71
	Tayburn Ron	B	B/R	F.T. Ch. Wilfred of Cromlix	Tayburn Borgie	The late Vice Admiral Sir David Gregory	Owner	16.1.70
1974	Exton Anna	B	Black	Exton Andrew	Exton Fickle	Mrs T.A. Watt	Owner	5.3.72
1975	Carswell Johnnie	D	B/W	F.T. Ch. Jimmy of Elan	F.T. Ch. Whisper of Corsewall	Earl of Mansfield	Mrs P.M. Badenach-Nicholson	14.7.72
	Carswell Zero	D	B/W	F.T. Ch. Danny of North Standen	F.T. Ch. Whisper of Corsewall	Mrs P.M. Badenach-Nicholson	Owner	17.5.71
	Tayburn Cockle	B	B/W	F.T. Ch. Carswell Zero	F.T. Ch. Tayburn Ron	Lt A.M. Gregory	The late Vice Admiral Sir David Gregory	9.5.74
1976	Beidlieston Speck	B	B/W	F.T. Ch. Jimmy of Elan	Carswell Wanda	Mr and Mrs G.W. Tickner	J.A. Wilson	7.4.71
	Concraig Skim	B	B/R	Jordieland Spot	Jordieland Lassie	W. Bremner Jnr	J. Windle	12.9.73
	Sonia of Templebar	B	Ln/W	F.T. Ch. Templebar Blackie	F.T. Ch. Speckle of Ardoon	Mrs R. Hall	K.A. Erlandson	1.4.72
1977	Helion Manor Tyhill	D	Black	Tweed of Elan	Helion Tamar	Mr and Mrs G.W. Tickner	Owners	2.10.72
	Exton Jemima	B	Black	F.T. Ch. Ardnamurchan Mac	Exton Jenny	Mrs T.A. Watt	Owner	20.5.74
	Jordieland Kit	B	Ln/W	Bunter of Jordieland	Jordieland Twiggy	W. Bremner Snr	J. Windle	1.6.75

	Sooty of Bellever	B	Black	Gwivernant Carcajou	F.T. Ch. Monnow Mayfly	R. Hill	K.A. Erlandson	26.7.72
	Tina of Helion Manor	B	Lr/W	Dengie Helion Tim	Headland Hazel of Monnow	Mr and Mrs G.W. Tickner	A. Wylie	16.5.73
1978	Beidlieston Spam	D	B/W	F.T. Ch. Ardnamurchan Mac	Carswell Wanda	Mr and Mrs G.W. Tickner	J. Wilson	5.1.74
1979	Bunter of Jordieland	D	Ln/W	F.T. Ch. Carswell Zero	Cavinia of Duchrae	M.J. Cottam	Lady Henderson	24.3.74
	Gwibernant Eel	D	B/R	Gwibernant Carcajou	Monnow Elizabeth	F.J. Cheney	P.L. Hayward	27.3.76
	Burnhatch Splash	B	Ln/W	Concraig Teal	F.T. Ch. Burnhatch Fly	C. Bremner	Mrs Hopkinson	6.4.75
	Diedre of Duchrae	B	Black	F.T. Ch. Carswell Zero	Davinia of Duchrae	Lady Henderson	Owner	26.4.77
	Exton Dickle	B	Black	Exton Danny	Exton Fickle	Mrs T.A. Watt	Owner	31.5.74
	Linswell Rosa	B	B/W	Wilfred of Hurryon	Carswell Della	Mr and Mrs K.J. Howell	Owners	2.6.75
1980	Rhu of Migdale	D	Lr/W	Southfield Sam	Ginger of Gwibernant	D. MacLean	K.A. Erlandson	22.5.76
	Sandringham Mango	D	B/W	F.T. Ch. Helion Manor Tyhill	Isherwood Medlar	W. Davidson	H.M. The Queen	27.5.78
	Lollipop of Anahar	B	B/W	F.T. Ch. Carswell Zero	Tayburn Johannie	Mrs D.J. Douglas	The late Vice Admiral Sir David Gregory	15.5.74
1980	Jinny of Anahar	B	Golden	F.T. Ch. Carswell Zero	F.T. Ch. Tayburn Ron	Mrs D.J. Douglas	Cdr Muir	17.4.76
1981	Lea Cross Thumper	D	B/W	Linswell Diver	Lea Cross Zara	C.D. Burrows	D.J. Evans	13.2.78
	Burnhatch Sprite	B	Ln/W	Concraig Teal	F.T. Ch. Burnhatch Fly	Hon Mrs F. Hopkinson	Owner	6.6.75
	Concraig Gyp	B	Black	Blackie of Jordieland	F.T. Ch. Burnhatch Splash	C. Bremner	Owner	30.3.79
	Tayburn Valentina of Anahar	B	Black	Lammerlaw Muffin	F.T. Ch. Tayburn Cockle	Mrs D.J. Douglas	Lt Cdr A.M. Gregory	14.2.79

	Name of show champion	Sex	Colour	Sire	Dam	Owner	Breeder	Date of Birth
1982	James of Anahar	D	B/W	Jordieland Tip	F.T. Ch. Lollipop of Anahar	D.J.B. Douglas	Owner	1.7.79
	Pixie Cala	B	B/T	Tayburn Fleet	Gwibernant Sly	Mrs P. Rhodes	M.J. Shefford	12.8.80
	Dale of Biteabout	B	B/W	F.T. Ch. Sandringham Mango	Eskendar Twiggy	W. Davidson	G. Smith	23.5.80
	Lady of Jenoren	B	Black	F.T. Ch. Morborne Tees	F.T. Ch. Linswell Rosa	E. Robertson	Mr and Mrs K.K. Howell	6.6.79
	Nancorrow Gypsy	B	B/W Roan	Burnhatch Brig	Morborne Tell	R. Tozer	H. Millington	23.9.79
	Gwibernant Snake	B	Black	Jasper of Gwibernant	Imp of Gwibernant	Mr and Mrs H.C. Gwynne	K.A. Erlandson	14.8.78
1983	Black Belle of Torbruad	B	B/W	Blackie of Jordieland	Moanruad Chuckle	C.B. Riddell	J. Styles	9.10.80
	Nancarrow Sooty of Craigfelin	B	Black	Burnhatch Brig	Gwibernant Ebony of Rawreth	R. Tozer	H. Millington	11.8.80
1984	Smut of Jordieland	D	B/R	F.T. Ch. Gwibernant Eel	Dacre Jet	J. Edgar	Miss A. Hill-Wood	20.9.81
	Gemma of Kenwunn	B	Black	Cimerv Ceiliog Brith	Headland Unity	W.G. Fox	G. Morris	4.3.80
	Lady Kings Thorpe	B	B/W	Linswell Diver	Tina of Linswell	S.D. Knight	Mrs A. Goodall	14.4.82
	Morborne Nese	B	Roan	F.T. Ch. Gwibernant Eel	Morborne Sheelin	E.J. Quince	F. Cheney	2.3.82
	Tayburn Brora	B	B/W	Gregory of Anahar	F.T. Ch. Tayburn Cockle	Cdr and Mrs A.M. Gregory	Owners	8.7.81
	Wellonhead Blondie of Elan	B	Ln/W	F.T. Ch. Bunter of Jordieland	Dynamight of Wellonhead	Lt Cdr E.A.J. Collard	Mrs A.C. Choat	17.4.80
	Wernffrwd Tylwyth Teg	B	Black	F.T. Ch. Rhu of Migdale	F.T. Ch. Gwibernant Snake	Mr and Mrs H.C. Gwynne	Owners	18.5.81
1985	Wernffrwd Bunterson	D	B/W	F.T. Ch. Bunter of	F.T. Ch. Gwibernant	Mr and Mrs H.C.	Owners	17.3.83

	Jade of Livermere	D	Ln/W	Simon of Kenstaff	Kim of Holcot	C.R. Colclough	Mrs N.B. Stearn	25.5.83
	Wernffrwd Jetson of Larford	D	B/W	F.T. Ch. Bunter of Jordieland	F.T. Ch. Gwibernant Snake	P.W. Clulee	Mr and Mrs H.C. Gwynne	17.3.83
	Weaverdale Twig	D	B/W	Tayburn Naver of Weaverdale	Migdale Liz	Mrs A. Tiplady	Mr and Mrs A.G. Nicholls	29.6.80
	Glenfernate Meg of Ormewood	B	B/W	F.T. Ch. Sandringham Mango	Martha of Glenfernate	P.E. Rawlings	Mrs S. Heathcote-Amery	18.7.82
1986	Carradog of Iarl	D	Black	Cimerv Ceiliog Brith	Headland Unity	G.B. Roberts	G. Morris	4.3.80
	Craig Felin Angus	D	Golden	Windmillwood Socks	F.T. Ch. Nancarrow Gypsy	D. Ormond	R. Tozer	2.3.82
	Migdale Ben of Weaverdale	D	B/W	F.T. Ch. Bunter of Jordieland	Migdale Liz	H. Millington	D. MacLean	19.1.79
	Swallow Law Snipe	D	Liver	F.T. Ch. Smut of Jordieland	Misty Law Katy	J. Dickson	Owner	13.7.84
	Heath Hill Lad	D	Black	Picklewood Oak	Spey of Spinning Loch	D.R. Hickinson	Mrs P.J.M. Wood	14.6.84
	Housty Solo	D	B/R	Tayburn Fleet	Gwibernant Sly	P.E. Jones	M.J. Shefford	30.8.82
	Norbeck Beaver	D	Liver	F.T. Ch. Rhu of Migdale	Norbeck Pip	J. Holloway	Owner	3.5.81
1987	Wernffrwd Pawn	B	B/W	F.T. Ch. Rhu of Migdale	F.T. Ch. Gwibernant Snake	E.E. Burchell	Mr and Mrs H.C. Gwynne	4.6.84

INDEX

Page numbers in *italic* refer to the illustrations